Footprints of the Capitol Astrologer

August 24, 2002

For Amy

It's all in the stars!

Best Wishes,

James A. Stott

Footprints of the Capitol Astrologer

Janice A. Stork

Dedication

In loving memory of my mother, Lillian Peterson, for giving me my first book on astrology when I was a teenager. She passed away while I was writing this book.

My mother also worked for the Legislature and together we enjoyed numerous parties and political events.

Acknowledgments

I want to thank Linda Beauregard-Vasquez for being such a good friend and editor. We learned many things together and spiritually grew in the process. She has a metaphysical chat channel called psychic teachings at http://www.psychicteachings.com.

I also want to thank cover designer, Cathi Stevenson, of http://www.bookcoverexpress.com.

For any questions, http://www.janicestork.com.

Prologue

Climbing the steps of the California State Capitol building, I noticed how well the granite had held up with time. Hundreds of tourists and politicians had been making the same climb for decades, leaving only the subtle hint of their footprints behind.

Pulling open the enormous mahogany doors, I hurried down the hall to check the clock next to the Governor's office like I once did before I retired. There was just enough time for me to stop and say hi to someone before meeting a friend for lunch. As I opened the office door, I heard the familiar voice of a woman with whom I used to work talking on the phone. She was repeating dates to the person to whom she was speaking. When she saw me appear around the bookshelf blocking the view of the door, her eyes lit up, and she gestured with her index finger that she would only be a minute. Then she pointed to an empty blue upholstered chair in front of her desk where she wanted me to sit.

"I really have to go," I heard her say. "Someone has just come into my office that I need to talk to."

"How strange," I thought to myself, "She wasn't expecting me."

"It's good to see you. You look fantastic," she smiled hanging up the phone.

"Thank you," I said, glancing at the old wooden desk I used to sit behind when I worked there. "I will be meeting a friend for lunch shortly, but I wanted to stop by and see you first."

She stepped away from her desk and came around the corner to give me a hug before retiring to the white couch a few feet away.

"That was the press on the phone," she said nervously crossing her picturesque legs and adjusting the clear plastic clamp that was holding her blonde hair up off her shoulders. "Your timing was perfect. I needed an excuse to get rid of them."

"I wouldn't want you to hang up on the press because of me," I teased with a smile remembering the political consequences a staff person sometimes faced when the press took something he or she innocently said and rearranged it to suit a story.

"Yeah right. You know how it is around here. Sometimes we forget we aren't supposed to talk to them," she sighed. "This Congressman Condit story is the talk of the Capitol. What do you believe happened to Chandra? Do you think Condit...."

"Chandra? Condit?" I questioned not knowing what she was talking about.

"Girl, where have you been?" she chided.

"Laying by the pool," I boasted. "You know I don't listen to the news anymore. It's too much like a soap opera for me. The suds build as the story line gets bigger."

I watched her give out a hearty chuckle. "But, Jan, this is big news," she offered trying to regain composure. "They claim Condit was seeing an intern that has disappeared. If you get a chance, look at his horoscope. Let me know if you see anything interesting."

I thought back to the days of the 'Gang of Five' when I had first seen Condit's astrology chart. My heart tightened at the thought of another intern story. For a moment I remembered Monica and President Clinton and how the public was so shocked when they learned what had happened between them. Then I wondered what would happen if people knew my story and what it was really like working for the Legislature. I was thankful my ex co-worker couldn't hear my thoughts. I nervously glanced up at the clock above the sofa.

"Now, I have got to run or I will be late for lunch," I said rising up from my chair.

"Next time stay awhile," she laughed teased as she got up from the sofa and walked me to the door.

That night when the news came on the Condit and Chandra Levy mystery was the lead story. I walked to the television and turned it off. The conversation I had earlier that afternoon about Condit was still fresh in my mind. Now I found myself relating to Chandra and remembering the days when I worked for the Legislature. In some ways it was an honor for me to witness political giants at work and play, especially since it was during one of the most notorious times in California's political history. However, during the 32 years I served there, sometimes the politicians played too rough, and I still had the scars to show for it.

Quietly, I reached for my diary....

Chapter 1

As a blonde-haired, blue-eyed, little girl of four, I remember the huge fourteen-acre chicken ranch I lived on in El Cajon, California. My home was white and trimmed in blue. The roof was covered with speckled tiny blue and white rocks that glistened in the sun creating the appearance of snow for those approaching it on the dusty road that led up to it.

My father built a cement fishpond under some gigantic oaks in front of our ranch house. It had live water plants that goldfish would hide behind when I tried to reach for them.

Behind the house was a canyon with a stream that flowed during the winter months. This is where my father killed our chickens that we would eat for supper. I still remember him taking the chicken's head and putting it face down through a large silver metal funnel that was nailed to a huge oak tree. Once its neck was stretched, he chopped off its head with an axe. The bird's body would hit the ground and dance all over the place, while red blood squirted out its neck brightly contrasting its white feathers. If we needed beef for our meals, a gunshot would echo through the canyon and somewhere on the property, my dad would be hanging a bull upside down from a tree, getting ready to skin it, gut it, and then cut it up for the freezer.

My favorite place to play and hide on the ranch was inside an enormous cactus patch. There was a secret room inside it for my dolls and storybooks that I carried there. Sometimes my fortress was covered in white flowers that grew into red cactus apples that I could eat if the painful thorns didn't discourage me when I tried to peel the skin. Cactus thorns were what protected me in my hideout from my annoying little potbellied brother who liked to follow me and from what I called the "night people."

1

The "night people" were people who terrified me when I was in bed and it was dark. My father's brother, Uncle Lee Roy, was one of the "night people." Once he came to visit us carrying a big blue stuffed monkey for me. He smiled a lot and looked handsome standing tall in his Army uniform.

That night, after he arrived, I remember lying in bed when someone entered my room. I didn't know who it was. If it were my mommy or daddy they would have turned on the light, but whoever the dark shadow was didn't do that, so I got scared.

"Don't be afraid," a male voice said and I recognized it as Uncle Lee Roy's. Suddenly, my dog King, a beautiful boxer, started barking outside my bedroom window. I remember my dad running into the room, carrying a big shotgun in his hand.

"Don't you ever set foot on this property again," he shouted pointing his gun at my uncle.

Lee Roy ran out the door and I never saw him again.

It would be many years later before I would really understand why I was so terrified of "night people" and why this incident with my uncle never left my memory, even though I didn't remember anything happening. Sometimes the night people were in my imagination when I thought I saw a shadow in the corner of my room moving but didn't, or when I heard the creaky noise a house makes which sometimes sounded like footsteps. However, these night people would appear off and on as I was growing up and each time they would be a male relative or a friend of the family that no one suspected.

When I wasn't hiding out in my fort I found comfort in playing with my dolls. Living on a ranch that had streams and fortresses added charm to the enchanting world I lived in. My dolls were a big part of my magical world. To me they were real and even though I was only a few years old I liked knowing that they needed me to take care of them. Sometimes my dolls "talked" to me and told me not to get frightened when my parents fought. Other times they kept me company and made me feel safe when I lay awake during the night. Now, I believe my imaginary friends were probably spirit guides or angels, that never left me throughout my journey in life, even though I sometimes found people along the path who seemed to sprout wings.

My father was a tall thin Irish farmer with dark wavy hair. He was raised during the depression by my grandmother. She was a woman who ran off with every Bible-carrying preacher man that showed up at the door. Not having much of a home because of it, my dad left home at age twelve, traveled on railroad cars, worked at odd jobs, and took care of himself. He was strong enough to butcher an animal for his family's food but kind-hearted enough to take us all to the drive-in movie and buy us popcorn or take a sticker out of my finger if I ever got hurt. Once, I even saw him take a rabbit out of a gopher snake's mouth in order to save its life. He was an honest man and never did give two cents about what the neighbors thought about us.

My mother, on the other hand, was a beautiful full-faced woman with long auburn hair and emerald green eyes. She also grew up during the time of the depression. As a young girl she and her three sisters always had to hide from their father who was always trying to make sexual advances on them.

One day my grandmother caught her husband getting too close to one of their daughters, and she ran him off the property with a shotgun, much the same as my father did with his brother. Needless to say, I never met my grandfather. This left my grandmother alone, raising four young girls on a hot run-down desert ranch in Imperial, California, which was in the middle of nowhere. All of this trouble caused my mother to carry an emotional suitcase full of clothes stained by poverty and left her with a craving to be seen and admired by everybody she met. This included men and women, even though she didn't trust the men. Her baggage affected me when she insisted that I take accordion lessons when I was only five so she could impress her friends and our relatives with my performances.

One day my parents got into a verbal fight that was worse than any of the others that I used to tune out. This time when my dad ran out the door and slammed it, the whole house shook. Suddenly, my world was crumbling and I didn't know how to fix it. I ran after him. I saw him jump into his red pick-up truck. Then he pealed out of the driveway unaware that he was gouging a wound of abandonment inside me that would never heal.

3

"Daddy," I cried out. "Daddy, don't go," I sobbed, feeling my heart twisting so tight that I thought the pain was going to kill me. The dust must have blinded his rearview mirror because his truck kept going further down the dirt road and no matter how fast I tried to run my legs couldn't catch up with him. Finally, I fell to the ground, legs hurting and sat sobbing as I watched the king of my fantasy world step down from his throne and hand me the job of looking out for my mother and my younger brother at the tender age of five.

Suddenly, I was yanked from my warm familiar fantasy world and put into a cold world that lacked friends, relatives, my dad, and my dog, King. In this case it was Galveston, Texas where my mother packed us up and took us to live. Life in Texas was a nightmare for me. The mosquitoes were so thick that they had to use smoke machines to clear them at the drive-in movies my mother sometimes took my brother and me to. Lightening storms were so violent and loud that they kept me awake at night and terrified by shadows of demons on the wall that seemed to have thunderous voices.

Schools in California were behind in comparison to the schools in Texas. Everyday I was getting sent to the principal's office for stupid stuff such as asking the teacher for a pencil and paper because I didn't bring them to school because my previous school provided them. If my brother wet his pants, which happened frequently since my parents separated, I was the one who got called into the principal's office. Once there, I was firmly told to take my little brother home, but first the principal would look me straight in the eyes and ask me if there was someone at home to take care of us until my mother came home from work.

While my father taught me the importance of my word and told me not to ever lie, my mother let me know under no uncertain terms, I was never to tell the school, or anyone for that matter, that my brother and I were home alone. She told me there wasn't much money and for me to just pretend there was a babysitter. So, I would lie to the principal and feel humiliated and ashamed as I walked my brother home. Once there, I didn't answer the phone or the door until my mother arrived. I hated the lies and the secrets, but it seemed I had no choice if I didn't want to get punished, which was also true later in life.

Then one day my father showed up unexpectedly to make amends with my mother. This may have been one of the happiest days of my life. I remember we all went out to dinner that night celebrated. Now we were a family again. My brother and I played in the back seat of the car as we left Texas and headed for California.

My father had purchased two duplexes that were like two homes connected in the middle. He moved us into one side of the one that faced the street. It wasn't the same as the ranch I remembered and to this day I have no idea what happened to King because I never saw him again.

Once we were settled, my parents got in yet another fight. This time when my dad stormed out of the house, I ran over to the couch and stood on it as I pulled back the curtain so I could see him out the window. There was an attractive petite woman with short black wavy hair sitting on the passenger's side of the car. She said something to my father when he climbed into it; then she turned and our eyes met. I watched the car take off down the road until it disappeared around the corner. When my father walked out on us the second time, it did many things to my childhood. It left the gate open to allow my hardest teachers entrance into my world.

One of the first men to arrive on the scene that would make a lasting impression on me was my stepfather, Ed. He was a tall lanky Czechoslovakian Naval Chief Warrant Officer. He had dull black wavy hair that he combed back and let fall into a slight bang on the side of his face. I only met him once when he treated my mother and us kids to a movie. The next time we met, he was returning from their honeymoon in Reno, Nevada. My brother and I stayed with a babysitter until he and my mother came to get us. When they arrived, my mother had popcorn Easter bunnies and a straw basket filled with brightly colored candy eggs for each of us. We quietly sat in the back of his station wagon, holding onto our goodies, while I wondered what life was going to be like now.

When we drove up in front of our new home, my eyes bulged out and my mouth dropped. It was a lovely green house that he had built on two lots. A cyclone fence surrounded the property and white lilies grew along the front of it. Ed jumped out of the car and opened a second gate so he could drive up to the garage and park along the side of the house.

5

I thought this tall stranger was going to make a great stepfather until I mispronounced his last name and he swung back his arm and backhanded me across the face when I got out of the car. My mother didn't say a word. Instead, she pretended it didn't happen even though I looked to her for help as tears swelled up in my eyes. I never cried when we left the ranch or when my father walked out on us the second time, but now it was hard to hold back the tears.

Ed treated my brother and me like military recruits in boot camp. We were to rise at a certain time every day, take a quick rinse off in the tub that didn't last more than three minutes, and then hurry to the breakfast table where we weren't allowed to speak. Before going to sleep every night, we had to say our prayers to God with him. This practice created a serious conflict within me spiritually since I felt this man was the devil himself.

My stepfather did everything possible to make sure our life was pure hell. He swore like a sailor but if we repeated a slang word we heard him say, our allowance of one quarter for the week was taken away. Saturday mornings when other kids headed for the beach, which was only a block away, we were required to sit along the fence with scissors and trim the tall blades of grass the lawn mower couldn't reach. Then we had to clean our rooms and spend an hour practicing music on our accordions that my mother taught us to play.

The community saw my family as a role model, the epitome of the perfect one. We were well dressed, well behaved, and well fed. In public we smiled and kept up the pretense but in private, my mother mended clothes and babysat to make extra money to make sure we had nice clothes. My stepfather's name appeared in the society column of the newspaper whenever we played our accordions at a social club or if someone from out of town came to visit us.

By the time I was a teenager, the house I lived in was a prison cell, and my stepfather was the warden. It got so bad that when I turned fourteen, I started climbing out the window at night to go see an older boy I was dating from school who would meet me in his car around the corner. I remember how my heart pounded each time I slipped through the cyclone-fenced gate because I knew my stepfather would lose his temper and kill me if he ever caught me. Once free, my boyfriend and I would go to the beach and make out for hours. I loved listening to the waves crashing and feeling our hot bodies snuggled up next to each other for protection from the crispy-cold ocean breeze, while music played on the radio.

It seemed I was living a double life, one in which I dated and one where I kept up appearances for my mother who was busy keeping up appearances for the neighbors. Part of doing that meant constantly being on a diet. If I didn't like something on the table, Ed made me eat twice as much. If my mother knew I liked what was on the table, she restricted my serving so I wouldn't get fat and embarrass her

From my formative years with my mother, which included a father walking out and a wicked stepfather walking in, I walked away knowing how to carry myself before the public. It also caused me to be highly tolerant of unacceptable behavior and that's what prepared me for the jobs waiting for me further down the road.

Though my journey in life began at birth, my spiritual consciousness wasn't aroused until I turned fourteen years old. It was then that my stepfather and my mom took us kids to see a movie called _Exodus_. It was about how badly the Jewish people had been treated by the Germans under Hitler's dictatorship. Never before had I seen such brutality from one human being to another.

I couldn't get the movie out of my mind. Other kids were at the beach having fun. Instead I found myself reading several books about the Holocaust, such as Hitler's book, _**Mein Kompf**_, and a book that told the story of Eichmann, a man responsible for murdering four million Jews. The book on Eichmann had black and white pictures in it that showed hundreds of people lined up to take showers. Mounds of dead bodies looked like they would have died of starvation if the gas from the showers didn't kill them. Shoes were piled high and so were the eyeglasses that had been confiscated from the victims.

My world felt like it had cracked wide-open exposing hundreds of questions with nowhere to turn for an answer. Sometimes I would ask my history teacher a question about what I was reading. But the question to which I couldn't find an answer, the one that triggered a spiritual search that would last a lifetime, was the one that asked why such cruelty existed in our world.

That was when I discovered one of my greatest tools in life. It happened one day when I walked into my mother's bedroom and sat on the floor pondering through her books that were on a wooden shelf beneath her television set. A red book, *Astrology for the Millions,* by Grant Lewi caught my eyes. Page after page unveiled a subject about which I had never heard before. Grant Lewi observed that the time a person is born is significant because it shows where all the planets were in the sky at that time and these placements would affect that person's personality and what he or she would experience during his or her lifetime. For example, if a person were born in the middle of August, his or her Sun sign was Leo because that is where the Sun was in the zodiac of the heavens at that time. This astrological placement would instill in that person's personality great leadership qualities, pride, and a need to be seen and loved by others.

It didn't just talk about the importance of where the Sun was. It talked about the position of the Moon, which changes signs every two-and-one-half-days. Its position in the zodiac shows the hidden side of every individual. Maybe an individual is born with her Sun in Leo, which causes her to crave the limelight, but if her Moon were in Cancer, symbolized by the crab, the person would also want to hide from all the attention she craved without knowing why. Retreating is what the crab on the ocean does when it hides in the sand or in its own shell if we get too close to it. If another planet were in Cancer, like Mars, a forceful planet, she would hold her anger in.

Soon I was having fun reading every book on astrology I could find. I learned that the position of Venus in the zodiac at birth showed me characteristics about the individual's love life. People born with Venus in Pisces are very compassionate. It is an ideal aspect for people who are nurses and care givers but it sometimes creates problems when they fall in love with someone because they see a weakness that they think they can fix. However, if Venus were in Aries these people would fall in love quickly and be very passionate but most of the time the romance wouldn't last. Venus in Taurus is different; it causes delays because these individuals want to be sure of themselves before they willingly give their heart away. This is why their relationships always last longer. By nature,

Venus in Taurus likes expensive things like nice jewelry, expensive cars, or a beautiful home.

Suddenly, it was as if an angel had handed me a velvet pouch full of stars to carry with me on my path in life. Up until now, I had been living in an insane world. My new knowledge on astrology gave me a second set of eyes that removed the masks that people wore. It also blessed me with straight "A's" in speech class whenever I got up before the students and gave a speech on it. They didn't know for sure what I was talking about, but they liked hearing about themselves and always wanted to know more.

Now I realized that my stepfather was a Scorpio like I was, so that was why everything he did felt as if I was getting stung. The Scorpion in the zodiac symbolizes Scorpio and it's known to have a stinger-like way of retaliating at real or imagined offenses. My boyfriend at the time, Bill, was an Aries. In astrology, the planet Mars, known as the god of war, rules the sign Aries. This explained Bill's attraction to the neighborhood gangs, fast motorcycles, and why he had a hot temper.

Being the Scorpion, I was probably had a lot to do with my finally rebelling against my life when I turned 17. I picked a powerful way to get even with my mom and stepfather for all the years I had been so suppressed and unhappy. When my brother and I went to visit my dad and stepmother on their ranch in Oregon, I begged my father to give his consent for me to marry Bill so I could leave home. He reminded me that I was a minor and refused to go against my mother. The next day, when I found him on the east forty chopping firewood, I handed him a letter my mother had sent me saying she hoped I was having a good time. She went on to say what a bitch my stepmother was for stealing my father away from us. My dad never said an unkind word about my mother, but this was all it took to get him to sign the papers.

What no one knew is that every night when I was back home, I would sneak clothes out of the house and take them to Bill when he met me around the corner in his car. My drawers were all empty and so was the closet.

Bill and I were secretly married in Ventura at his grandparent's home with many of his relatives present. I didn't have any friends or family there. It was a simple ceremony that took place by a waterfall in the back yard and I wore a beige corduroy suit. A couple of weeks later, I called my mom and told her we had gotten married. She was both furious and heartbroken.

For me, marriage was like playing house. Eight months and three weeks after we were married my son William was born. I loved dressing him up like a little doll in clothes the family gave us. The following year my son Jeff was born. Both boys were darling with their blond-hair, fair skin, and playful smiles. My mother adored the children and so did Bill's mother. Each one took turn lavishing the boys with gifts and affection.

However, my husband and I were too young. Instead of going to the movies or out to dinner once in awhile, all we did is argue about bills we couldn't afford. It wasn't long before our marriage fell apart and ended in a divorce. This made me wonder if my mother knew something I didn't when she begged me not to get serious about Bill, or anyone, while I was so young.

Chapter 2

While at first I felt a little guilty about leaving my husband, I soon realized that I preferred my freedom. However, my divorce didn't make life easier for me. Instead, it landed me on welfare and going to night school to make up two years I missed in high school. It wasn't easy because I had two toddlers that had to go to a babysitter every morning. Then I raced off to a welfare-training program at the Economic Opportunity Center (EOC) where I worked during the day. In the evenings I picked up my boys, fixed them dinner and then took them back to the babysitter so I could go to night school to get my high school diploma. My lunch hours were spent doing homework from the night before.

Once again, I was confronted with a principal who called me into his office to talk to me. He was upset because I was moving too fast through the system, even though I was making outstanding grades. When he explained "the state was paying the school to teach me, therefore, I needed to take my time," I retorted that the state was paying me as well and I needed to hurry up and get off welfare. My defense left him speechless and he conceded to let me study at my own pace as long as I kept my grades up.

At the EOC I was to learning how to work in an office, so that I could get a real job. The County Welfare Department paid me one dollar a day towards lunch for being on their work program. It was only a matter of weeks before the people for whom I was working at the Center noticed the quality of the work I was doing in their office, so they assigned me the responsibility of doctoring up statistical reports for them.

Apparently, the center had to justify its existence and the government required them to turn in tallies of their work each month. I would watch staff from the Crisis Center within EOC leave the office and go door to door in the community looking for a crisis. As I filed papers away, I saw the salaries of the people running the Center and realized how important it was for them to find a crisis in order to keep their jobs and high paying

11

salaries. If someone came in off the street needing change for a newspaper, I was told to mark down that I helped someone look for work.

What I enjoyed at EOC the most was a man named Victor who said he was born in Haiti. He was a dark-skinned man who stood over six feet tall. Victor told me that he had realized his life long dream when he became a Catholic priest, but that life wasn't what he had expected it to be. He loved people and listening to their confessions, but the church frowned on him getting too closely involved with his congregation, so they would transfer him to a different church every time he became too popular. When his superiors realized that he enjoyed listening to confessions and helping people, they told him he couldn't do confessions anymore. Finally, he left the church feeling disillusioned.

Victor told me what it was like when he lived in Haiti. I sat on the edge of my seat listening while he talked about the witch doctors practicing voodoo. He said he saw many things happen that most people wouldn't believe.

One of Victor's stories was about a young man who went to a witch doctor to get help passing an exam. The witch doctor agreed to help him. The young man was having a lot of trouble with his studies but didn't want to work at improving himself. When it came time to take his tests, he passed. Of course, the young man was quite pleased and a bit smug about it all – never knowing what the witch doctor had done to help him. A few days later, however, a car that hit him killed him while he was crossing the street.

I gasped, speechless, with my eyes wide open.

"You pay-to-play in this world. The man got his wish about the exam but it had a price tag – his life," Victor said smugly looking straight into my blue eyes with his dark brown eyes. "Of course, it was also the man's karma to get hit by the car."

"What is karma?" I dared to ask.

"It is the law of cause and effect that travels with us from one life to another until our actions make restitution for something we once did."

"Then you think we've lived before?" I asked.

"Of course, my child," he said with a smile.

I immediately excused myself from Victor's office and went back to my desk where I sat quietly all morning thinking about what he had said. Later, a phone call came in while Victor was out to lunch. When he walked past my desk I deliberately didn't hand him the message, so I could deliver it to him personally in his office.

"You came back for more stories?" Victor teased as he looked up at me from his desk.

"A call came in for you while you were at lunch and I just wanted to make sure that you got it," I said trying to keep a straight face as I handed him a pink slip of paper.

"Thank you," he replied reading the message.

"But while I am here," I added boldly trying to get his attention.

Victor looked up and smiled. "Yes?"

"I have to know something. Why did it work?"

"Why did what work?" he asked puzzled.

"Why did the Voodoo work?"

"Let's see if I have this right. You bring me a phone message in one hand and then simply ask a question that sages haven't been able to answer for centuries and expect me to have an answer?" He laughed.

"Seriously, you were there. What made it work?" I begged.

"Energy makes everything work. The intent of the witch-doctor is one part of it," he answered softly.

"What do you mean by intent?" I asked spellbound by his every word.

"Intent is powerful. The intent is the end purpose or goal you seek. The witch-doctor simply activated energies necessary to manifest in reality what the young man needed done but couldn't do for himself."

"I don't understand any of that. It's mumbo jumbo," I frowned.

Victor laughed even louder at me, causing my supervisor to look into the room as she walked by.

"What don't you understand?" he asked, lowering his voice in a serious tone.

"The witch-doctor activated what energy?" I asked desperately.

"It's so much more complicated than poor Victor can explain," he grinned. "Hmmm, well, let's think of it this way. There are realms within realms in our Universe, all controlled by energy and energetic forces. It took many things to make the Voodoo spell work."

"What kind of things? That's mumbo jumbo again," I snapped frustrated.

"Let's see," Victor looked up to the ceiling for a moment then looked straight into my eyes. "The witch doctor was trained to focus the powerful energy of his thoughts on one end and one goal. When the young man came to him asking for his help, the young man gave the witch doctor his own power or energy. This made the energy of the witch doctor even stronger. Then the one thing that could have made that energy even more powerful was if the witch doctor didn't do what you call 'mumbo jumbo' with a bunch of words but actually visualized in his mind a picture of what he wanted. Then he could put the strength of his energy and the energy the young man gave him onto that picture until it exploded into an action which was the desired result in the physical world."

I sat there speechless. Victor was speechless too. We just stared quietly at each other for a moment.

"Energy is that powerful and that easy to use and access?" I whispered still in distant thought.

"Sounds simple but it's not that easy. Yet, all things go philosophically around the Universe and come back to that one simple fact. Whether you are a witch working with a spell or a minister doing faith healing, you are combining energetic forces and beliefs that can create results and each one will believe that theirs is the only one that works. Each one will believe theirs was done for a good cause."

"So, can we use the energy to heal?" I asked.

"Oh, yes. Also, remember that things contain the energy they are given from their inception unless that energy is changed."

"What do you mean?" I asked intently. "How does that relate to healing?"

"I visited New Orleans once. I talked to some people there who told me many stories of people practicing what we have been talking about. But one story that was fascinating was the story of a baby who was deathly ill. The small child was just old enough to stand in his crib. Doctors didn't know what was wrong with the toddler who was burning up with a fever. The child kept pointing to a corner of the room where there was an old empty hive that wasps had made out of mud. The father reached for it and handed it to the child. The boy ate it, mud and all, and got well. The energy of the wasps was still in it and this supplied the boy with whatever he needed and helped him get well."

"I have never heard such stories as that before." I paused for a moment. "Why does everyone think that theirs is the only religion that is right?" I asked.

"Their consciousness is limited to what they believe in and you, my dear little one, ask far too many questions."

"Thank you, Victor," I smiled affectionately knowing he had work to do and that my time with him was up.

"You have a hungry mind, little one," he cautioned. "Just make sure that it never takes a bite out of you. We can get lost in our intellects. Don't make that mistake."

"Yips," I thought to myself. "What if Victor opened a door to me that held demons and devils and blood and...." I scrambled out of his office lickety-split, hearing his laughter trailing behind me as I hurried back to my desk for safety.

I was being shown a world I never knew existed. Somewhere in the Universe there were forces that affected us, forces that could be manipulated or forces over which we didn't always have control, and my new love for astrology had something to do with it.

It wasn't long before I left EOC to take a different training job. The Welfare Department reassigned me to a local legislator's district office. It was 1967, and Ronald Reagan was in the Governor's office. He had been elected Governor of California by a margin of a million votes in 1966; he was re-elected in 1970. Little did I know then that my "training" programs would lead me to cross paths with this future president and lead me into the dazzling world of political smoke and mirrors.

All I really knew back then was that it was exciting to be asked to work in the political arena, even if it was only in a member's district office. Now, my salary was going to be increased to two dollars a day for lunch. Nonetheless, I never wanted to stay on welfare and was probably one of the few people who used it in a way it was originally intended.

15

One thing that happened about the same time I went to work in the members' district office is that I came across the name of an astrologer who was listed in the phone book and doing business close to where I lived. Her name was Dawn. I decided to order my astrology chart from her since I had read so many books on the subject but had never seen a chart. I really wanted to know where all my planets were when I was born and what she thought their placements meant.

When the chart I ordered arrived in the mail, I was glued to every word. It said I loved to study philosophy and religion because my Mercury and Venus were in Sagittarius, which also meant a lot of travel during my lifetime. I would attract attention before the public, but I would have problems with children, pets, and loved ones unless I learned patience because my karma in those areas was carried over from one of my previous lifetimes. High honors were also shown to be ahead for me due to the position of Jupiter and the Sun when I was born. The report went on to say that I loved my freedom and would be interested in astrology and other metaphysical studies because my Moon was in Aquarius. The chart seemed to know more about me than I did. It nailed me.

Impressed with my chart, my mom asked me to order a chart for my stepfather and her, so I did. Then I went to see Dawn one evening to pick the horoscopes up. As I drove there I wondered what an astrologer looked like. Dawn had short auburn hair and was a rather large woman in her late fifties. She was attired in a long black skirt and a long flowing silk blouse that covered her large breasts. Her home was beautiful and she had a servant to wait on her. She looked like a typical upper middle class woman, but when she talked the words that came out of her mouth were strange to my ears, stuff about lions appearing at her feet and visitations by aliens from outer space.

I decided I loved the astrology charts, but I thought she was nuts. However, I did notice a book that was sitting close to her that she seemed to refer to a lot. It was called, ***The A to Z Horoscope Delineator***. When I left her home, I went out and bought it. Then I noticed everything I had read in the astrology reports I had ordered from Dawn had been copied out of the book. Whenever I wasn't working, I found myself reading it.

Life was exciting working in the political world. Constituents called all the time voicing their concerns about government. Sometimes they called because they needed help unraveling the inevitable government red tape. We had a vivacious young man working as the administrative assistant to whom we referred all of the constituent calls. He was tall, dark-haired, and very handsome.

I also worked with Katie, a large framed, middle-aged woman with short red hair who was the legislative secretary. She taught me everything I needed to know.

"Jan, if the press calls I don't want you answering any of their questions. Forward those calls to the administrative assistant. If the boss is in town, don't give the calls to him until his assistant talks to the reporter first and sees what they want," cautioned Katie.

"Why's that?" I asked innocently.

"Because they twist the things you say around and then say the legislator said it," she answered adamantly with a stern look on her face.

"Thank you for warning me," I said while slitting open another envelope from a stack of mail sitting on my desk.

I knew Katie wasn't upset with me because we became friends right away, especially when I said I was studying astrology. I was able to tell her a lot of things about her personality. She was a Gemini. They are all restless and intellectually curious about everything and love to gossip. They epitomize the phrase, "jack-of-all trades but the master of none."

Katie liked me so well that sometimes she closed down the office and we took off for the horse races. That was always more fun than working but we had to make sure the boss wasn't going to be in town. His schedule was fairly easy to figure out. He flew into town late on Thursdays then flew back to Sacramento every Monday morning. So, at the end of the week we had a lot of freedom to talk and go to lunch together.

I always felt nervous whenever our boss called to talk to a member of his staff. Part of my nervousness was because I knew that he was calling from the State Capitol building. I knew what he looked like because one of my jobs was to cut stories about him out of our local newspaper. Often times his picture was in the article but I still wanted to know what he looked like in person. Then one day I finally got to see him.

17

He wore expensive tailored suits with nice ties. His wavy brown hair was combed back. Everyone wanted to see him or talk to him on the phone. He carried a white three-by-five card inside his coat jacket that told him where he was supposed to be at all times. I knew this because sometimes I helped Katie type it up.

One morning he called me into his office. He was sitting behind his big wooden desk. By the way he was eyeing me, I knew he was very pleased with what he was seeing.

"Have a seat," he grandly gestured with his hand to the seat across from his desk.

"Thank you," I smiled, sitting down.

"How do you like your job so far?" he asked.

"I like it a lot," I answered, smiling broadly. "It is interesting and exciting work."

"How much do you make working here?" he boldly questioned.

"Two dollars a day for lunch," I mumbled, feeling embarrassed.

"I think you are worth a lot more than that," he smiled. "How would you like to go to work in the State Capitol building?"

"Well, I don't know what to say... Sacramento? You want me to work in Sacramento?" I stammered with brightly-lit eyes.

"Yes. Go to work in Sacramento. Would you like that?" he asked with sparkling brown eyes.

"But how will I...?"

"Don't worry about all the details just yet," he interrupted. "I have already talked to the Chief of Personnel in the Capitol. You need to set up an appointment with the employment office downtown. Once you pass the typing test, you need to fill out some forms and then you will be on board. It's as simple as that," he explained.

"Oh, thank you, sir," I grinned from ear to ear. "How can I ever thank you?"

"It's not necessary. We all appreciate the work you have done here," he answered standing up to escort me out of his office.

That night when I went to pick up my two sons I was overjoyed until I got home. Tacked to my front door was a notice from Edison, my electric company. My electricity had been shut off for non-payment and wouldn't be turned back on until I went down to their office and paid the bill in person with cash.

I opened the door, letting Billy, then Jeff, go in first. I walked over to the phone and called my mother.

"Hi mom," I grumbled softly when she answered.

"What's wrong? You sound upset," she coaxed.

"I need help. The Electricity Company shut off all the power and I can't cook and it's going to be dark pretty soon. They close in about 30 minutes. Do you think you could help me out with the money? I'll pay you back on the first when I get my welfare check," I pleaded.

"Well, I don't have a lot of..."

"Oh, I forgot to tell you that the legislator I have been working for offered me a job working at the State Capitol building," I interrupted with excitement.

"Are you serious?" she replied with enthusiasm. "Come right over. I will take you down personally to get that electricity bill paid," she said. "Hurry before they close."

With that paid and out of the way, I was free to concentrate on the typing test, which was not as easy to pass as I first thought it would be. Driving downtown from the neighboring city where I lived made me nervous, especially since I had to get my sons ready and off to a babysitter first. I was also nervous thinking about what my life was going to be like when I did pass it.

"How's your test coming?" my good-looking boss asked one morning when he passed my desk walking towards his office.

"I've gone down there a couple of times to take the test, but each time I was too nervous to pass it because I have had to fight traffic and I just got my driver's license," I said disappointedly.

"When are you scheduled to take it again?" he asked.

"In two weeks," I answered.

"Well, keep trying," he said looking back before disappearing into his office and closing the door.

I didn't think any more about our conversation until I went to take the typing test again at the State Unemployment Office like I had several times before. Only this time something different happened.

19

Several people were gathered about waiting to take the typing test when I arrived.

A woman walked out of the testing room and looked around. "Is there a Janice Stork here?" she asked.

"Good. You stay here and wait. Would everyone else please follow me?" she announced before leaving the testing room.

"Why was I singled out?" I wondered as I waited. "I need to take the test too."

Ten minutes later everyone who went in to take a test started coming out of the room and racing past me to leave.

The woman administering the test returned and looked at me with a smile.

"Please come with me," she said before turning to lead the way back into the empty room.

"I don't understand," I said with a puzzled look.

"Someone called from the State Capitol. They said you are to take the typing test until you pass it, so I am going to give it to you. If you fail it, I have instructions to give it to you again... and again. You aren't leaving here until you pass it," she explained. That day I learned the power of the Legislature. With one simple phone call, I was suddenly given an opportunity others never even knew existed.

"Wow," I thought as I made myself comfortable at the typewriter.

"This is a five minute test. You may start now," the lady said clicking her stopwatch before sitting down to wait.

"Ring," went the bell, bringing me out of deep concentration.

"You may stop now. Bring me your test and wait while I grade it. You need to type 55 words a minute after all errors have been subtracted."

"Okay," I said hoping I didn't have to take it again.

I watched quietly as she graded my paper. I saw her mark an error, then another and still another. Then she looked at me almost in horror.

"What's wrong? Did I fail it?" I sighed.

"You typed 75 words a minute with only three errors. I will have to double check this score."

I could tell she was very nervous. Apparently, she didn't expect me to type that fast, especially since I had failed it so many times before.

Instead of needing to help me, I flew through it and got an embarrassingly high grade because I wasn't nervous.

"It's correct. You typed 75 words a minute. Congratulations, you passed the test and may leave now," she smiled. "I wonder why on earth anyone would think that we needed to help you? You did just fine – in fact, better than anyone else that took it – all on your own."

That day my life changed. My mother was ecstatic when I told her I passed the test. It did secure me the job in Sacramento. However, a few nights before I was supposed to leave, I stayed awake most of the night thinking about my sons, their father and his incredible family that was so supportive. My future was frightening. I had never been away from home or had a real job. I didn't know what dragons waited so far away in a land called Sacramento and I was still a minor.

It was then that I made a decision that would haunt me for the rest of my life. After only six months since our divorce, my ex-husband, Bill, had already found someone he wanted to marry someone that his family had liked and known for years. I remember sitting in the kitchen with a photograph album, staring at picture after picture of Bill's enormous family. I knew my ex-husband would have lots support that I wasn't going to have when I moved.

It was then that I decided to let our oldest son, Billy, stay and live with his father, while Jeff came with me to Sacramento. Agonizing over the decision, I finally called my ex-husband and asked him about it. He agreed with my decision and said Bill could come and live with him.

No one could see the tears I was hiding, but I knew Billy would be safe as I watched his father put him in his car and drive off. Quietly, I packed up Jeff and drove to Sacramento.

Chapter 3

Everything I saw and experienced when I went to work in the State Capitol was foreign to me. I had outstanding grades in civics in school, but none of it applied once I stepped into the political arena. For example, in a district office a secretary spends their time answering calls from constituents, writing letters, tracking the boss' legislation and cutting out newspaper clippings. In a district, one thinks that is what they do in Sacramento. But working in a member's Capitol office was a lot more glamorous than I ever imagined.

My job with the Assembly was working in a secretarial unit where my supervisor assigned me to different legislative offices that were short-handed. Going in and out of offices throughout the building let me see what was really going on. While district staff worked directly with constituents and tried to keep them content, the staff in Sacramento worked with powerful lobbyists who brought us boxes of candy and took us out to lunch in exchange for getting in to see our boss on some bill they were interested in for their clients.

Despite the fact that I knew absolutely nothing about politics, suddenly I could see everything that my mother had taught me coming into play, including my playing the accordion before large numbers of people at age five. Even the make-up lessons and insistence on how I dressed helped me enormously, even though a part of me still felt insecure and out of place.

I didn't know anyone in Sacramento but all its trees impressed me. In the evenings I could see the State Capitol building from most of the freeways surrounding the downtown area. Lights helped silhouette the majestic white building against the night sky sprinkled with tiny twinkling stars. It reminded me of an enormous white wedding cake and I was proud my fate had served me a piece of it every time I saw it.

With each month that passed, I was beginning to see the mystique of the powerful energy that flows through the Capitol halls and draws to it any souls needing external validation from it. I noticed that once a member was voted into office by over 400,000 constituents, which was the case with the Assembly, a peculiar kind of schizophrenia sometimes developed in the member's personality, where they presented one face for the public and yet another for staff.

Immediately after smiling for the cameras, or greeting groups of constituents on the Capitol steps, some members of the Legislature frequently retired to their offices where they sometimes verbally abused staffs for any of a variety of offenses. In a classic example, most members pulled rank by snapping at staff for not recognizing other members on the phone when they called. The members didn't say whom they were when they asked to talk to our boss, but resented it when we questioned who was calling. It didn't happen often, but when it did, my heart pounded for fear of losing my job. It was a strange world in which to find myself.

In still another incident, one day I was waiting a long time for an elevator. Suddenly, a prestigious member of the Legislature raced toward the door as it opened. "But it is going the wrong way," said the well-dressed gentleman following him. "It's not now," said the member when he got on, knowing the elevator operator would immediately change the direction it was going in or else risk losing her job. She looked at me apologetically, knowing that I was the one who had pressed the button that had called her. During such times you learned to roll with the punches.

Meanwhile at home, I was getting heavy lessons from the Universe on what it was like being a single mother who had to work. Evenings were spent at the local Laundromat, washing and drying clothes or else grocery shopping. After paying for a babysitter there was little money left for food and rent, so I didn't spend extra money on a nighttime babysitter or go to parties like other people my age did. Instead I just stayed home and played with Jeff and read my astrology books after he went to bed.

Slowly I was learning that studying planetary placements at birth revealed a star map of our life on Earth. I was born with Saturn conjunct

Pluto in my 10th house in the sign of Leo. My karma, shown by Saturn, was my children, loved ones and my father who left me as a child. It was also my work that would cause me to sacrifice my home life for it more than once. The Moon, a planet that changes signs every two-and-a-half days was locked into these two slow-moving planets, Saturn taking twenty-eight-and-a-half years to complete its orbit through the zodiac and Pluto that takes approximately 248 years. This combination explained my difficult birth when I struggled to be born to my mother who was suddenly paralyzed on her right side.

Digging deeper into the subject I learned if a transiting planet hit this grouping of natal planets that I had, it felt like solitary confinement until the hovering planet moved out of aspect. I would suffer from this astrological checkmate my whole life in seven-year increments, lasting a year to eighteen months each time it happened. Texas was my first incident. That is the state my mother took my brother and I to live when she and my father got a divorce until we later returned to California. Another similar planetary pattern occurred when I was a teenager facing a spiritual crisis. Later, it happened when I filed for a divorce, which left me alone raising my sons and trying to go to school while also working.

My mother was a perfect teacher for me because she made me feel the burden of these planets without my knowing anything about astrology. For example, I truly believe what made raising children so difficult for me was watching how my mother raised me. If the doorbell rang when I was little, my mother would panic while she hurried to clean up the house or put on make-up so everything would be presentable when she answered it. "What would people say?" was the constant question that she asked, and somehow it became my question too.

It was all about what other people thought, so much so that I couldn't claim an identity of my own. If my son sucked on a pacifier I felt as if people were actually scolding me with their eyes as they smiled and said what a cute baby he was. Somehow it seemed mandatory that a child say at least one word and take his first step by age one. Everywhere I turned I felt my mother's eyes watching me, and when I didn't feel hers, I could feel other people's as guilt always set in to suggest that I might be doing something wrong as a mother.

But despite all the guilt, I was learning some powerful spiritual tools. Sometimes, today, people ask me when it was that I first started hearing spirit guides talk to me. It began back in 1968, which was over 30 years go. I remember because one morning I dropped Jeff off at the babysitter's house. I had driven a mile down the road when it started raining outside.

"Roll down the window," I heard a soft voice in my mind say.

"It's raining outside. People will think I am nuts and I will get wet," I reasoned, not really knowing with whom I was carrying on a conversation.

"Roll the window down and feel the cool fresh air," it said gently.

I rolled the window down. One block later a diesel Peterbuilt truck slammed into me while I was making a right hand turn. It tore off my rearview mirror and badly smashed in the side of the car where I was sitting. Had the window been up, the shattered glass would have badly cut my face. I was pretty shaken up but still tried to go to work. At work my co-workers warned me that I didn't know how badly hurt I was and they told me to go home. Reluctantly, I went. Sure enough, the next day my neck was frozen in pain. I had suffered a whiplash.

Not too long after that my son, Jeff, got into my purse while I was on the phone and took a handful of the pain pills that had been prescribed for me for the whiplash. Immediately, I rushed him to the hospital where I watched as they pumped his stomach. A few months later he swallowed some cleaning fluid that was under the sink and had to be rushed to the hospital again where the doctor feared he might catch pneumonia from the fumes. Then a few months later he fell off the front porch when he was walking on its cement wall. Fortunately, the padded fur inside the hood on his blue corduroy jacket cushioned the blow. Once again, I rushed him to the hospital emergency room where they took x-rays and said he suffered a mild concussion.

Those incidents only added to the doses of guilt and fear of being an "unfit" mother I already had. To make matters worse, I still hadn't healed yet from the auto accident. For a long time after the accident my neck would freeze up and I would have trouble moving it from side to side. Even back then, I was interested in holistic healing. In order to get back to work, I decided to go see a foot-reflexologist that a friend recommended. A foot reflexologist is someone who treats the body by applying pressure to special centers in the foot. This person was also able to adjust my neck so I could move it again.

Raising my son alone kept me busy after work. Instead of getting better I found myself going to bed exhausted and waking up tired. It was around this time that I convinced myself that it had been a mistake to separate my sons. They had always been close, and I knew that they were both suffering by not being able to live together. My fear of being an unfit mother only played into the situation even more. I was positive that Billy and Jeff's father would be a better parent than what I was. Once again I faced the torment of deciding to give up a child.

"What kind of person are you?" I silently screamed at myself. "How can you do this?" And this was no spirit guide yelling at me; it was me.

Later, I would think, "How can you not do this if it is for the good of the child?" Then I would reason, "Perhaps letting him live with his father will give him the love of a family you never had."

I will never forget the plane trip that would take me to the southern part of the State, with my two-year-old sitting close by. Tears swelled in my eyes. For me, making the decision to let him go was the second most difficult one I ever had to make, Billy was the first. I didn't know where the journey in life was going to take either one of us. I discretely wiped the tears from my eyes so he couldn't see me crying.

In the months that followed I started having nightmares every night about letting both my sons go and doses of guilt from the Universe grew even greater. I knew I had failed as a mother, and I accepted the consequences of what I had done. However, as fate would have it, in time the Universe would show me that it wasn't about to let me get out of any of my karmic lessons that easily.

Suddenly, I found myself single in a world of tinsel and glitter. I focused all of my attention on my job and learning new skills to help me advance in my career. Life in the Legislature was fun especially having just turned twenty-one. I had never dated anyone other than my ex-husband or been to any parties before. Now I went to all of them as if making up for lost time.

Free liquor flowed at gatherings and so did the dinners that lobbyists were willing to pick up the tab on for staff, especially if they were attractive females. I still didn't have much money but fortunately my mother, still married to Ed, loved living her life through me so she handmade all my clothes. Soon I was a social butterfly, holding court at various political functions with men and women who went out of their way to make me feel special while I entertained them with my astrological insights that mesmerized them.

I recall one dinner that was held in the basement cellar of the Firehouse restaurant in Old Sacramento, a place where gangsters once hung out. I was invited to attend because I was helping out the committee secretary who was putting the dinner together. I remember an influential lobbyist walking into our office and asking the attractive blonde woman I was assisting to order whatever she wanted and he would make arrangements to have the tab covered so that the committee chair, her boss, would never see the bill.

At this particular dinner, there were about thirty people seated around the linen-covered table that went from one end of the room to the other. The women wore beautiful dresses and their hairdos were bouffant, which was in style in those days. Dates, husbands, and legislators wore tailored suits and stylish ties.

A waitress from the bar took orders for drinks. While one waiter served dinner, another one walked around the table asking whether we wanted red or white wine. Then he poured us a glass. After the wine had been served, the open bottles were placed on the table so people could freely help themselves to more. I don't remember what was served as the main course, but I do remember the hearts of palm salad, which I had never tasted before. For desert we were all served grasshopper pie, which was the most delicious chilled pie I had ever eaten. It was lime green, made with Creme de Menthe liquor and a chocolate cookie crumb crust. After desert, more wine was served.

I had fun entertaining seatmates by drawing astrology charts in blue ink on small white cocktail napkins. Everyone listened while I told people what I saw about their personalities or future in their charts. They would look surprised and verify what I was saying while at the same time asking how I knew that about them. Then someone else would eagerly yell out a birth date and ask me tell them something about their chart. By the time dinner was finished and all the liquor had been consumed, the planets sometimes looked like they were three dimensional and orbiting around my head.

It wasn't just my astrological skills that were attracting attention now. Members of the opposite sex started chasing after me when I started coming out of the shell I had hidden behind for so long. That is when an attractive blonde secretary for whom I had been working decided to sit me down and talk to me about the birds and bees of the Legislature. The man she talked about that caught my attention the most was Jessie Unruh, the Speaker of the Assembly. That evening I went home and cast his astrology chart so I could learn more about him.

Assemblyman Jessie Unruh was born September 30, 1922 in Newton, Kansas with his Sun in the sign of Libra. As I write this I am looking at the picture that he once gave me. It reads, "To Janice: Who looks at the future, from a friend of the past, Jess Unruh."

On the top of one of the twin state buildings in front of the State Capitol are the words, "Give Me Men to Match My Mountains." Jessie Unruh was such a man. When he walked down the halls of the Capitol, his presence was known, and when he entered a legislator's office, people stopped what they were doing at once to greet him.

I remember the early days when Jess Unruh first arrived on the political scene. He was a big man who swore, told a lot of jokes, and enjoyed eating whatever he wanted. He was so friendly and outgoing that people felt like it was easy to get close to him; in fact, he was fondly known around the Capitol as "Big Daddy." One day he decided to clean up his act and went on a diet of nothing but steak and salad. He lost a lot of weight, but his personality changed with it. It was never as easy to get close to him after that. He was born with his Moon in Aquarius, which told me he had numerous friends but loved his freedom so much that he was actually close to very few people. This planetary placement would also make him independent but a good humanitarian.

When the secretary for whom I had been working told me about the sex life of the Legislature, she warned me to watch out for Jess. I asked why and she said he had been keeping a scorecard on the number of women with whom he slept that worked in the building. As an astrologer I could see from his planets that he was a die-hard romantic, but the placement of his Venus in Scorpio told me he was probably an insatiably sex-driven sensationalist behind closed doors. For certain, he was definitely a charmer. This caused me to seek out even more information on him.

Jess Unruh grew up in poverty in Texas and was the youngest of four siblings. He often referred to the economic difficulties he witnessed having been raised during the depression. He served in the Navy in World War II, and then he came to California where he finished his studies at the University of Southern California. He ran for office in the State Assembly the same year he graduated, but it wasn't until he ran again in 1954 that he won the election to the State Assembly.

As a politician, he was downright shrewd. Upon coming to work in the Legislature, he chose to listen and learn until he had something to say. Once he did have something to say you had to just get out of his way. Eventually, as Speaker of the Assembly he became one of the most powerful political figures in the State of California, second only to the Governor.

I understood how Unruh was a force to be reckoned with both in and out of the Legislature. From an astrological standpoint, I could see Mars opposed to Pluto, which squared Saturn in his natal chart, all three major malefic planets, which created a forceful personality. A voter would have had to have been hesitant to vote for Unruh because she wouldn't have known if Jess's political force was going to make the State or break it.

As for me, I made sure I gave him a wide berth. It was around this time that I began to date a married legislator whom I will call Mark. He had been interested in me for several months. At first, our encounters were innocent enough – a lunch here, a dinner there. So many men were chasing after me and pressuring me to go out with them that oddly enough, he seemed like the safest. He was always concerned how I was doing on the job and conversations with him over dinner were delightful.

Soon our times together occurred more and more often. Eventually, it became clear that we were actually getting involved romantically with each other. I remember one evening when we were having dinner at the Neptune's Table. Jess came up to the table and Mark introduced me to him. Jess smiled when he looked at me and took my hand to kiss it. For a moment I sensed from his eyes that he approved of Mark's date. When he excused himself to leave, I watched him disappear to a nearby bar where lobbyists flocked around him as if he was their best friend. Each one fought over who would buy him the next drink.

I asked Mark about Unruh. Then the conversation turned to some of the duties the Speaker of the Assembly has. I was fascinated when he said that sometimes the Speaker had to call a member back to session who had left it if a vote was needed. He said on one occasion that the Sergeant-at-Arms was asked to call a member's home to find him. When he did the member's wife said her husband was at the State Capitol, but he wasn't. The Sergeant-at-Arms tracked the missing member down and found him on a boat on the Delta with his girlfriend. The missing legislator was quickly, but secretly, escorted back to the chambers. Mark laughed when he finished the story and so did I. Then he took my hand and held it near the flickering candlelight as we waited for our dinner to be served.

I thought of our conversation that night much later in my career when someone I was working for was in the hospital. The Sergeant-at-Arms called our office looking for him. I said that he was in the hospital. The Speaker immediately ordered that he be taken by ambulance from the hospital to the airport where he was put on a plane headed for Sacramento. He voted on the bill and was flown immediately back to his district where he was transported back to the hospital. That was the kind of power the Speaker, and the demands of the Legislature, had over a member's life.

At one time when lobbyists wanted to help a member, they gave the money directly to that member. When Unruh became the Speaker of the Assembly, the lobbyists gave him the money instead. Then the Speaker would dole out the money to each member, which kept him or her beholden to him. He was still doing this when he became State Treasurer. On July 13, 1986, Paul Jacobs reported in the *Los Angeles Times* that Unruh transferred $200,000 from his campaign coffers to other campaigns in the Legislature to help members of the Democratic Party and to also oppose a reapportionment initiative that might threaten the Democratic majority in the Legislature. Unruh once said, "Money is the mother's milk of politics," and his actions proved it.

Unruh also led John F. Kennedy's California delegates to the 1960 national Convention. Later, he was the California campaign manager for

Senator Robert F. Kennedy's presidential bid. He was at the Senator's side when he was assassinated in Los Angeles on June 5, 1968. It was common knowledge throughout the Capitol that Unruh was heartbroken when this happened because he was the one who had talked the young Kennedy into running for President. Unruh once served as Chairman of the Assembly Finance Committee, and then later as chairman to the prestigious Assembly Ways and Means Committee. His experience there served him well when he ran for State Treasurer and won.

In the same article, Paul Jacobs further that the 63-year-old son of a sharecropper, ridiculed as a boy because his family couldn't afford money for haircuts, had officers of major investment houses, banks and other firms that did business with the State Treasurer courting him with Rose Bowl and Super Bowl tickets, lavish meals, chauffeured limousines, flights in private jets, and accommodations when traveling Europe, not to mention political fund-raising receptions.

Jessie Unruh died of cancer in his home in Marina Del Rey, California on August 4, 1987 while still serving as State Treasurer. He was 64 years old.

But to be honest, my mind wasn't very focused on politics or the role of Speaker in those years. Instead, I was caught up in the thrill of dating Mark who always made be feel special when he introduced me to his colleagues and various other political leaders such as the Speaker. Because I was assigned to the secretarial pool, I occasionally had to work for Mark. This added even more spice to the relationship. Frankly, being involved with a member carried a lot of prestige in those days. If we went to lunch, for example, I could leave work early to spend the afternoon with him and staff wouldn't say anything because he was the boss.

Being wined and dined by him was exciting. Tucking my arm under his, he would escort me to expensive restaurants and teach me how the Legislature functioned over dinner. He talked about issues that troubled him. These were issues where he had to choose to vote the way his constituents who elected him wanted or to vote what his conscious and religious upbringing was. At other times I sat spellbound as he explained other things to me, like how the Speaker's Cabinet worked.

His attention was intoxicating and so were the glasses of liquor he made sure the waiter kept full before me because he knew that if I had too much to drink I would get passionate and he could have his way with me. However, there was a darker side to it for me as well. He made it clear that neither his wife nor anyone I ever worked for should know about us, even though people always recognized us as a couple whenever we went out together. When we made love, it was almost as if he had to trick me into it. I would push him away over and over again, only to give in to him because I had had too much to drink or didn't want to be alone.

I tried not to notice that whenever we slept together he took off his wedding ring and then put it back on afterwards. The next morning he would always go to mass and confess his sins, which always made me feel cheap and dirty inside. Each time he left I was reliving abandonment all over again because I knew that we didn't really have a real relationship at all. We each had our own guilt. He had his, which he relieved in those confessions, and I had my own private hell of self-recrimination.

We also shared our respective hidden agendas. I wasn't passionately after his body. I was passionately after safety. I wanted Mark to be my "cactus patch" like the one I had known as a child and keep all the other men away from me. But of course he couldn't really be that. He had a hidden agenda as well. I realize now that what he craved with me was calmness. My voice could put him to sleep as we talked and he forgot his day. I would be very attentive to him, rub his back, take off his shoes, and fix him his favorite Scotch on the rocks, and dress nicely for him when we went out. He was proud to show me off wherever we went. Many times he would call me from a political function out of town or out of state just to ask what I was doing and if I still loved him as an escape from his hectic life away from his real home and the people he cared about.

At the same time, I noticed that Mark had a dual nature. He would nod like he heard every word I was saying, but his mind was always somewhere else. Other times he was outright angry with me for "endangering" his career. Something that really scared him happened one July evening in 1969 when we were going out to dinner. As a rule I never asked him to do anything for me but that night I asked him if I could stop by Levitz Furniture store so that I could give them $25 on a piece of furniture they had on lay-away for me.

On the way there, we drove down the freeway, listening to the sound of the rain pounding on our windshield and to the news playing on the radio. Suddenly, the announcer stated that there was a breaking news story that began the night before. Horrified, we listened as the announcer stated that Sen. Edward M. Kennedy had driven his Oldsmobile off a wooden bridge on Chappaquiddick Island, drowning his passenger, a young campaign worker named Mary Jo Kopechne. When the news anchor added the fact that Kennedy had returned to his hotel and contacted police only when he "fully realized" what had happened almost 10 hours later, Mark began to sigh a deep breath. He tried to act like what he was hearing on the radio didn't bother him, but I could tell it was by the way he was clutching the steering wheel with both hands.

Suddenly, he turned and looked at me. Just then another driver changed lanes and cut in front of our state car. He gasped when his eyes swiftly turned back on the road and he saw how close we had come to being in an accident, one in which he wouldn't be able to explain me. Then I quietly watched him fall apart.

"Oh, my God," he said. "We could have been in an accident. This could have been just like Kennedy at Chappaquiddick. It would destroy my career... my marriage."

I watched him play out different scenarios of the same scene over and over in his mind. He looked at me angrily, as if blaming me for being his "other woman" that everyone found out about, never once worrying that I too had nearly died.

That night dinner was quiet, no issues, and no insights, just silence. My heart ached for allowing myself to get into this situation with Mark to begin with. It was incidents such as these that caused me to both love and hate him. Soon, I walked a tightrope, trying to maintain emotional distance yet still desperately craving a real relationship.

While all of that was going on, my popularity as an astrologer was growing not only at dinner parties to which I was invited while helping out in different members' offices, but at other gatherings as well. One incident that stands out in my memory is when I went to a dinner party at the Hotel Senator for the San Diego delegation. The delegation was comprised of all the legislators in both the Senate and the Assembly who represented the City of San Diego. Since I had been helping out in a member's office that represented San Diego, the secretary invited me to attend the function with her.

Once again I was having fun entertaining people at the table where I sat drawing their astrology charts on cocktail napkins. A lobbyist, Bud Porter, was hosting the gathering. Then he started introducing elected officials that were present. He turned toward me and called out my name as he introduced me as "The Capitol Astrologer." I stood up, bowed, and blushed. I turned to him and smiled as if to say thank you. As a young woman, I got to taste the intoxication of being in my own spotlight. At the time I never realized that being "The Capitol Astrologer" was part of my spiritual quest on my journey in life, nor how difficult it would be to find peace and sanity in a political environment where survival was the order of the day.

By this time, I was also growing increasingly dissatisfied with accepting the "sloppy seconds" that were the inevitable result of dating a married man, much less a married member of the State Legislature. It meant that I couldn't see him on holidays. I never knew if he could get away for weekends or if he did whether his wife would be in town. Too many times I would watch him in the legislative chambers during session, knowing that a part of me cared deeply about him, but also knowing I wouldn't be allowed to really be a part of his life, so I shut my feelings down and tried to cling to what I hated about the relationship. How easy it was to feel victimized and used, especially when I thought about how he always signed a lobbyist's name to his dinner bills that made me feel like I was being served on a silver platter as his dessert whenever we went out. There was no doubt in my mind that our relationship had a "dead end" sign posted at the end of the road on which we found ourselves traveling.

One day I picked up a brochure I found on the sidewalk on my way to lunch. It talked about career opportunities working for the State Department in Washington, D.C. I wandered down to the Personnel Board, a few blocks from the State Capitol, and talked to someone there about it. He gave me another brochure that showed people taking free classes on different subjects. Shorthand was one of the subjects listed. I had been studying shorthand on my own for months during the evenings when I was alone, but it was too difficult for me to grasp by myself. I asked how to apply for a job with the State Department. He handed me a form and I filled it out on the spot then handed it back to him.

The next time Mark and I went to dinner I proudly told him what I had done. He was pretty upset with me at first. He spent hours trying to talk me out of my decision, never realizing that he was the main reason I wanted to leave. No matter what I said about wanting a new life, he promised that he would visit me there on a regular basis, unwilling to let the distance kill our relationship.

It took a full year for me to get the security clearance I needed, and the pressure he tried to use on me to convince me not to go was incredible, only making me more determined than ever to get out from under him. Once that clearance was in place, I headed off for Washington, D.C., with the hope of one day going to Africa where I dreamed of working for an embassy as an Ambassador's secretary.

Chapter 4

In the beginning I loved Washington, D.C. I met a lot of new people where I worked and in time I was invited to embassy parties that members of the State's Department's foreign service attended. I was even introduced to the Ambassador of Nigeria at one of the functions.

Of course, life in Washington, D.C. wasn't my answer to happiness, nor was it what I had fantasized it would be. Instead, I found myself completely alone again in a strange city. The shorthand classes I was looking forward to taking were not available at the time I arrived, but it didn't stop me from trying to learn it. On my lunch hours I would walk over to the basement of the main State Department building. I would flash my security pass, then check out some shorthand tapes, and study them quietly on my own.

Once again, everything at work also revolved around secrecy. Typewriter ribbons were put in burn bags every evening and locked in file cabinets that had combination locks hanging on them. There were about twenty-one file cabinets and a secret book that held their combinations. I was told over and over again that if someone found the secret book that person could be fired. Later someone who had worked in one of the embassies abroad said the Marines played a dirty game on secretaries to see if they could catch them being careless. A Marine soldier would tell a secretary that the Ambassador wanted to see her. The secretary would leave her desk to see what the Ambassador wanted. Meanwhile, the Marine officer would search her desk to see if she left anything out in the open that was classified as secret.

One member of the foreign office staff told me they got a demerit because she left out a confidential memo in which the Ambassador had sent some flowers to a dignitary's wife who had been sick in the hospital. I also heard stories from single women who proudly said they hid liquor in their thermos jugs. When I listened to their stories, all I saw were a bunch of lonely women, traveling from one assignment to another, without a place to call home. There was such sadness in their voices and such a sense of being rootless that it haunted me. Knowing that Mark was still trying to maintain our relationship made it all worse.

These stories plus waking up in the middle of the night looking for microfilm under my sheets made me think that leaving the job I had with the Legislature in California might have been a bad decision. Therefore, after having been gone for only five months, I decided to move back to Sacramento.

This time when I consulted my astrology chart I noticed transiting Saturn was playing havoc in my 6th house, which represents health and work. This planet was moving into a difficult aspect in which it was about to square and oppose many of my planets that were in the sky when I was born. While I didn't know with certainty exactly what that planetary placement would specifically do to my life, I did know that the lesson approaching me was karmic and it would relate to work, my home, and possibly my children, and it would be frustrating and restrictive.

Knowing that these aspects were affecting me, I made the decision to break it off with Mark who visited me in Washington, D.C. and wrote letters all the time. Since moving from one end of the United States to the other didn't end the relationship the way I had previously hoped it would, I decided that I simply wouldn't tell him where I was when I moved. I kept that promise to myself although once I moved back to Sacramento, I did think about calling him. In the end, though, I decided against it and didn't call him.

Busily, I tried to reestablish my life in California, which included trying to get my old job back. However, no sooner had I moved back than I noticed something was wrong with me. Whenever I tried to do exercises like sit-ups my stomach would knot up and contract into a tight ball. I mentioned it to a friend of mine, Dorothy O'Malia, who was a popular astrologer on *KCRA* radio at that time. It was Dorothy's simplified approach to astrology taught me how to cast horoscopes on cocktail napkins at parties I attended. We were such good friends that we taught astrology classes together, and it wasn't unusual for us to stay up most of the night charting out horoscopes of the state or the nation trying to figure out what was going to happen before it did. We both took opposite stands on President Nixon when the Watergate scandal broke out. She thought he would be shot in office. I didn't. I knew if Nixon's chart was as bad as his was, it meant he was going to have to live through it and feel every bit of the pain.

Dorothy looked at my horoscope and said it looked like my health problem was a movable tumor. My stomach knotting up made me nervous, so the next day I decided to go see a doctor. Dorothy was nice enough to go with me. The physician did a physical on me; then he left the room for a while. When he came back he said certain signs suggested to him that I was five-and-a-half-months pregnant, but he wanted to do some tests just to confirm it. I sat on the edge of the examining table in shock. He couldn't understand why I didn't know sooner, but I said I had been under a lot of stress from all the changes going on in my life and whenever that happened in my life, Mother Nature didn't visit me every month like it did with other women.

For a moment everything that was happening seemed so surreal. One minute I was living a normal life and then the next minute I was told I was going to have a baby in fourteen weeks. I know my face was blank when Dorothy walked up to me in the waiting room and asked me what the doctor said. All I could do is shake my head back and forth in disbelief as I headed for the exit to get some fresh air.

When I got outside the doctor's office, I told her that he said I was about five-and-a-half-months pregnant. Together, she and I walked forty-eight blocks back to her house that day, stopping only long enough to get each of us an ice cream cone at Baskin Robbins along J Street. It wouldn't be until much later that I would realize the karmic tie we shared with each other and the unborn baby.

Suddenly, with a few words from the doctor that sunny afternoon, that his tests later confirmed, I was an unwed mother and going back to work for the Legislature was no longer possible for me. It was 1970 and the backlash of gossip in the halls of the Capitol would never do, so I had to figure something else out, quickly.

I walked around in a daze for several days. I couldn't talk to anyone. To make matters worse, when I knew I was leaving Sacramento to go work in Washington, D.C., I went to a party where I ran into a handsome lobbyist I knew from work. Since I had wanted to break the bonds with Mark, I agreed to go out with the man. We had several drinks while we talked and laughed. Then later we went to dinner and made love when he took me home. It was the sixties. We lived to have fun and sex was no big deal. So, I really didn't know for sure who the father was. Immediately, I denied any possibility that Mark could be the father; instead, I chose to believe someone I barely knew might be although that was the only time the lobbyist and I had been together. Even that was the way my karma was supposed to play itself out.

Stunned and hurt, I remember humbly walking into the Catholic Cathedral on the K Street mall, located a block away from the Capitol. I wasn't Catholic, but I needed help and there was no place else to turn. I placed a quarter in a silver metal box like Dorothy once showed me how to do. Then I took one of the candles and lit it in front of a statute of Saint Jude that towered over me. I don't recall the exact words of my prayer but I am sure the word "HELP" was used over and over and maybe "PLEASE."

That's when I learned God answers our prayers even if we aren't Catholic because the next day when I called my mom, she had all the help I would need. She contacted a male friend of hers who sent me money for a plane ticket out of town. Then he helped me find a place to live that was within walking distance of doctors' offices and the hospital.

Interestingly, I never went to see the doctor again after learning I was pregnant until I was almost eight-and-a-half months along. The reason I didn't was because I didn't have any money and since I had already had two children, I didn't figure it was that important to do so. It turned out that wasn't a good idea after all. When I moved, I had to apply for emergency welfare, and they insisted I see a doctor immediately. The doctor said I had a severe iron deficiency and feared it was going to be a breach birth.

Carrying the child was not easy for me. Since I had already had two children, my body was sending out false contractions almost every night. Then when the baby was due, he never came. Fearing the baby might be in danger, a large needle was inserted into my stomach where fluid was extracted to see if the baby was getting what it needed. Then labor was induced but nothing happened. Later, when I was dilated like I was supposed to be but there was still no labor, the doctor told me to come to his office where he again induced labor. After several hours of shots every so many minutes, the doctor told me to walk over to the hospital so he could break my water.

As long as I live I will never forget how lonely I felt as I walked to the hospital that afternoon without a friend or loved one in sight. I realized from the planetary placements that I could see in my mind that once again my karma was at work. The one thing I held onto that kept me going was getting to see my baby who had been entertaining me with its forceful kicks when I tossed and turned at night wondering what was going to happen to us. In those days we didn't know if it was going to be a boy cr a girl, but that didn't matter to me. I knew this child was different from my other two because I would no choice but to raise it since I was all that this baby had and in some ways it was all I had too. Somehow I felt as if I had been given a second chance, but I worried how I was going to raise the infant without an income.

When my son, Jonathan, was born I remember doing something few women have ever done. On that day in December of 1970, I mentally cast his astrology chart on the ceiling of the delivery room. The planets revealed that many of his planets were conjunct mine which confirmed that I would raise him because he would have my traits. It also told me that he would be a strong-willed, natural born leader or a rebel that wanted his own way. Sure enough, when the tiny boy was born he was already fighting mad as he cried and cried while he waved his tiny arms and feet in the air.

The next day a strange thing happened. My doctor came to see me while I was holding the baby.

"There were some cops here asking questions about you earlier today. Do you have any idea why?" he asked with a puzzled look on his face, reaching for my wrist to take my pulse.

"I haven't done anything wrong that I can think of and no one knows I am here except for a friend who helped me move here," I said.

"You might want to check into it after you are feeling better," he said. He scribbled some things on my chart at the foot of the bed and then left the room.

I figured maybe it was a mistake and they had the wrong person.

When the baby and I were released, I called Mark, who had lost track of me.

"Hi, it's me," I began softly, after I wiggled through his secretary's questions in order to get through to him.

"Honey, where are you? Where have you been all this time? I have missed you," he whispered so no one would hear him.

"I just got home from the hospital a few days ago. I had a baby," I said.

Mark was silent. Finally, he asked me where I was living and said he was canceling all his appointments in the district office that afternoon and coming right over.

Shortly afterwards, I heard a knock at the door.

"Hi! Mark," I greeted, feeling grateful to see someone I knew after all I had been through.

"Hi Honey." He took me in his arms and hugged me.

Then he turned and saw the newborn in the bassinet. Suddenly, tears came into his eyes when he looked back at me because of the difficult situation in which he found me.

"Look, I will help you get your job back, but you have to give up the baby," he warned. Then he put his arms around me and tried to get me to kiss him, but I angrily pushed him away. I hadn't expected him to say what he did.

We never talked about the possibility of him being the father. Somehow having a friend and someone whom could help me get my old job back seemed more important at the time than wrecking someone's marriage because of something I had done.

Suddenly, Mark looked at his watch and said he had to leave. He said he would make some phone calls to Sacramento and see what he could do to help me get my job back. Then he walked out of the apartment leaving me stunned that he would suggest my giving up the baby, which might be his.

Sitting on my faded gray couch, I looked at my astrology chart to see what it said about this new development and my moving back to Sacramento. My planets said what they had all along, children and issues of the heart were part of my karma and I knew raising a child was part of what I was seeing in the chart. Then I remembered Virginia Gagnon, who is a gifted psychic and one of my dearest friends. She once told me she saw me dragging a cross like Christ did, but my cross was my children. "Were our lives so predetermined," I wondered. "If so why bother living it at all?" I questioned.

I picked Jon up from his bassinet and held him in my arms. Then I walked into my bedroom and laid him next to me on my bed. He was so small and so helpless. He wrapped his tiny little pink fingers around my little finger. Suddenly, he heard a loud motorcycle go by outside. I watched as his eyes widened, even though they were shut. I wondered what kind of karma we shared. Then I remembered the Virgin Mary and baby Jesus because I walked to the hospital on December 23, 1970 and took my son home from the hospital on Christmas day wrapped in a flannel blanket, and tucked inside a huge red Christmas stocking some hospital volunteers had made. I couldn't help but wonder if the Virgin Mary was watching over me.

At first it seemed that God or the Universe was giving me a second chance to right an old motherhood wrong. It made me want to dance around like the Irish girl I was and toss white daisies into the heavens like a blissful offering. But what followed in my life was like taking sand and trying to wash the stained blood off a mistake attached to my soul.

The year was 1970. Transiting Saturn had moved into Taurus forming a perfect adverse square to my natal Saturn, Pluto, and Moon while opposing my Sun and Jupiter in Scorpio. Something I had done in a past life needed retribution. The issue would be a child or my job, and since the transiting Saturn was moving into the 7th house, which ruled legal matters, that was tossed in too. Right on cue, the police really were looking for me.

To make matters worse, Saturn was moving into Taurus, the sign that rules money. Since the planet was in adverse aspect to so many of my planets, there was no money and that was part of the lesson. Sure enough, everywhere I turned I had problems to face. The Chief Executive Officer of the Assembly Rules Committee, who does the hiring for the Legislature, told me there was a warrant out for my arrest and I couldn't come back to work until it was cleaned up.

Suddenly, I thought that the God who answered my prayers when I lit a candle in the Catholic church was now trying to punish me for my inability to raise my other two sons, my naiveté`, and my looks which had gotten me into so much trouble. At times I hated my life and wanted to abort the mission to Earth I must have originally agreed to undertake. I thought of committing suicide but knew my soul would return lifetime after lifetime until I learned what I was supposed to learn. There was no way out. It was like being in checkmate on Earth while the planets currently transiting in the heavens checkmated my planets at birth.

Eventually, I scraped together some money to hire an attorney who helped me clear up the matter with the police department. Apparently, it turned out that I had forgotten that I had cashed two checks, which bounced when I learned I was expecting. One check was to help buy food for a lady friend and me with whom I had stayed before I moved out of town. The other check was cashed to buy flannel fabric to make baby clothes that I would later need for the infant I was carrying.

Once the attorney learned I was going to return to work for the Legislature, he jacked up his fees and I felt as if I were selling my soul to try to get my job back. But get back to work I did, and Saturn stopped nailing me to the wall as it slowly started moving away. Fortunately, I learned enough from studying shorthand that I was able to finally pass a test on it that reclassified me as a secretary instead of just a clerk typist, which increased my salary. I found a babysitter for Jon and shortly thereafter, Assemblyman Wadie Deddeh hired me to work in his office, which gave me another salary increase. It was 1971. My world looked brighter. However, I wasn't the same woman anymore. The innocence was gone and the responsibilities I shouldered were many.

Working for Assemblyman Deddeh was a learning experience. I remember how I eagerly did his astrology chart the night before I went to work for him to see what I was up against. He was born on September 6, 1920 in Baghdad, Iraq. His Sun and numerous other planets were in Virgo. This configuration showed me how critical to detail he could be. It also revealed how much he loved to lose himself in his work and how personally insecure he was, which created a lot of self-induced worries for him. His Moon in Gemini revealed an interest in education and also a mind that needed to be intellectually stimulated on a constant basis. He was one of the shrewdest politicians I ever encountered while working in various offices of the Legislature.

While working for him was exciting, my life as a single mother was difficult, but I found a comfort inside me that only a mother understands.

I wasn't alone any longer. My friend Dorothy, who stood by me when I first learned I was pregnant, now embraced my son like a genuine grandmother. She loved to hold and rock him. She even bought him cute clothes and stuffed animals to play with which helped me a lot. When Sundays came, I put my son in a stroller and walked him to a park several blocks away where I broke out a brown paper bag full popped popcorn that I cooked so Jon could watch the ducks gather to eat it. Later, we would go to a nearby restaurant and share breakfast together.

I needed to earn extra money now to raise the child, so I started seeing astrology clients during the evenings after Jon went to sleep. Word spread fast that I was an astrologer and an extremely accurate on at that. Once, when I applied for a loan at the Golden One Credit Union, I told someone what I did on the side because I didn't know if I should declare it as income or not on their loan application. The female loan officer made an appointment to see me and in the weeks that followed I saw at least a dozen people from the credit union. Secretaries working in members' offices were also making appointments to have their horoscopes read. Then they would tell another secretary who would in turn make an appointment to have me read her chart. Quickly my role of "Capitol Astrologer" returned. While I no longer ran with the political wolves of my early legislative days, I could never completely escape people recognizing me at the endless Capitol caucus gatherings, fundraisers and receptions.

One Capitol caucus party was particularly memorable. Caucus parties such as this took place once a week so that staff members, legislators, and lobbyists could get together and mingle in the prestigious Senator Hotel that was located across the street from the State Capitol. When I walked into the room I spotted Senator Mills, who was the President Pro Tem of the Senate, surrounded by reporters asking him questions.

Senator Mills noticed me watching him, excused himself, and started walking towards me. He had seen me several times before when I had worked in the San Diego legislator's office, which was where the Senator's district was located. But it was my reputation as an astrologer that seemed to interest him the most.

"So, you are an astrologer," he laughed as we got to talking. "What can you tell me about myself?"

Laughing, I asked him what his date of birth was. He said he was born on June 6, 1927, which meant his Sun was in Gemini. I will never forget the look on his face when I told him that being a Gemini meant he was intellectual and an educator. He laughed and shared a memory he had of his college days when he and some classmates tried their hand at table tipping. We both laughed.

Then he asked me if I was hungry and I answered that I was. He smiled and in his deep voice that I really liked said he knew of a nice Chinese restaurant nearby.

"Want to join me for a bite?" he asked.

"I would love to," I answered enthusiastically.

We both discretely left the caucus party and started walking towards the restaurant he wanted to take me to. I remember what a gentleman he was. He took my arm as I stepped down from a curb, then held on to it when I stepped back up again. It made me feel very special along with the fact that I was still in awe of being in the company of one of the most powerful men in the State of California.

While at the restaurant, we talked more about my beliefs in astrology. Then Senator Mills demonstrated with his fingers how to eat with wooden chopsticks. He was patient while I awkwardly learned how to do it. After dinner, he walked me home to the Lupe Apartments that have since been torn down and replaced with the Sacramento Convention Center. When we got to my apartment, I invited him in for a glass of wine. Looking back, I laugh knowing that I served the President Pro Tempore of the Senate a glass of Boone's Farm Strawberry Hill wine. He was probably an expert on wines but being the gentleman that he was, he acted like he enjoyed his drink while we laughed and talked some more. Shortly afterwards, I walked him to the door and thanked him for a lovely evening. I never talked to him alone after that, but I still smile when I think of him.

I watched with amazement in November of 1980, when Senator David Roberti, a Democrat from Los Angeles, succeeded in successfully getting enough votes from his colleagues to replace Senator Mills as President Pro Tem of the Senate. Interestingly enough, Mark Arner reported in *The San Diego Unon Tribune* on May 16, 1994 that in 1975 Senator Jim Mills introduced legislation that established the Metropolitan

Transit Development Board (MTDB). The MTDB "was designed to ensure that the San Diego Trolley was given priority over a competing high-speed rail project." Ironically, when Senator Mills left the Legislature he went to work as chairman for the Metropolitan Transit Development Board in San Diego. Characteristic of the Gemini he was, Mills went on to author such books as *Memoirs of Pontius Pilate* and *San Diego: Where California Began.*

Life in the State Capitol never ceased to fascinate me. No one surprised me anymore in those days than my boss, Assemblyman Deddeh. Wadie Deddeh was the first Democratic legislator elected to his then Republican district in San Diego. He secured the votes because he was extremely conservative, so much so that as I watched him over the years, he reminded me of a seagull sitting on a fence, looking in both directions to see which way the political climate was blowing before flying with the prevailing wind and casting his vote.

He spoke five languages and had a photographic memory. His speeches, on four-by-six-cards, were only outlines of what he wanted to say; yet he always delivered them eloquently. I remember how he once criticized me for not putting a stamp high enough on the envelope I was mailing and I thought, "What a Virgo!" because those born under this zodiac sign can be so critical and nit-picky. It was also extremely important to him that staff answered all mail within twenty-four hours of the date it was received. On numerous occasions he would walk into his outer office and declare, "If I were the Chairman of the Assembly Rules Committee, there would be a lot of changes in the staff of this Assembly," reminding us of how inefficient he felt all staff members in the Legislature really were in his mind.

I remember an incidence in which I looked at his astrology chart and told him that he would be in the hospital in June of that year. When June rolled around, he was in fact hospitalized. This prediction astounded him. Years later he asked me to predict exactly when the Assembly was going to pass their budget. I predicted a date for him, and lo and behold, I was right. He was so impressed that he announced my precise prediction to the staff at our next staff meeting. But Assemblyman Deddeh was not a fan of astrology. He just found it surprisingly accurate.

Still, he had enough things happen in his life that took the form of a prophecy that he respected what I did and never discouraged it. For example, long before he was elected, he would go to Sacramento to visit his in-laws as a young man. While he was staying with them he would stand on the steps of the State Capitol building looking up at it in awe. He wondered what it would be like to be a legislator working inside it. Each time he did that he was more and more drawn to it, convinced that somehow he would be a part of that life. Somehow, without his having an understanding of metaphysics, he was exercising a Universal law that I understood, that powerful thoughts held in the mind long enough would manifest as concrete reality.

One thing that stood out about this man was his political mind. I vividly recall an example of how shrewd Deddeh was. It was getting close to election time. Since he was a Democrat running in a predominantly Republican district, he always worked hard to gain the confidence and votes of his constituents.

Early one Monday morning I walked into his office to take him a cup of coffee. Classical music was playing in the background and he was reading the stock market quotes in the **_Wall Street Journal_**, which he did every morning. Interestingly enough, he didn't take risks politically but he did when it came to gambling with cards and dabbling in the stock market.

He asked me to sit down and take some notes from him for a letter he wanted me to draft. He said the letter was to go out as soon as possible that morning. I excused myself from the room long enough to get a writing pad and a pen. When I returned, he started dictating his letter. Apparently, he had attended a church service the day before in his district. Deddeh was sending out a letter to the minister to thank him for the inspirational message the minister delivered during the service, which as he had me write in the letter, "moved" him and "truly touched" his heart.

At first I was impressed by his eloquent words and thought it was really nice of him to send such a nice letter to the minister. However, I started questioning his gesture the following week when another letter to a different minister went out, especially since I knew Deddeh was such a devout Catholic. These letters to different ministers went on for several weeks prior to the election. Finally, I asked him why it was so urgent for each letter to go out every Monday morning. He answered by saying he wanted it to get to the minister in time for him to read it to his congregation on Sunday morning. I silently gasped.

Though I left his office to work for other members, I kept an eye on what he was up to over the years. In time his destiny became very clear, and it wasn't what he had expected. I watched how his astrology played out his karmic lessons, most of which were focused on money.

Deddeh experienced a lot of poverty when he first came to this country while struggling to get his education. He sometimes told his staffers stories about his mother having to sell his deceased father's wedding ring in order to put food on the table for the family. In later years, he lived on potted meat and crackers as he struggled financially while going to college in Michigan. Food was scarce, but his hunger for an education was greater. Ultimately, playing with money became both his favorite obsession and his greatest lesson.

For example, in one of his election races, an opponent who was running for Congress accused Deddeh of taking $800,000 in contributions from the insurance industry and then introducing legislation for them. He was never proven guilty of it and the electorate in his district never found it to be significant enough to vote against him, but it was an example of karmic lessons related to money that were trailing after him whether he did something wrong or not.

Eventually, Deddeh was elected to the Senate. He loved to play poker and frequently got some members together to play poker with him in a back room at Frank Fats' Chinese restaurant. He also loved to invest in pieces of property with business partners. His gambling on the larger scale is what eventually cost him his seat in the Senate. He told me how he had purchased a very expensive piece of property with some investors during a time when the real estate market was failing throughout the State. When the property couldn't be sold for what it was worth, he and his partners were sued for the difference. This lawsuit wiped him out financially, and the courts eventually took away whatever assets he had, including his lovely home in San Diego with its ocean view. After that he had to find a home for himself and his wife to rent – a huge karmic blow to a man who had struggled to rise above the financial hardships he experienced earlier in his life.

Years later, on August 17, 1993 Senator Wadie Deddeh, a Democrat representing Chula Vista, California resigned from the Senate. I watched from a distance as controversy followed him yet again when he returned to his position as an instructor at Southwestern College in Chula Vista. Although he had actually taught less than ten years there, he was given credit of over 30 years worth of tenure due to the number of years he worked for the Legislature. John Marelius reported in _The San Diego Union-Tribune_ that Deddeh's resignation from the Senate would "now benefit Assemblyman Steve Peace who wanted to run for Deddeh's position." Assemblyman Peace's stepfather was G. Gordon Browning, President of the Southwestern College Board, which left people wondering if there was something shady about this arrangement. Later that year, Steve Peace won the election for the Senate seat vacated by Deddeh.

All of this Senator's losses were devastating for the gambler that risked too much, but it was the transiting planets that were in aspect to planets he was born with that triggered the lessons he was born to learn. Even the fact that he was a Professor of Economics and knew more about money than most couldn't erase what he had come here to experience. Of course, part of my karma was to experience many things including working for him.

It was also during this time that my karmic tie to my son's father once again reared its ugly head. Somehow, without really realizing it, we had slowly drifted back into the pattern of seeing each other. A part of me despised him for it. I tried not to get too close to him, focusing my attention on my work instead. Little did I know that my karma with him, and all the time I spent alone, would afford me the time I needed to embrace my real passions – my spirituality and my astrology business. Soon I started teaching astrology at a recreation center in South Sacramento, little realizing I would work with a future President to professionalize astrology in California.

Chapter 5

During my early years of working for the Legislature, Governor Ronald Reagan was in office. One evening I studied his astrology chart based on the information I found about him, not realizing at the time what an important role he and I would play in the practice of astrology in California. The Governor was born February 6, 1911 in Tampico, Illinois under the sign of Aquarius. I noticed that he had the planets of Saturn and the Moon in Taurus opposing Jupiter in Scorpio. This combination told me that his karma in this lifetime related to money. Politically, money was obviously a concern for him because he made drastic budget cutbacks as Governor in the early 1970's.

Most Aquarian men need a spouse or a partner to help them make their dreams a reality, and Ronald Reagan was no exception. He had his wife Nancy to help him. There were numerous stories on how devoted she was to him. She would call in the evenings and tell her husband he would have to bring his meeting to a close because it was getting late and time for him to come home.

While I worked for the Legislature, I saw many protests and marches on the Capitol steps, but I always felt there were more protests during Reagan's reign as Governor than at any other time. While many people continue to revere him to this day, many people in California were furious about his actions when he was Governor. He raised tuition for students, made cutbacks in education, stopped dental services to most people on welfare, and closed down mental health outpatient services without ever fully informing his constituents on what the ramifications of such actions would be. He did all of these things because he was driven to save money no matter what the consequences might be.

His need to save money and not tell all didn't stop there. I remember the time I was working for the Assembly Public Employees and Retirement Committee. The committee secretary had taken ill and couldn't travel out of town. She asked me if I would fly down to San

Diego and serve as committee secretary for an unemployment hearing that was to be held there. I agreed to do so. It was the first time I had ever been put in a position where I was the one that would be responsible for catching a plane out of town to assist the Chairman and other members of the Committee. It was my job to make sure the members had pertinent reading materials that they needed and to assist the Sergeant-at-Arms who would be recording the hearing.

The purpose of this hearing was to find out what percentage of unemployment existed in the State of California at the time. Several key workers with the Department of Unemployment came to testify. From their testimony we learned that if a person collects unemployment, that person counts as an unemployed statistic. When his unemployment runs out, or when he's working part time, he would no longer be tallied into the percentage of people unemployed in the State. As a result of the hearing, we found out that the rate of unemployment in California being reported to the federal government was far lower than what it actually was. This facade aided Governor Reagan's image while he was being groomed to run for President of the United States, but it meant less money coming into the State from the federal government.

On a more personal note, when I think of Governor Reagan the picture that always comes to mind are the numerous times I stood near him at a gathering. He was the first man I ever saw wearing make-up and it was obvious that his hair was dyed brown. Sometimes I would get distracted trying to figure out what shade of lipstick he was wearing or the color of his eyebrows. Then I would miss most of what he was saying.

In those days security was much more relaxed around the Capitol. On a cold winter night in December of each year we would find the Governor in front of the Capitol building watching the lights being turned on for the first time on the giant Christmas tree that had been harvested for the special occasion. There by his side would be his wife, Nancy, smiling, with her eyes looking up adoringly at him.

It was public knowledge that Nancy Reagan was an ardent follower of astrology. It came out in 1988 when America was shocked to learn that Nancy Reagan frequently consulted Astrologer Joan Quigley on important events or dates that would affect her husband when he was

President of the United States. She said she had been consulting an astrologer since 1981 when an assassin had threatened his life. The truth is that Nancy was interested in it long before then.

Nancy and Ronald Reagan weren't the only people who consulted astrology charts to gain information about opponents. As a secretary, it was sometimes my job to work for the Democratic Caucus. Both parties, the Democrats and Republicans, have their own caucuses, which exist for the sole purpose of looking after their own party's members. In the office where I was assigned to help, they kept extensive files on what the Republicans were up to. Back then; before there was the Internet, legislative offices used a clipping service, which charged a monthly fee to cut out newspaper clippings on whatever subject we were interested in. Then the service would mail the articles to us with a little orange tag stapled to the top of the clipping stating the date and the name of the newspaper it appeared in.

In front of me one morning were a bunch of clippings that needed to be filed. I walked to the room where the file cabinets were and started thumbing through the files. To my surprise, I noticed a file the Democratic Caucus was keeping on Governor Reagan. I opened the folder and found a computer generated horoscope that someone had ordered with the hope it would give him or her some insight into what each day of the month foretold for the Governor. It didn't seem to fit in with the high profile office on which I was working. As an astrologer, I knew a computer-generated report would be too vague in comparison to what a professional astrologer could have told them. Nonetheless, I found it interesting to see how far one party would go to find out something against the other.

Even though Nancy was interested in astrology, I don't believe she ever imagined what a significant role Governor Reagan would play in the future of it in the State of California. When I first moved to Sacramento, I learned that it was illegal to practice astrology here.

One day I walked into Weinstocks department store, across from the State Capitol building and saw an astrology display on one of the glass counters. When I got back to work, I called the Police Department and asked them if astrology was illegal and they said that it was. Then I called Weinstocks and asked to talk to the store manager. I told him what the police department said and questioned the astrological display in their store. By the end of that day it had been completely removed from the glass counter.

The newspapers were full of daily horoscopes and several astrology magazines were on the newsstands, yet Sacramento banned the practice of it. I got together with a group of other concerned astrologers who took it upon ourselves to try to change this law. We testified before the Sacramento City Council and the Board of Supervisors, but we were told they weren't going to legalize astrology because the Sacramento Police Department was against it. That's when I registered myself with the Secretary of State's office as a lobbyist for the Astrological Research Society and probably became the only person who ever worked for the Legislature and was a registered lobbyist at the same time.

I talked to Assemblyman Ed Z'berg and got him to introduce Assembly Bill 3503 relating to astrology. Assemblymen Deddeh, Garcia, Bob Wilson, and Senator Gregorio agreed to co-sign the legislation. (Co-signers on a piece of legislation give the bill some clout when it appears before the House to be voted on.) The bill passed both Houses of the Legislature.

This legislation was significant because it took astrologers out of the realm of fortunetellers and said the State would permit cities and counties to regulate the practice of astrology for compensation. On August 30, 1974, Governor Ronald Reagan signed this legislation into law, which became Chapter 583, and added Section 50027 to the Government Code, relating to astrology. After this legislation was passed, Sacramento issued business licenses to astrologers and allowed them to practice for compensation.

When Governor Reagan was elected as President of the United States, it was a well-known fact that the date he was sworn in was one for which an astrologer carefully calculated the proper alignment of the planets. I smile when I think of his inauguration because I know what his chart looked like and how he helped me to legalize astrology as a business.

While all of that was going on, life with my little boy was different for me now. I was 27 years old and a little more mature. My work at the Capitol kept me busy. Instead of going to wild parties or thinking I was missing something I mostly stayed away from the political events. I tried to disentangle myself from Mark, mostly unsuccessfully. For a time, I did start dating a lobbyist who was good to Jon and I. Our evenings were spent eating gourmet food that I cooked for us and watching television. But a serious, committed relationship wasn't possible with him. A part of him was very domesticated but another side of his Gemini nature made him a flirt. One day a rumor got back to me at work that he was seeing someone else on the side, so I broke up with him and just concentrated on my work at the Capitol and my growing astrology business, seeing Mark on an occasional basis.

During this time, I astrologically watched Jerry Brown. Edmund G. "Jerry" Brown, Jr. was born April 7, 1938 in San Francisco, California. His Sun was conjunct Saturn in Aries and squared his Moon and Pluto in Cancer. Numerous planets were in the sign of Taurus. I sensed that this man was born with a tormented soul, who felt guilty perhaps for what he might have done to his fellow man in a war in a past life even though he wouldn't know why he felt so guilty. His planets showed me that he was too rigid, cautious, and stubborn. He was also very opinionated.

Jerry Brown was elected Secretary of State to California in 1970. I remember going to a birthday party for him. His cake was a large two-layer white sheet cake that was carved in the shape of the State Capitol building. He was laughing with his fellow workers. I remember looking down and noticing his pant legs were too short; they were "high water" pants, which seemed out of place for someone elected to that position.

Later, Jerry Brown was elected Governor in 1974. It wasn't unusual to see him walking through the park on his way to his two-bedroom apartment where he lived across the street from the State Capitol on "N" Street. It was a plain old white building that sat next to the "gravel pit," an unpaved parking lot where employees that worked for the Legislature parked their cars. The building was very modest in comparison to the Governor's mansion that his father, Edmund Brown, Sr., lived in while he was Governor of the State from 1959 to 1967.

To this day I can remember going the airport to join many other people in greeting Jerry Brown when he flew into town on his way home from Southern California where he had been campaigning for his re-election. I shook his hand and it was like shaking hands with a feather that was barely there. I also looked down and noticed his pant legs were the right length now, which meant someone had groomed him well for this office.

There was something else that happened while Brown was Governor that is burnt in my memory. His press secretary came into the committee office where I was working one day to visit a consultant she knew. She told him she had just come back from a speech that the Governor had given to a small group of agricultural people inside the Hotel Senator and needed to borrow the phone to call her office. When she made the call, I overheard her say that on a scale of 1 to 10 when the Governor said whatever he said about farmers, the audiences' reaction was 7. She went down the line and gave the person on the other end a quick list of every single audience response the Governor's speech had received. Then I knew she was actually talking to a fellow staff person in the Governor's office who was discretely monitoring how audiences reacted to him, so that his speechwriters would know what he should or shouldn't present to farmers statewide.

I thought this tactic was very clever and very frightening at the same time. Later, I would discover that almost all of the politicians in Sacramento and Washington, D.C. used polls to define their positions prior to having one. Not only would they require staff to conduct the polls, but they would also hire outside firms to do it. In fact, the people who conduct these polls created a big business for themselves.

Something that attracted a lot of attention to Governor Brown back in March of 1984 was the unveiling of his portrait that was hung in the State Capitol building. The portraits of all of the governors of the State hang in stately precision, each face carefully arranged in the most statesmen-like fashion possible. Each portrait also lists the dates that person was in office. Governor Jerry Brown, however, wasn't willing to settle for such traditional art. When a person turns the corner and sees his portrait hanging on the wall, it is a shock to the senses. Brown's portrait is so radically different that it is like taking a blow to the stomach. In an abstract modern art attack, the strokes of the artist's paintbrush are blunt and the expression on Brown's face is one of great pain and concern. In fact, the portrait is full of splashes of orange skin color and dashes of red around his head. His portrait stands out, so much so that tourists, who to this day continue to wander throughout the Capitol daily, never fail to comment about it. Sometimes they even stop to take a picture of the portrait with their camera. A postcard of the portrait is sold in the gift shop located in the basement of the Capitol.

The Governor always fascinated me because he had an almost schizophrenic nature: He almost obsessively sought out the limelight, yet he would retreat from it at the same time as if it would burn him. For example, as Governor, it was a common practice to give a copy of one's autographed picture to members of the Legislature who requested it, so they could hang it up on the walls in their offices. Brown didn't like giving his picture to legislators or anyone else for that matter.

One day, a legislator for whom I was working took a couple of children from his district into the Governor's office. When he introduced them to Governor Brown, he offered them the chance to take their picture with the Governor with one of the cameras their teacher was carrying, but Jerry Brown didn't allow it. At a later time, I watched his father, Edmund Brown, Sr., on television at a Democratic Convention with his radiant energy flying throughout the room, while in a marked contrast his son, Jerry, was practically sitting under his seat, unsuccessfully trying to hide from the cameras.

It was during Jerry Brown's reign as Governor that Proposition13 passed, which was the largest voter-imposed tax cut in the history of the United States. Despite the fact that the Governor originally spoke out against Proposition 13, he later froze the salaries of the State's 190,000 employees, and new hiring was totally forbidden once the voters passed it in June of 1978. In 1984 Pete Wilson defeated Brown and Brown later sought the 1992 Democratic Presidential nomination.

Governor Jerry Brown was well known for having studied for the priesthood at Sacred Heart Novitiate, a Jesuit seminary in Los Gatos. In the years that followed his retirement from the Legislature, he worked with Mother Theresa in India and frequently attended Zen retreats for meditation in San Francisco. Brown went on to host a popular radio program, "We the People" that airs on *KPFA*, in Berkeley, *KPFK* in Los Angeles, *KPFT* in Houston and *WBAI* in Manhattan. His commentaries were aired nationwide on a daily basis.

As for me, I was just trying to be a single mom and to raise my son. Fate would have it that my income would come from working for the

Legislature. I tried to do whatever was expected of me in an office. However, as a naive woman who had been raised as a child on a farm, I saw many things that surprised me.

For example, in the years I worked in the Legislature I saw countless freebies such as television sets delivered to various offices, members taking expensive trips out of the country, and receiving lavish committee dinners, football game tickets, theater tickets, clothing, trips to the Academy Awards in Hollywood, cases of expensive wine delivered, gorgeous baskets full of fruit to staff, cases of oranges, grapes, apples, and individual cases of candy delivered to staff members. There was so much See's candy in members' offices that if a secretary from our Secretarial Unit went to reach for a piece and the one she wanted wasn't there, she could work in another member's office the next day and it would probably be in that box. Naturally, what I saw was small potatoes in comparison to the deals that were being made when a member walked past my desk with a lobbyist and went into his office and closed the door.

The deals were interesting and the game intriguing when I learned how they played it. Naturally, I was always asking questions, but it would take years to see the magnitude of the power plays. For example, a member could accept a favor from a lobbyist in exchange for introducing a bill. But what the lobbyist wouldn't realize if he was new to the Capitol, is that the member had the power to have the bill killed in the committee to which it was assigned to be heard in just by talking to a few colleagues or putting in an amendment here or there. Technically he honored the original agreement to the "special interest" person, which was to introduce the bill, but he never intended to actually get it passed.

There were many, many of those incidences when the member didn't mind introducing a bill because he knew it would be killed. A member could also make money, known as an honorarium, just for making a speech.

Of course, that kind of corruption and graft couldn't last forever. One morning in June of 1974, I arrived at work to find everyone gossiping about what was going to happen now that California voters passed Proposition 9 by a 70% majority at a time in history when the Watergate crisis was at a peak in Washington, D.C. We didn't have to wonder long. The freebies were gone.

Proposition 9 created the Fair Political Practices Commission (FPPC) and gave it a $1.1 million budget. It would be FPPC's responsibility to interpret the new 20,000 words Political Reform Act. It would also be its responsibility to enforce the strict campaign financing provisions set out in the law that affected legislators, lobbyists and staff.

Every staff person working in the Capitol who ranked Committee Secretary and above, including legislators, was going to be accountable for all free gifts he or she received from lobbyists and special interests groups. Now these specified public servants had to file a Conflict of Interest Form 700 Statement of Economic Interests every year. Eventually, when I became a Committee Secretary, I also had to fill out the form. It was so personal that it made me question whether or not I should have accepted the position that qualified me to have to file one. It asked for the value of my home, what year I bought it, and what it was worth now. It asked whether I owned stocks, had money in the bank, had outside sources of income, and other personal questions. If a staff person was married the same information was required on their spouse.

Suddenly, there was a $10 limit on a gift that a lobbyist could give elected state officials, members of the Legislature, and certain staff members during a calendar month, and the total could not exceed $320 in any given year. There were restrictions on how much money a lobbyist could loan out to specified persons according to the new Act, and honorariums were prohibited, although there were some exceptions.

Penalties ranged from cease-and-desist orders to heavy fines and even jail terms. In the years that followed numerous legislators, lobbyists and special interest groups would end up in violation of Proposition 9 requirements. For example, Daniel C. Carson, reported in *The San Diego Union-Tribune* that Assemblyman Terry Goggin agreed to pay a total of $13,500 to the State of California to settle charges in connection with 14 violations of the Political Reform Act. Carson also reported in *The San Diego Union-Tribune* that lobbyist Grant Kenyon agreed to pay $10,000 in fines for illegally distributing campaign contribution checks to lawmakers in the Capitol building.

In 1992 Paul Jacobs, reported in the *Los Angeles Times* that Senator Dianne Feinstein agreed to pay $190,000 to the State Fair Political Practices Commission for failing to comply with campaign finance rules when she unsuccessfully ran for Governor in 1990. Jacobs also reported in the same story that Governor Pete Wilson agreed to pay a fine of $100,000 to the FPPC for reporting violations.

Chapter 6

While the politicians worried about the FPPC, I finally got up enough nerve to discuss my son with Mark one day when he invited me to join him for lunch across town. He denied that he was Jon's father and threatened me with my life if his family ever found out about the child or me. He said he didn't want some woman knocking on his door claiming her child was his in front of his wife. Right away I backed down and understood his fears because of his political position before the public, completely disregarding how what he was saying impacted the lives of my son and me and how his cruel words were making me sick to my stomach.

Soon I became two completely different women with him. I was a woman who cared about him and that he still took out to dinner once in awhile and the mother of a child Mark refused to acknowledge. I thought I handled it well, though, because not only was I known for doing a good job at the Capitol, I was also known for my discretion at work. While we would exchange looks and even kisses behind closed doors when I slipped away from the office in which I was working to go see him; no one else ever suspected what was really going on except his secretary. In some ways it was a total thrill, stimulating and exciting. In other ways it was degrading and made me feel cheap.

One day, however, I reached my limit when I was called out of the Assembly Secretarial Unit where I worked to help out in Mark's office because his secretary was out sick for the day. Mark's wife called the office and I answered the phone. Though I had talked to her many times over the years, this time I reacted badly. She was excited about an exotic vacation that she and Mark had just returned from and wanted to talk to her husband. The happiness in her voice galled me. While they had played in the sun on some luxury liner at sea, I had been forced to work twelve-hour days and then go home to stay up all night caring for my son who had been sick the whole time. My son's father was not there to help me. He was off gallivanting to foreign countries and leading a life of luxury while denying that he was the boy's father and still trying to see me.

After listening to her gush about how wonderful a trip she had and how much she and her husband had enjoyed their time alone, I forwarded the call to Mark. I could hear him lovingly talk to her, even though it was me he made love to the night before as he told me how much he missed me while he was gone. Now, listening to him talk to his wife, it was as if my son and I didn't exist; yet I was the one who was keeping his and her world safe by not saying anything. It didn't seem fair.

As I sat there fuming about the injustice of it all, I realized that one of the primary reasons I hadn't said anything to anyone was because I didn't have proof. Proof would have meant blood tests that the press might get wind of. One whiff of news like this back in those days would have made headlines in every newspaper throughout the State, especially with Ted Kennedy getting in trouble with his affairs all the time in Washington, D.C. And that was what the Legislature was all about, secrets. Information was powerful, and so were the secrets.

I kept my secret for a long time, too terrified to do anything about it. But that single phone call, from Mark's wife, rocked my world so hard I couldn't remain in denial about my anger and pain any longer. Jon was two years old now. The more I thought about it the more I stewed at the injustice of all. My son and I needed his help and just because he was in denial didn't mean I had to stand for it any longer. I decided right then to do something about it. I would get Mark's blood type no matter what. The pediatrician I had when Jon was born told me my son had AB negative blood which wasn't that common and said it would be impossible for his father to be type "O."

I had shared that information with Mark over dinner once. He used it against me the one and only time we talked about the possibility of him being Jon's father. He blatantly said he was type "O." Now, I wanted to know once and for all but I wasn't sure how I could find out without attracting attention, losing my job, or maybe even ending up in a dumpster somewhere. Suddenly, I had a brilliant idea.

Determined, but frightened that I might get caught, I pretended I was from the State Capitol Emergency Medical Unit and called the hospital

Mark had just been released from for some routine minor surgery. I said I was updating my records on members working for the Legislature and Mark forgot what his blood type was and asked me to call their hospital to find out since he had just been released from there. I guess the nurse felt honored someone was calling from the State Capitol building in Sacramento because she immediately pulled his record and gave me his blood type. My heart sank when I heard the words I hadn't been able to accept since the birth of my son two years prior. I thanked her and then hung up the receiver, frozen with pain and shock.

Finally, I half-ran to the Assembly Floor and looked around the room to see where Mark was. The first thing I noticed were the gargoyles in the ceiling of the Chamber leering back at me, mirroring my own feelings of desolation and danger. Prior to this moment, these golden gothic monsters had always fascinated me. Whereas the Senate had one, the Assembly had three of the leering monsters. One was concealed on a ledge high above the Speaker's rostrum. Today, its red tongue seemed to slap me in the face as I went on my mission to confront the real monster, my son's father who had lied to me about his blood type.

I remember looking around the Legislative chambers, watching the members struggle on a particularly difficult bill up for consideration. No one seemed to notice me. Once again, I was the invisible woman. Growing more furious with each passing second, I testily asked the Assembly Sergeant-at-Arms to get Mark and let him know I was in back of the gallery waiting to see him.

When Mark approached, he could tell by the look on my face that something was wrong.

He tried to calm me down, so I wouldn't make a scene. He kept saying, "Honey, what are you talking about?" in a condescending tone of voice.

"You lied about your blood type. It isn't type 'O' like you said. You are 'B negative.' I have proof you ARE Jon's father, you lying son-of-a-bitch. You knew how important this was to me and you still denied me and my son," I raised my voice, causing people to turn and see what the commotion was about.

He just kept telling me we could talk about it after session adjourned for the day, but I wasn't about to be shut up any longer.

"I can prove you are his father now, and I am going to do just that!"

But once again he turned on his charm and convinced me to leave, which I reluctantly did, but I couldn't return to work. I was too angry and too hurt. I told his secretary, who was a friend of mine that I was going to see my attorney about filing a paternity suit. As my friend and his most trusted employee, she was the only one who knew our little secret.

Dazed, I left the Capitol building and went to see the lawyer I had just called from inside the Capitol building. He was the one who had helped me clear the bad checks I wrote when Jon was born. When I arrived, his secretary escorted me into his office where he stood from behind his desk and extended his hand to greet me. Then he motioned for me to have a seat.

"I want you to draw up a paternity suit against a member of the Legislature," I told him. "I tried to keep quiet up until now but I can't do this alone any more. My son was born with a collapsible wind pipe and has been hospitalized for it more than once, and the man I have been protecting is not more important than my son and I."

The door opened and in walked the attorney's secretary. She said there was a call for me from the State Capitol. It was Mark's secretary.

"Jan, you have got to come back. Mark is suicidal. You can't involve him in a paternity suit. He is a married man and he knows it will destroy him, his career, and his family. He begs you to come back and let this be taken care of in-house," she pleaded.

At first I hesitated. After all, he had lied to me. How could I be sure this wasn't just another ruse to shut me up?

"He wants you to see a friend of his who chairs one of the committees. You will be taken care of. He promises. Honest if you go through with this, he will commit suicide. He said so," she warned.

By then, I could see the attorney's eyes lighting up at the bucks and press he might rake in on this case, so I agreed to at least speak to Mark's friend in the Legislature, especially since the attorney had charged me so much money for removing the warrant for my arrest the last time I retained him. As a matter of fact, I still owed him on it.

I told the attorney I was dropping the suit.

"You have legal rights to child support and an education for your son. If you walk out of this room, you might be jeopardizing all that," he cautioned, with a look in his eyes that let me know he knew they had gotten to me and were ready to buy me off.

I nodded that I understood. I got up and left his office, knowing I would meet with Mark's very powerful legislative friend the next day.

Mark's secretary went with me to see Mark's friend whom I was supposed to talk regarding paternity. The night before I had carefully written this man a letter so he could hear my side of the story since I knew this particular political giant could mow someone like me down in a heartbeat. When we met, I handed him my letter for him to read.

"What's this?" he asked taking the letter from my hand.

"I've listened to you on the squawk box in offices where I worked while you debated the merits of a piece of legislation on the Floor during session. No matter what my view was on an issue debated, I ended up changing it to yours after you presented your argument. The letter is my way of getting my two-cents worth in before you speak and I change my mind," I explained.

He laughed while sitting down behind his well-varnished mahogany desk to read the letter while Mark's secretary and I took a seat in two empty black leather chairs that faced him.

Inside my letter were well-chosen words explaining that Mark and I were not a casual one-night stand. We had seen each other for many years before and after my son had been born and how I went to see the attorney because I wanted this matter of paternity settled once and for all. It also described how Mark used to park his car behind in a tree near my apartment when he came to pick me up for dinner, so no one would see his white state car. This story and other little quips made him laugh aloud while he read it, obviously recognizing similar cautious traits his colleague had. Mark once told me that he bailed this member out of a difficult situation once with a vote he needed. I figured seeing me was the political pay back he was doing for Mark because of that incident. I also mentioned our blood types and how my son's was rare.

"Did anybody ever tell you that you are a gifted writer?" he asked when he looked up from the letter he laid on his desk.

"No," I said smiling, already being captured in by his charm.

"What do you want from all of this?" he asked.

"Child support to help raise my son," I spoke up.

"How about my giving you seventy-five dollars a month every month at someplace we agree to meet," he offered.

"That won't work," I said noticing the surprised look on his face.

"This isn't the first time this has happened where a woman has been in your situation and come to me. That's what was done then. Why doesn't this suit you?" he questioned with a curious look on his face.

"You might die and then what? I came to you instead of the attorney I was going to see and I went out on a limb. Now you want me to settle this whole thing by meeting every month with someone who might die," I said straightforward.

"What?" he said shocked that I was talking about his demise, which he obviously hadn't considered. "That's all that would have happened if you filed a paternity suit with the attorney you went to see. You would have gotten monthly payments."

"Wrong. All this would have been legal and I would have known for sure that the outcome was fair and not all one-sided. That's the difference," I boldly countered.

"How do I know you won't turn around after we take care of you and see the attorney anyway or spend it all and say you need more?" he said studying my eyes.

"Because I know how to handle money and my father taught me that a man is only as valuable as his word is," I said proudly, "And I don't lie!"

"Good father," he smiled. "Good advice. Okay. What amount sounds fair to you?" he asked, looking at this watch, getting back to the subject at hand.

"Take the figure you offered and multiply it to age 18. That will be fine," I said thinking how shrewd I was being before the political wolf that I still wasn't sure I could trust.

"That's a lot of money. If it is settled in a lump it needs to be for a WHOLE lot less and I need to break it down into three payments. You can meet me in the rear of the chambers the next time we go into session," he said. "When your son is older we will talk about his education," he added.

"Very well," I agreed, getting up from my chair and reaching out my hand to shake on our agreement. My friend that had been sitting close by bid him goodbye as she got up to leave.

Two days later, I waited for about an hour for Session to get under way before I went to the rear of the Assembly chambers to meet him. He spotted me right away and walked off the Floor towards me. He reached for my hand as if to shake it, and then slipped several one hundred-dollar bills into it that were rolled up into one big wad.

"Who is paying this money to me?" I asked softly searching his eyes.

"Well," he paused for a moment looking into my eyes with a warm smile. "I collected it from a few members here on the Floor," he replied.

"What did he contribute?" I asked.

Suddenly, his smile was gone which answered my question. Despite being so suicidal and desperate to shut me up, amazingly enough, my son's father didn't contribute a single penny. This guy had covered for him right to the end.

"But don't worry," the committee chairman said, whispering that I was to meet him again here in three weeks. I looked around for Mark, but he was nowhere to be seen. Intuitively knowing what I was doing, the committee chairman said that Mark was giving me time to cool off about the paternity matter before he tried to talk to me.

I didn't know what to do. I was completely unprepared for the whole situation. He could see from the look in my face that I was still hesitant because Mark hadn't contributed.

"This will help you, but let me warn you that if you ever tell anyone about this, I will deny I even know you."

The look on his face told all. I knew in that moment that my job and reputation were on the line. If I didn't keep quiet, I would lose everything that mattered to me. I was no match for the power of the Legislature, which obviously protected its own. Once again, the gargoyles stared back and me, and in my mind I could see the red tongue of the one hidden on the ceiling behind the Speaker's rostrum flicker menacingly at me. I was trapped between these two powerful men. They had me where they wanted me, scared to death. Besides there was a part of me that wanted to believe them – needed to believe them – when they said they were just trying to help my son and me.

With a final glance at the gargoyle in the ceiling above me, I took the money and shut up. While gargoyles stir our imagination of gothic mystery and danger, many believe they are protectors, keeping evil away from both the people and the buildings on which they are placed. Perhaps the myth is true.

For a brief second I thought back to one day many years ago when one of the three chandeliers valued at $25,000, anchored in the ceiling of the Assembly chambers fell and crashed onto the floor. While no one was hurt that day, I remember looking at the heap of broken glass. Now I found myself thinking, "More than just objects get shattered here. Peoples lives do too."

I walked to the closest restroom and locked the door to one of the metal stalls, so I could count the money. It would be barely enough to pay for the attorney I still owed for writing a bad $50 check for baby clothes when I found out I was pregnant, let alone medical the bills I still owed for when my son was in the hospital and I didn't have insurance.

Despite the fact that I was raising Jon whom I loved dearly, it had been burnt inside my soul again and again over the years that the identify of his father had to be concealed because if the news of it ever hit the press it would destroy both Mark's family and his political career. In my mind, I didn't matter and the child had to be protected. I also felt guilty about being a single mother and for having had the affair in the first place, but being so young left me incapable of fully understanding the ramifications of my actions until much later.

Now, of course, I realize how much I had lost to the political giants who played a game with me to win my silence. Some would have handed over their gems, gold watches, and fat wallets just to be in the same room with such power and intelligence let alone to play in the arena for even one day and surely some had done just that when they mortgaged their homes to run for a political office and lost. I shouldn't have been surprised when Jon's education was never brought up again nor taken care of as promised. Instead, he had to borrow money to pay for his education.

Despite my loyalties over the years, when I was caught in political battles that one party wages against another, I was left to die or dance fast with survival skills and resumes my lengthy tenure with the

Legislature afforded me. My feelings of betrayal extended to everything I once believed. I felt as if everyone had lied to me. That is except for the only truth I found that never let me down. It was my Ephemeris that showed me the formation of the planets, which had honestly foretold there would be trouble involving a loved one, my health, a child, my job, and money. Now the planets that had squared once again began to move away and let me breathe for a little while before I would have to face another karmic lesson down the road.

It wasn't unusual for me to work for a member for a while and then return to the Secretarial Services Unit because I needed a change or perhaps the member lost an election, which is what happened when I was working there in 1983. I loved being assigned to different offices during the day and then going home and taking care of matters there. Rather than being tired to one member's office, the secretarial pool seemed to give me the space I needed to be a working mother.

As the years flew by, I saw how working in the political arena had a spiritual purpose for me beyond being an employee. It was like being in a graduate school that gave me an opportunity to meet and study many people. Sometimes my evenings were spent pondering what I had seen and experienced during the day. Many consultants and secretaries working inside the State Capitol were caught up in the political games that were being played, while I mediated on the karmic implications of everything I saw.

For instance, I thought about the woman for whom I once worked who had married a blind man. Out of all the men she could have married, she chose him and not someone else. This kind of thing made me wonder why we pick a certain person with whom to spend the rest of our lives out of so many that cross our path. The woman who married a blind man had a child that was severely mentally retarded. Yet, she didn't give up her child or her man and walk away to live a life that would have been more comfortable. Woven into these questions that I pondered about life was the one that had me asking why I never left Mark. Karma, and facing the lessons we had come here to learn, seemed to hold the only answer for me.

In time I noticed the Universe seemed to be sending me to offices where my spiritual and astrological insights were needed more than my secretarial skills. One office I was sent to many years ago still stands out in my memory. The secretary was frantically getting ready for a hearing that was coming up. Agendas needed to be finalized, travel arrangements made, materials sent to print, and speakers who were going to testify had to be confirmed. After we put the finishing touches on the meeting, one of the consultants to the committee who had been out of town walked into the office. The secretary introduced me to her.

She was a beautiful young Hispanic woman with dark eyes and long brown hair. When she spoke her eyes sparkled. It was so many years ago that I don't remember her name, but I can still recall the essence of her vibrant energy. As time passes we sometimes forget dialogue, but burnt in my mind are her words as she looked me straight in the eyes and asked, "What does it feel like to be different?"

"Different than what?" I responded, somewhat caught off guard by her reference to me.

"You know! That astrology stuff you do!" she replied.

While the phones continued to ring off the hook with people asking questions about the upcoming hearing, I still managed to answer the consultant's questions on astrology, a subject that seemed to fascinate her. I mentioned a couple of interesting cases in which I found myself involved at one time.

My favorite story was about a friend of mine who owned a detective agency in Sacramento. He came to me asking if his beautiful new wife was having an affair. After looking at his wife's astrology chart, I told him if she was, it was on Wednesdays. The man said that was impossible. Now that she had become a Catholic, she went to church on Wednesdays. A week later he peeked in a diary he found of hers and saw the words, "We made love," in blue ink on every Wednesday. Apparently, she was sleeping with the priest. The man confronted the church, and the priest was sent back to Ireland.

"How could you see the affair?" asked the puzzled consultant.

"His wife's chart showed she was sexually aroused and feeling romantic when the transiting Moon went into her fifth house. Each house describes a different area of our life. The fifth house rules love affairs," I explained

"Amazing," she shook her head.

The consultant and I finally went our separate ways to finish the work that needed to be done for the hearing. That night when I went home something unbelievable happened. Each night before I went to bed I always meditated. On this particular night I was sitting in a yoga position on the floor with my back leaning against the wall for support.

The meditation was very deep. Suddenly, in my mind's eye I clearly saw a woman in a market place. Two women were hovering close to her sides as she slowly walked on the street that was made of uneven stone. The woman was in her fifties and slightly plump. There was enough hair sticking out from under the wool shawl she wore to see that it was dark with contrasting gray hair silhouetting her slightly bronzed face. What was bizarre was that she was looking up at me looking back at her, and I knew from within the depths of my soul that she was me.

Suddenly, I was sitting in my bedroom once more realizing that I had just seen one of my past lives. It appeared that I must have lived in the Middle East. I felt that might have explained why I had numerous friends and acquaintances that were from that part of the world that always paid me such great respect.

As I came out of the meditation further, a voice within me spoke firmly, "Take your books to work and do an astrology chart for the consultant you met today," it said.

"The consultant?" I argued with myself, remembering the young Hispanic woman I had met earlier that day. "We may have talked about astrology, but she never indicated that she wanted her chart done. Anyway, I never take my books to work. I would be busy full time and never get my work done if I did." After years of meditation I finally learned to hear an inner voice that frequently guided me. In time it sometimes told me what to say to my astrology clients as if it were talking to their guides.

"Take your books to work and do her chart," I heard once again.

There was something about the firmness in the request that made me feel like the spirit guide knew what it was saying. Early the next morning, I looked for my large *Ephemeris*, a book that had the positions of all the planets in it for a person born from 1900 to 2000. This book would show me where the consultant's planets were when she was born.

However, for the life of me I couldn't figure out why someone who appeared to be so happy that she glowed, needed to have her chart done.

When I arrived at work, I found the consultant's door open to her office. She was editing some papers. I told her I brought a chart and my books in case she wanted me to do a quick reading for her. The consultant was pleased with my offer, and said she would call her mother and get back to me on the break at ten o'clock so that we could do it then.

I vividly remember telling the consultant that I saw she had recently moved and left a loved one behind. It also revealed that if she didn't make the break with this person she cared about, she would eventually be forced to do so. The consultant reached for a handkerchief to wipe the tears now streaming down her face. It was then that she revealed to me that she had left Los Angeles to move to Sacramento recently. There was someone there with whom she was in love, but they broke up. A doctor had just told her that she was pregnant and carrying that man's child. Then she added that she was contemplating suicide the night before. A cold chill ran down my body because it was at exactly the same time as she was having suicidal thoughts that my spirit guide had spoken to me to do her astrology chart. Something had stopped her, she said, but she couldn't figure out what.

"God has already given each of us everything we need in life to do whatever it is that we need to do. It's just a matter of silencing ourselves and reaching inside to see what is right in front of us," I explained to the young woman.

Then I explained how planets forming difficult aspects, which we see as challenges appearing in our lives, move forward in the zodiac where they will later form favorable aspects. So, however difficult a situation appears to be, it can sometimes gauge how beneficial life will be for the person in that same area of their life a few days, months, or years down the road, depending on how long it will take for the transiting planet to move into a more favorable position.

The consultant graciously thanked me over and over for doing the reading for her. She kept saying it was a wonderful gift I had and it had given her some insights and hope. Then she got up and put her arms around me and gave me a hug that warmed my heart.

That afternoon at lunch I was reminiscing about the astrology reading when another strange thing happened. For two years I had been in search of a blue ring that I knew was supposed to be mine but nothing I ever saw felt right. It was then that I could hear the same inner voice talking to me, which had spoken the night before. It was if it were dancing on my shoulder whispering something in my ear, "Your ring.... It's around the corner at the pawn shop."

"But I have been to that pawn shop before and I didn't see any blue ring that I wanted," I argued.

"Your ring. It's around the corner at the pawn shop," the voice grew more insistent.

Since I still had thirty minutes left before I had to get back to work, I decided to pay the cashier and venture around the corner to peek at the jewelry in the pawnshop in case the voice was right.

A ring did catch my eye. It had gold spirals that reminded me of the spirals of the Universe that I had seen in a recent dream. In the center of the gold casting was a 1-karat blue stone. I couldn't get the jeweler who worked there to identify the stone, but he did say that it wasn't Aquamarine or Blue Topaz. I bought the ring and a few days later had the stone tested at Roper's Jewelry store. A young woman working there took the ring into the back room and tested it. When she returned she said it was Tanzanite, which comes from Tanzania. The answer fascinated me because of the vision I had the night before, of the woman in the market place who lived somewhere in the Middle East, which I felt was me in a past life.

The following morning I got a call from the consultant for whom I had done the chart. She said she went home that evening after talking to me to find that the jewelry her former boyfriend had given her had been stolen. Then later that night she had a miscarriage. She said she called to let me know that what she learned from my reading helped her get through it all.

In time she eventually left the Legislature, fell in love again, and got married.

Life wasn't so easily resolved for me. By this time, Jon was twelve years old. Just as my astrological chart had predicted, raising my son was a delight but also my greatest challenge. This child was truly a wise old teacher who had come to teach me about my karmic lesson of motherhood. By today's standards I would say he was a hyperactive child and probably should have been on three different drugs to calm him down, but that sort of treatment wasn't available back then. Ultimately, Jon was also a wayward child, so he kept me on my toes.

For instance, one morning I let my then twelve-year-old Jon off restriction long enough for him to go collect money from his customers on his paper route. After a couple of hours of waiting for him to come home to no avail, I started calling around the neighborhood and learned that he and another boy had taken a Greyhound bus from Sacramento to Great America, which is an amusement park almost a hundred miles away.

That was not the worst of it. When he became a teen, Jon continued to misbehave. Once the police showed up at my door saying that he had been lighting M-80 explosives in the shopping center behind our house. A few weeks later the police came back and said that they found him ditching school and rafting down a draining ditch behind some homes nearby.

My son was like a modern Tom Sawyer, always on some risky adventure out on the streets. Clearly his father not only refused to acknowledge him, but he also refused to help support him and any small sum of money I had previously received in the rear of the chambers was long gone doing catch-up on bills at the time. So, I had to work really hard just to pay the mortgage and keep food on the table not to mention having to come up with money for repairs on the car or house. To help cut corners, I learned how to replace the garbage disposal, plaster holes in walls that my son would accidentally inflict on the house, do electrical wiring and some minor plumbing all by myself.

As the years passed and Jon got older, it was getting harder to do what the Legislature required of me. My career had advanced from clerk typist making crumbs while my son was really young to that of a Committee Secretary making $53,000 a year by the time he was a teenager. To make that kind of money meant being able to track as many as 450 pieces of legislation flying through the Assembly and Senate Houses of the Legislature and frequently working until the wee hours of the morning. For me, it felt like I lived in a world where I was plugged into an electrical socket that was fully charged all the time. Since approval was still important to me, I did my job well, but the price was pretty high when it took a bite out of my private life. Slowly, I began to develop an attitude of "every man for himself," including my son, while I was riding the wave of legislative deadlines.

However, I wasn't the only one selling my soul and energy to the powerful legislative vacuum. The Legislature, by its very nature, sucks up the energy of every staff member with whom it comes in contact if they are as dedicated as I was. I saw staff work until 2 or 3 a.m. only to go home for a few hours to get some sleep and then hurry back to work to analyze bills that were going to be heard in committee or in time to brief their member prior to session the next morning. All too often staffers ended up running to emergency rooms at nearby hospitals after a deadline passed or session ended because they didn't have time to go see a doctor or to take proper care of themselves. Divorces were common and so were the constant fears that information would leak and it would cost them their jobs.

Many workers' compensation lawsuits were quickly settled behind closed doors over stress-related injuries people's bodies sustained. There were also lawsuits staff filed against members for stress or harassments that were also settled outside of the courts. In some cases there were no formal lawsuits filed but suddenly staff members would be making larger salaries, which we all knew was hush money. Sometimes getting a prestigious committee assignment, one that he might even chair, silenced a member.

Chapter 7

As exhausted as I sometimes was, I continued to work full-time and to do my astrology business on the side. As my skills as an astrologer progressed, I began to compare one political figure's chart to another political figure when they stood out in the political arena I found myself sharing. When an attorney goes into practice, he chooses a specialty. Astrologers have specialties in their field as well. My specialty was comparison charts between two people to determine compatibility based on the energies the planets brought to the relationship.

How comparisons are done is really quite simple. We take favorable planets from one person's chart and arrange them on top of another person's chart, which shows what support and positive things this person will bring to the relationship. We can also put the malefic planets, ones that are more challenging, over the chart to see what things might need to be worked out in the relationship between the two individuals or if it is dangerous for there to be a relationship at all. Since one person's planets differ from another person's, one person could bring out the best in us, while being with a different partner might bring out the worst. This was true whether the relationship being compared was that of lovers, a marriage, a business partnership, or even two members of the Legislature.

While working for the Legislature I learned a lot by studying the comparison charts of the various politicians. Without these member's realizing it, which legislator they would clash with and which ones would support them could easily be seen in their astrology charts.

An interesting member that raised my astrological curiosity was Assemblyman Tom Hayden whose spiritual journey began on this planet when he was born on December 11, 1939 in Detroit, Michigan. When Tom Hayden was first elected in 1984, I watched as he attracted a lot of attention because he was married to Jane Fonda, a famous Hollywood movie star who had been active in protesting the Vietnam war. They were both freedom-loving Sagittarians that had Mars in Pisces in their horoscopes. I suspect that it was the "humanitarian cause" that kept them together; later, not sharing the same cause is what ended their marriage. Seeing Mars in Pisces also revealed to me that Hayden was a caring man who had a heart that reached out to the underdog in a situation. If he were a sports fan, he would probably have backed the team that was behind.

During his term in office, I watched Senator Hayden fight against tuition increases in schools in California and fight to have sweat shop workers compensated for lost back wages. Despite his accomplishments, one could hear frustration in his voice whenever he expressed how dysfunctional the political system was in California.

Little did Tom Hayden know that when he was elected to the Legislature he would meet someone he knew from a past life and karma would kick in. It would do so in such a way that the entire Legislature would be affected, which it sometimes was when karmic wars were waged in its political chambers. His arch-rival was none other than Assemblyman Gil Ferguson who was born April 22, 1923 in St. Louis, Missouri.

To the world it appeared as if Tom Hayden was a peace-loving man fighting against war. However, the truth might have been quite the opposite due to his Saturn in Aries, which told me that Tom Hayden was born with a karmic debt that related to war. I felt it was his purpose to speak out and do what he did because of his involvement in the war in a past lifetime when he might have been a soldier who had taken many lives.

What became most fascinating was wondering about Hayden's karmic relationship to Assemblyman Gil Ferguson. Assemblyman Ferguson was born with his Sun in Taurus, which made him stubborn like a bull to say the least. I could see in the astrology charts how these two men's planets interacted with each other's and clashed out into the Universe like two symbols coming together with a loud bang. To make matters worse, Ferguson's Moon and Saturn were making aspect into Hayden's Saturn, which only reinforced what I suspected about the karma they shared. The verbal attacks came from the adverse aspects between Mars, known as the god of war, and Mercury, which rules communications, in their charts. If they could have killed each other with words, they would have. Furthermore, there was a distinct possibility that they might have killed each other in a past lifetime.

How strange it seemed to see two people struggling in a political arena over something they had no idea was controlling them; in fact, it was the past life energy that each still carried that caused them to hate the other. In other words, although they didn't consciously know it, they remembered on some subtle level that they had once been enemies. Suddenly, it was as if they both were in a war such as a Vietnam with guns pointed at each other, not realizing that in truth their battle may have originally been fought in Rome or even China centuries ago. Only Tom Hayden's soul knew if he had to make amends in this lifetime for lives he may have taken in a past one, but as I observed him, I knew there were karmic implications and debts that had to be repaid.

These karmic forces had a field day in 1985 as I watched Assemblyman Gil Ferguson, a high ranking military officer during the war in Vietnam, go after Assemblyman Tom Hayden like a badger for aiding and abetting North Vietnam at a time when we were at war with that enemy. *The Los Angles Times* carried numerous stories that year about what was going on inside the Legislature between these two men. On September 5, 1985, Kenneth Bunting, a reporter working for *The LA Times,* quoted Hayden calling Ferguson, "a retired Rambo having a mid-life crisis, who had no grounds whatsoever to demand that he (Hayden) be ousted."

On June 24, 1986 Ferguson's attempt to oust Hayden from his seat in the Legislature went down on a vote of "41-36." It was ruled out of order and never passed, yet taxpayers in the private war that he had been waging spent thousands of dollars.

I remember working in Assemblyman Ferguson's office on his first day of session. He left his office like a soldier proudly going to do his duty. However, when he returned he seemed quiet and subdued as if to he were suddenly disillusioned. Perhaps it was because military life was orderly and the Assembly Chambers are anything but that. Members walk around talking to other members while a member presents his bill. The Speaker is always banging his gavel to try to get everyone's attention. Members never show up on time, which causes members who do to have to wait around the Chambers until enough members are present to get a quorum so the House can be called to order.

As time went on I, too, would eventually get caught in horrible political battles that were to come. What were at the root of the battles were the Republicans' attempts to oust the Democratic Assembly Speaker. I would come to call him "The Unsinkable" Willie Brown, Jr. because he set the record for holding the title of Speaker longer than anyone else in over two decades; he reigned from 1981 to 1995. When I first encountered this charming and persuasive politician, I naturally had to peek at his astrology chart to see the man behind the mask.

Speaker Willie Lewis Brown, Jr. was born March 20, 1934 in Mineola, Texas. He was the first African American elected to be Speaker of the Assembly in 1981. When he was born, his Sun was in the sign of Pisces, which was conjunct Mars in Aries. Several planets were in Aquarius. As an astrologer these astrological aspects of his chart told me that Willie Brown, Jr. was a humanitarian who fought for the underdog and those less fortunate than himself. His Moon in Gemini with its aspects to other planets in his chart revealed that he was well read, restless, and a keeper of many secrets. Friendships were cherished and were also a part of his karma.

The Willie Brown I first got to know was not entirely the same man he would eventually become. In my possession is an autographed picture Willie Brown gave me back in the '70's. It is autographed by him and it reads, "Jan, Good luck in Washington, D.C., Willie B." What makes the picture so unique is that Brown is wearing a suit that looks like he bought it at K-Mart to match an ugly striped tie. He looks like a young man fresh out of college, sporting plastic glasses, a mustache, and a short Afro hairdo. Today this man is well known for the beautiful suits that he has tailor-made for him in San Francisco for hundreds of dollars apiece.

Willie Brown, was one of the few men whom I came across while working for the Legislature whose essence and presence were strongly felt when he entered a room. He commanded attention just by his presence. I can still remember his laughter and twinkling eyes. He acknowledged everyone that passed his way, but if he were angry, the same eyes could lash out like a whip across one's back.

Although the relationship had begun to be more and more on again-off again, I distinctly recall going to dinner with my son's father, Mark, and asking him to tell me about the "real" Willie Brown. I was curious to see just how closely he would match his astrological chart. Not surprisingly, it was a perfect fit. The legislator told me that Willie wanted to be Speaker early in his political career with the Legislature, but the Democrats felt he was too impulsive, so they waited until he became more seasoned as a politician and less excitable before they turned him loose. Once they did, he steadily rose up the political ladder. Prior to becoming Speaker of the Assembly, Brown was the Chairman of the Assembly Ways and Means Committee. This Committee was responsible for deciding the fate of all bills that have been introduced in the Legislature that require a financial expenditure. As the chairman of "the" money committee, a person becomes very powerful.

Another thing that I learned over that dinner was that the Speaker had cabinet members who worked the Assembly Floor for him and met with him on a routine basis. As to be expected, it was the job of the cabinet members to "work" the legislative floor, voicing the Speaker's desires on certain bills or other matters and sometimes applying pressure to members reluctant to vote the desired way.

Eventually, I learned about another asset this Speaker Brown developed as part of his arsenal. Since both the Republicans and Democrats played a ruthless information game, one morsel of information could be worth a lot, so much so that Willie Brown, Jr. had women known as his "lieutenants" who reported to him on people's every move, watching carefully both staff and other members alike. Most people didn't even know about them. These women, most of who were paid handsomely for their work in various positions within the Legislature, reported to Brown any information they felt he would be interested in. Typically these women were assigned to a member's office, the secretarial pool or even as a consultant to a committee. Nevertheless, they would still report to Speaker Brown behind their bosses' backs.

Not surprisingly, Speaker Brown had a way of charming these women and making them feel so special that they would work even harder to please him. One day, when I was working for a committee, one of the consultants went into her office and put hot rollers into her hair. She made it obvious that she was having lunch with Brown and that it was a "special occasion," requiring one's best foot forward. She was not unusual in this attitude. Other women with whom I had worked over the years who served as Brown's lieutenants also lit up when his name was mentioned or he asked to see them. This was partly because his position was so powerful, but also because he went out of his way to make whatever the women told him seem so important and useful to him that inevitably the women felt honored and worked even harder to get him more "information."

As for me, as an astrologer, I knew it was a karmic cosmic playground, not much different than the times of Rome. There was always scme lieutenant or member of the Legislature who was willing to throw staff or especially a fellow member of the Legislature into the den of lions. Many walked away penniless and disheartened. The press watched closely, so they could report on various members' fall from Willie's grace in newspapers that would go throughout their districts. Then the constituents could "boo" or "cheer."

However, it wasn't until the Secretarial Services Unit sent me on an assignment for three weeks into Speaker Brown's office that I fully understood the tremendous responsibilities this man carried. Many of the incoming calls were from people who, like him, were black. One call I took was from someone concerned about a brother in prison that needed special medicine and felt Brown could help him to obtain it. Another was a call from a woman who called herself "a sister" who needed Brown's help with her children who had been expelled from school in his district.

These were only typical examples. To me, it almost seemed unfair to place so much burden on one man, yet he did what he could and balanced it all really well by still being there for all the people who came to him needing his help but who didn't share his same race. Spiritually, I always felt this was the secret to what gave Willie Brown the tremendous protection he always seemed to have from his enemies. The energy of the good deeds he did for the hundreds of "little people" seemed to create a swirl of positive energy around him, which served as a protective barrier whenever he was in harm's way.

However, his burdens, about which he never complained, didn't stop there. For many years this man had a problem with his vision that most of his colleagues never knew about. All materials he needed to read were retyped in a large font by his staff. He never complained about this handicap. Instead he used his razor sharp mind, which was excellent at processing and retaining information presented to him, to help him. There was one occasion I recall when I was in a newly elected legislator's private office, sitting on the floor updating his government code books. We started talking about Mr. Brown and I mentioned the problems with his sight. The member said he appreciated me telling him about it because it explained why Mr. Brown didn't read the document that he handed him when he went to see him a few days earlier.

When Willie Brown became Speaker of the Assembly, I saw many changes taking place in the manner in which the Assembly would conduct its business. In the past we typed on stencils that could be mimeographed to produce numerous copies. I would be assigned to the Assembly Revenue and Taxation Committee, for example, where all analysis had to be typed by hand. Whenever there was a mistake in one of the lengthy analyses, the secretaries would cut the error out, type the correction, then paste it in, and copy it off. Realizing this, Willie Brown, Jr., brought in state of the art computers and insisted that staff learn how to use them. He no longer wanted consultants so dependent on secretaries and asked that they type their own analysis on the computers and demanded that the analysis be condensed down to two pages instead of the 10 to 20 pages that they sometimes were.

During Brown's reign as Speaker I watched as the political parties became more divided. If the Republicans wanted staff or furniture they went through their respective leaders, and the same was true for the Democrats. This division of parties was very evident to me when I would later serve as committee secretary to the Assembly Reapportionment Committee when reapportionment was actively taking place in the State, which only happened once in ten years after the census figures were released.

Someone wanting to run for a political office would come into our office to try to figure out what cities and counties were going to be in the new district. If he were a Republican, the staff would tell him to go buy a Thomas Map and figure out the boundaries of the district in which he wanted to run. If the person were a Democrat or a Democratic incumbent, a private concealed office had been set up with a staff person that could cut the maps for them. It's a small thing, but it was a valuable tool for a member of the party in power and it weakened anyone trying to run for office in a district for which they had trouble identifying the boundaries.

Although I wasn't exactly as in awe of him as his "lieutenants," when Willie Brown asked me to do something for him, I always felt happy to do it, especially when most consultants had never even met him. Once he asked me to call the Sergeant-at-Arms' Office and instruct them to have the locks changed on a member's office where I was working. Additionally, he told me to make it a policy that he wanted all locks changed within 48 hours whenever a Member vacated an office in the future.

On another occasion Brown appointed a legislator to serve as chairman to a new committee he had just created by splitting one committee into two. Chairing a committee was something the legislator had never done before. The Speaker then asked the chairman to talk to me regarding what needed to be done by his staff members. Of course, I agreed to meet with the new chairman, who assembled his staff together in his private office. I talked for almost an hour, and pencils in the staff's hands flew across the pages on which they were taking notes. Because I had worked for the Legislature so long, I knew every aspect of a committee including the rhythm of the workload.

On still another occasion, at the beginning of a new session, Speaker Brown called me into his office without my knowing what he wanted. When I entered, I noticed his room was full of tall white boards standing on legs. Each board contained the name of a committee. On it were magnetized nameplates of legislators, which he could move from one committee to another as he decided how the memberships would be assigned. It was then that he told me he wanted me to go work with an African-American legislator that he had just assigned as chair to the committee for which I had been working under a different member. Then he looked me straight in the eyes and said, "And this Chair may not like whites, so you might have your hands full." I chuckled as I left his office. As time would bear out, he was right – the member didn't.

Splitting committees and creating new ones was a specialty of Brown's. By doing so, he had a way to repay political favors by assigning several legislators to the new standing committee. One of the more interesting of the Speaker's techniques was to make full use of his power by creating "Select Committees" and "Task Forces." While Brown did not invent the idea of these, he certainly made full use of them. They were on a variety of topics, some of which were created just for the "name recognition" it would earn its members because ultimately members would go to Brown to request a committee on whatever they thought would help win them the most votes in their district. For example, if a Democrat needed to appear to be "tough on crime," or "pro-aerospace," or "anti-pollution" or whatever the issue, Brown could appoint that member to a new select committee dedicated to researching that topic. The member would then instruct his secretary to throw out all of his stationary and design new letterhead that acknowledged his new appointment to his constituents. These committees would conduct hearings, many of them in the chairperson's home district. Of course, these select committees had no real power or effectiveness. No legislation could be heard for a vote there; instead, it had to go to a regular standing committee.

Later, Brown would be highly criticized for his use of these committees. For example, the commentary entitled, "Will Orange County rebound with reform?" which appeared in _The Cal-Tax News_ newsletter on January 1, 1995, states, "There are a number of joint and select committees that do very little and cannot be justified on a cost-benefit basis." Interestingly enough, however, the select committee and task force system is still in place today, remaining a favorite tool of the various Speakers of the Assembly as a way to bestow favors to members of the Legislature.

While I worked for the Legislature during the Brown era, there were certain individuals I ran across whose lives were so dramatically affected by their own karma, with its twists and turns that hearing stories of them brought me down to my own knees humbly once again questioning life, karma, and what was expected of us. Perhaps the most dramatic example of this involved the life of three people whom one would never expect to even know each other much less be so strongly connected at the soul level.

One of the central figures in this karmic dance was Congressman Leo J. Ryan, who was born May 5, 1925. His Sun was in the sign of Taurus, and Uranus in Pisces squared Mars in Gemini. His Moon was in Libra. Since Saturn was in Scorpio it meant that his karma related to that which was mysterious or hidden behind the scenes and also to life and death issues. The Moon foretold how important fairness was to this man. The position of Mars said he couldn't be intellectually satisfied, and he always had something to say or teach people. In life, if he needed a weapon, his words would be it. Since Neptune and Saturn squared his Venus it was plain for me to see that children and loved ones also related to his karma, and somewhere along the line loved ones had hurt him.

I can personally attest to the part about Leo Ryan always having something to say. It was 1968 when I first came to work for the Assembly that I met him. Leo Ryan had been elected to the position of Assemblyman in 1962. I remember how bubbly this good-looking man was as he walked proudly down the halls of the Capitol, sometimes stopping to see the legislator for whom I worked. My job in those days was to open the mail. There was so much mail that came in stamped "Compliments of Assemblyman Leo J. Ryan, 27th Assembly District" that I finally asked the secretary with whom I was working about it. She said he was just that way, always having something to say. So, I told her that his motto ought to be, "Publish or Perish." She laughed.

Assemblyman Leo Ryan attracted a lot of attention, which was probably due to the way he radiated pure energy and enthusiasm wherever he went. He was known for liking to get personally involved in whatever subject attracted his attention at the time. For example, in 1970 he served eight days as a prisoner in a cell in Folsom Prison, so he could experience first-hand what a prisoner experiences. I didn't realize it until later, but already he was living on the edge and tempting his fate by being locked up with violent energies.

A woman who was tied to Ryan by karma was Jackie Speier, who came into the picture when Assemblyman Leo Ryan chose her out of a political science class at a local university to become his aide. That was the beginning of a journey for her that would intertwine her fate with his.

The third person whose fate was woven into the fabric of both Speier's and Ryan's lives was the Rev. Jim Jones, cult leader of the "People's Temple."

In San Francisco, a hugely popular minister, the Rev. Jim Jones was busily organizing political rallies and letter-writing campaigns for his favorite causes. He was so successful at supporting candidates, in fact, that Mayor George Moscone decided to appoint Jones to head the San Francisco Housing Authority in 1976. As *The Associated Press* noted in its November 20, 1978 news wire story, the appointment to that position was clearly "in appreciation for the minister's help in Moscone's successful campaign."

When reports that Jones was allowing beatings of his temple members and questions about how he was raising money began to surface, Jones abruptly resigned the position that Moscone had given him and departed suddenly for Guyana.

In November of 1978, while serving as a United States Congressman from San Mateo, California, Leo Ryan flew to Jones' commune in Guyana with reporters and an aide, Jacqueline Speier, who joined him a little later to investigate Jones and the alleged abuse taking place there. The fact that the congressman's own daughter was a member of the cult and was there at Jones' commune certainly had to be another reason for Ryan's desire to perform the investigation. On the morning of November 18, 1979, Representative Ryan tried to assist several defectors, including his daughter, to escape the settlement by putting them aboard two planes at a nearby airstrip in northwestern Guyana.

When fanatic followers of the cult saw the attempted defection, Ryan was ambushed. Gunfire broke out, and Leo Ryan was shot and killed; his aide, Jacqueline Speier, was critically wounded. When Jim Jones learned that Ryan had been killed, he gathered over 900 of his followers and preached to them for hours about the better life that awaited them when they left the evilness of this world. Then they died when they were given fruit punch laced with cyanide to drink. At that point, Jim Jones put a gun to his head and shot himself to death.

Ironically, a year and a half earlier, Jones had staged a huge protest on the Golden Gate Bridge demanding that a suicide barrier be erected to prevent future suicides because more than 600 people had leaped to their deaths from the famous bridge since it had opened. According to a November 20, 1978 *Associated Press* news wire story, Jones called the suicide victims "realties of society."

As the article further noted, "Hundreds of those in the audience were members of the People's Temple and had arrived for the speech in buses" and "many of them could have been among the nearly 400 persons found dead in the temple's Jonestown farming settlement in Guyana."

The connection between Jim Jones and the California State Legislature was not limited to that of Leo Ryan alone, however. According to the *New York Times* article of Sunday, December 17, 1978, by John M. Crewdson, former members of Jim Jones's cult claimed that Jones "ordered an organized campaign of fraudulent voting practices that included importing busloads of illegal voters to cast ballots in the 1975 San Francisco municipal elections, which included candidates such as the late Mayor George Moscone and Supervisor Harvey Milk, District Attorney John Freitas, Lt. Governor Mervyn Dymally, State Senator Milton Marks and State Assemblyman Willie Brown Jr."

In an article by Ellen Uzelac that appeared in *The Record* on Nov. 15, 1988, the connection between Jones and Willie Brown, Moscone, and Milk was even more important than most people realized. In her article, Uzelac noted that, "Willie Brown, the influential Speaker of the California State Assembly, was one of the People's Temple's greatest supporters, and the late San Francisco Mayor, George Moscone, appointed Jones chairman of the city's housing authority. Moscone and city Supervisor Harvey Milk were assassinated at City Hall a few days after the Jonestown massacre."

The interconnectedness between Jones and political leaders was extensive. For example, in 1977, Democratic Governor Edmund G. Brown Jr. attended a memorial service for the late Rev. Martin Luther King, Jr. at Jones' temple. A Republican State Senator, Milton Marks of San Francisco, once sponsored a legislative resolution praising Jones and his church.

As an astrologer, there are some things I can see, like what the transiting planets were doing in Ryan's astrology chart on the fateful day of his death. What I found was that on a personal level, Ryan's chart indicated he was devastated about something that was happening in his life that related to a loved one or perhaps a child. What he was going through was very painful and very much on his mind during his entire stay in Guyana. Certainly having a daughter caught up in the whole cult business couldn't have been easy for him.

What's interesting is that we don't know what other emotional issues were at work in his life, but we do know that whatever was going on was huge to him, so much so that it almost overshadows the astrological aspects that show his death. To clarify further, on the day he died his chart's aspects were what one would see if one suffered a devastating rejection by a lover or mate. Love stood before Ryan, but he couldn't be happy; instead, he was saddened beyond words – a kind of emotional near death experience that in this case became a real death. While a person's impending death may not always seem to be indicated in an astrology chart, Leo Ryan did have the aspects of someone who had the potential to be shot if one examines the natal chart with which Ryan was born.

Jones, too, had a chart that would reflect his future actions. The Rev. Jim Jones was born on May 13, 1931, in Lynn, IN at 6:57 p.m. He had Scorpio ascending. His Moon, Venus, and Uranus were in Aries at birth. Saturn was in Capricorn where it made a wide square to all three planets. Saturn also opposed Pluto and Jupiter in Cancer, which were also squaring his Moon Venus and Uranus in Aries. This arrangement of planets made up what is known as a T-square in his birth chart. A square aspect is when a planet is within 10 degrees of being 90 degrees away from another planet. It represents difficulty in a person's life, which is spelled out by the house in which it falls. When planet's transit and form a square aspect to natal planets, there will be difficulties as long as the planets remain squared. The crisis will then let up as the transiting planet moves on. In Rev. Jim Jones' case, there were six planets squared in his birth chart.

That chart tells me that Jones was an aggressive man, a born leader who experienced great restraint and control in his own life, which most likely came from his childhood or a mother that may have been too strict. His ego was enormous because Mars was in Leo. His karma in this lifetime related to money, children and loved ones, and something having to do with life and death issues because of his natal Pluto and Jupiter in his 8th house at birth, the house which rules life and death matters. As far as I am concerned, no matter how reprehensible his actions may have been, this man chose to incarnate in this lifetime for one purpose – to live out his negative karma. He did exactly what he came here to do at precisely when he was supposed to do it.

The chart further tells me that on November 18, 1978, when Jones ordered everyone to drink the poisoned punch, he felt a great surge of energy and was moved to do what he did because the transiting Mars and Neptune were forming a trine to his natal Mars in Leo in his 9th house of philosophy and religion. When this occurred one more thing was going on. Transiting Pluto, for the first time since Jones was born, moved into Libra and formed an added arm to the T-square of planets that he had in his birth chart, forming a CROSS. On the day the mass suicide was ordered, the Moon moved into Cancer, and ignited the planets that were now squared in the cross formation.

As an astrologer, I can tell that Jones knew exactly what he was doing, felt he was in complete control, and felt no remorse whatsoever. Since the natal Saturn was locked into this squared off cross, what happened was karmic – again something he came to this lifetime to do.

Another interesting thing about Jones is that he had the Sun in Taurus and Mercury in Taurus. Taurus placements like these suggest that survival of the family means everything. For Jones, the people in his cult were his family and somehow the maniac thought he was protecting them or taking them to a safe place where they would be together. Interestingly enough, Adolph Hitler was a Taurus by Sun sign. He wanted survival of the family as well in the form of a "pure" German race. Both men found strange ways to act out this intense desire for family unity.

I go one step further and say that due to the planets in Aries when Jones was born (the ones that made the T square) it was very likely that Rev. Jim Jones was a military officer in a previous lifetime and dealt with the deaths of masses of people then. In any case, as horrible as it was, Jones lived out his karmic destiny – and had to take on all of the negativity that went with it, if not in this lifetime, then certainly in the next.

Congressman Ryan was laid to rest at Golden Gate National Cemetery in San Francisco. Pursuant to his request, the 'Navy Hymn' was played at his funeral and he was bid farewell with the words he loved of H. L. Mencken's, "When I depart this vale of tears, if you have some thought to please my ghost, forgive some sinners and wink your eye at some homely girl." The world and the people who knew him saw his life was over and that he was now dead and gone. For me, however, yes, he had died, but now he was going to review the life he had lived and then later would reincarnate as a baby to start all over again. Whenever I thought about these three people and their shared karma, I would have to sit down and think about my life – and the lives of all I knew. The more I studied spiritual matters, the more I realized just how significant karma is to us all.

At the same time as I mulled over the way karma worked, I stayed busy working for as a standing committee secretary. In those days, what little strength I had left after working all day was taken away when I got home. It was easy to let things my son was doing slip by. But little demons become bigger demons in time if we keep feeding them the wrong food or energy. Obviously, I wasn't giving my son what he needed, and as a result his behavior problems escalated out of control.

At age fifteen, my son Jon's charm and persuasion had landed him a job as an assistant cook for the International House of Pancakes which was around the corner from where we lived. I told him that I didn't mind him working if he did his homework and kept his room picked up. When I went to put some clothes away in his room one night, however, I noticed that it looked like a cyclone had hit it. Food was strung out all over it, clothes were on the floor, and his bed was unmade.

I called him at work and asked him to come home right away. He came running home to see what was wrong. I told him he couldn't keep his job unless he could keep up with school and his responsibilities at home. They came first. He brushed it off like it was no big deal and warned me not to call him at work like that anymore.

Jon was acting weird. I seldom let my son know what I was seeing astrologically, but my mind took a quick look at his chart and I saw a ruthless aspect by a transiting planet was being made to his natal Saturn. However, there was nothing I could do or say that he would understand.

Ever since he was born, whenever that particular aspect formed in his chart something bad had always happened, and this time was no exception. Little did I know how much worse things were about to get.

Later that night, I remember rolling over and looking at the clock. It said 12:30 a.m. Suddenly, there was a loud knock at the door. I waited to see if it was just my imagination playing tricks on me like it had all evening, but the knock came again. This time it was even more forceful. I peeked out my bedroom window. Red lights were flashing on a squad car from the Sheriff's Department. I grabbed my robe and stumbled sleepily to the door.

The officer told me he had my son in the back seat of the car. I raced past him towards the vehicle.

"Who do you think you are? You had no right arresting me," he was shouting at the officer trailing behind me.

The officer tried to calm him down. "I've brought you home. But if you keep it up I will have to take you to Juvenile Hall!"

"Take me. See if I care, "he shouted disrespectfully.

"Stop it," I pleaded with my son.

His eyes were glaring like a frightened wild animal that had been captured. The officer tried to help him out of the car, but Jon struggled and shouted foul language. Suddenly, the officer threw him up against the car. I couldn't take any more. I ran into the house and closed the door hoping against hope it would all just go away like a bad dream. But it didn't. I opened the door again, but this time it was worse. The officer had my son face down on the sidewalk beating his fist against Jon's back, my son's hands cuffed behind him. A second officer standing close by looked up at me and told me Jon took a swing at the other officer. He added that Jon was drunk and they were taking him to the Hall. They shoved my son into the back seat of their squad car and drove off.

The following day I went to work feeling exhausted from not getting any sleep. Once I got there I received a call from Juvenile Hall saying I could go pick up my son. It was hard getting away from work. Recently I had accepted a new position as committee secretary. It was February, and the new Legislative session had just begun.

All the way home from Juvenile Hall Jon talked about what happened and what it was like being locked up. He told me stories abut a kid urinating on another kid's pillow, fights that had broken out in the chow line, and how the food that wasn't fit for a dog to eat. Deep inside I was grateful that he experienced what he had, especially since he said he was going to change now. Once again, I wanted and needed to believe him.

Later that night I went to the corner grocery store. When I got home, I was greeted by two burly plain clothed officers sporting guns in their holsters, flashing a search warrant under my nose, and demanding that I let them search my house. Shocked, speechless, and terrified, I stepped aside and let them in.

One of the officers informed me that my son was suspected of being involved in multiple crimes that had happened the night before. Then a few minutes later the officer returned, with my son in handcuffs, and said they found traces of marijuana on his dresser. He looked at me and asked me if I knew my son was doing drugs. I shook my head "no" in disbelief as I looked at Jon who refused to look me in the eyes. The officers booked him and took him back to Juvenile Hall.

Not long after that I learned Jon had also stolen a new truck, which just happened to belong to a retired sheriff. My son found a loaded gun in the back of the truck and pumped the vehicle full of holes. Then he busted the glass doors at the recreation center near where he abandoned the vehicle in a small creek.

Every time I got another call at work from the D.A.'s office, the Sheriff's Department, or the Hall, I wanted to cry, to die, or to have a way out. When I thought I couldn't take anymore, something would always happen to test me further. For example, when Mother's Day rolled around, I had to bail my dog out of the dog pound when he dug beneath a fence and got out. Then I had to visit Jon at the Hall. That was good for two more doses of guilt and many tears. No one, not anyone, knew what I was going through, especially anyone at work. Secrets built upon more secrets until I felt as if I would explode from the combined weight of it all.

I remember having turbulent dreams throughout this time. One dream stood out because I remember seeing a funeral in it. I thought it was my grandmother's. I called my stepmother and asked her if someone had died in our family. She said no. We talked about my grandmother and my Uncle Lee Roy's name came up in passing, a name I hadn't heard in years. The feeling of the dream wouldn't leave me, though, and I kept thinking about how I felt such an awful sense of grief and how emotionally exhausted I was when I woke up the morning afterwards.

A few days later I got a call from my stepmother.

"Jan," she said anxiously. "You won't believe what happened."

"What is it, mom?" I questioned.

"Your Uncle Lee Roy...."

"What about Uncle Lee Roy?" I spoke up interrupting her.

"We've been wanting to call you, but we were too busy with all that happened ...all so suddenly...."

"I don't understand. What's going on," I demanded to know.

"Remember when you called and asked if someone in the family had died?"

"Yes."

"Your Uncle Lee Roy wrote a note to your father, and then shot himself. It happened the night you dreamed a family member had died."

"I am sorry to hear that," I said trying to comfort her and feeling the pain of her loss.

"Oh, that's okay, he was no good anyway. He deserved to die," she said in her southern accent.

"What was in the note?" I asked wondering if he said something to my dad about the night he ran him off the property with a shotgun when my father caught him in my room with me.

"Don't know. Your dad wouldn't say," she said. "He just tore it up, but I could tell he was pretty shook up about it. He hasn't said a word in several days. He just goes out to his shop and works."

After I hung up, I thought, "Why me? How are our souls connected? Is it from a past life? How could I have known that someone had died, let alone him?"

That made me wonder who my son, Jon, had been in a past life. What had I done to deserve the difficulties I was having with him? What had he done to deserve the difficult life I gave him? Had I abandoned him at one time? Who were my other two sons in a past life and why had they chosen me to be the one to abandon them in this life when they were so young and I let their father raise them? I struggled to understand.

Eventually, Jon ended up being sentenced to the Boys Ranch. I sounded like Gandhi every time I went to visit him on weekends. I came with my arms full of pizza or sandwiches, sodas, and his favorite candy bars.

"Don't take on the guards," I tried to tell him. "They have a life sentence to this place whether they know it or not by the career they have chosen. Most of them have been here long before you were born and will be here long after you leave it."

I tried to explain that his biggest problem was his thinking. Over and over I would try to talk about cosmic laws, never knowing if Jon was merely acting like he understood or if he really did. "If you steal something, it won't stay in your life. You will lose it. It will disappear or worse, something will be stolen from you," I would explain. It seemed so important for me to try and get him to understand that our thoughts create our realities and what we think is what we make happen. If we fear something, suddenly we will be staring it straight in the eyes. However, he seemed to pay attention when I said, "If you kill someone, someone will kill you. It is the law of karma."

"There are plenty of people who have killed someone who didn't get killed, mom," he would say.

"If you don't get killed in this lifetime, then you might in the next," I answered. "It has to do with some kind of cosmic score card that some mysterious force keeps track of," I added.

It was like talking to a thirty-year old that was slowly reverting back to that of a seventeen-year old, but on some level I knew he was listening to me. I could also tell that he was extremely depressed. Each time our visiting time was up, his head of long brown hair drooped as he walked away, dragging his feet. My heart was breaking, but the authorities had my hands tied as his mother. He now belonged to them and since he was a part of me, so did I.

Chapter 8

With my son now in detention, work once again became my refuge. I remember decorating the Assembly Secretarial Unit in which I was working with Christmas decorations. I noticed my supervisor waving her phone and pointing to a phone outside her office to let me know I had a call. It was 1985.

"Hi, Janice. This is Rusty," said the cheerful voice on the other end of the phone.

I was silent for a moment.

"Assemblyman Rusty Areias," he laughed boyishly, thinking I didn't understand him.

My heart pounded. I didn't know why a legislator was calling me personally. Right away I wondered what I had done wrong in his office the last time I had helped out.

"Hi, Mr. Areias," my voice fluttered as I responded. "Where are you?" I knew the house was not in session because of the holidays.

"I am calling from my ranch. I want to ask a favor of you."

"What's that?" I asked while feeling honored that the most handsome bachelor member of the Legislature was calling me.

"I want you to come to work for me. I have a committee secretary and a legislative secretary position open. Take your pick and it is yours."

"But I have always only been back-up a secretary with a committee. I haven't been a committee secretary or a legislative secretary before," I spoke up.

"It doesn't matter. I have seen your work in this office, and I want you working with me," he said.

I was quiet for a moment. Then as I sat listening to him go on and on about why I would be perfect for the job, I remembered working in Assemblyman John Vasconcellos' office, which was the chairman of the Assembly Ways and Means Committee. All bills that relate to money coming out of the budget must be heard before this committee. One day I had gotten a call from the Assembly Rules Committee, which does all the hiring and firing and takes care of House business along with the members' personal requests. The woman who called said I was to forget my assignment to the Ways and Means Committee and go at once to Assemblyman Areias' office to help him out. I mentioned that he could have someone from the Speaker's Office of Majority Service. The female executive officer said, "Rusty wants you and no one else."

Now, here he was again, requesting me specifically.

"I enjoy doing committee work the most," I hedged as the member waited for my response. I realized that somehow I had impressed him previously with my work with him but still wasn't sure I could handle the job.

"Wonderful, the job is yours. I will give you a ten-percent salary increase no matter what you are making now," he added.

"Thank you, sir." My head swam when I thought about getting a ten-percent salary increase from Rusty, and another ten-percent because I would be working for a member. They were also giving out cost-of-living increases in a few weeks, which meant another five-percent increase. Suddenly, I was making thousands of dollars more a year.

"Have a nice Christmas. I will call the Assembly Rules Committee and make sure all the paperwork is taken care of immediately, so you can start to work in January. Welcome aboard. We will see you then," he said before hanging up.

"Thanks Rusty," I answered. I saw my supervisor looking directly at me. I could tell she was anxious to know why a member had called me personally. I walked into her office and said I had taken the job.

Of course, I had looked at his chart long before, but I quickly looked at it once again just to refresh my memory. Assemblyman Rusty Areias was born September 12, 1949, in Los Banos, California. His Sun was in the sign of Virgo conjunct Saturn and he had a lot of planets in Libra including Venus. This natal chart told me as an astrologer that he was hard working and a worrier but also an incurable romantic who wore rose-colored glasses. Whenever I see a lot of planets in Libra, including Neptune, it shows me that the individual lives life as if it were an art gallery – he wants everything to be beautiful and perfect. For people with these placements, their work, partner, kids, and money resemble pictures in an art gallery that must look a certain way to them, and when reality sets in and the circumstances don't match the pictures they painted, it often times creates pain and disappointment to the idealistic person. Areias was no exception.

Areias was elected in 1982 but he was still trying to get a fix on how the system functioned. It was overwhelming to someone newly elected. I remember he wasn't fond of talking to the lobbyists, but I explained to him that they were important because they knew the background on the issues. Besides, he needed their support if he expected to raise any campaign money. Gradually, he started warming up to them.

What made Rusty stand out so much in the Legislature were his incredible good looks and his young boyish manner. In jest, a female friend of his submitted his picture to *The Farm Journal* to nominate him as the magazine's "Bachelor of the Year." *The Farm Journal* turned around in January of 1985 and not only published his photo but also did in fact name him "Bachelor of the Year."

In the photograph, Rusty was sitting on a fence wearing a dark suit, a maroon tie, and a big smile. His eyes seemed to twinkle, almost portraying mischief. The caption read, "Two-term State Assemblyman Rusty Areias, 36, is also a third-generation dairy farmer who enjoys skiing, collecting Indian artifacts, and 'athletic, articulate women who have their own sense of style.'" It also listed the address of his family farm in Los Banos. Some time later, Rusty told me the reason he was sitting on the fence having his picture taken in the first place was because a bull was mating with a cow in the background, so a friend jokingly snapped the shot with their camera.

The sexual energy of what was happening in the background must have created a certain kind of sexual lure to the photo because, as a result of his picture being published, Rusty received over 1200 letters from women throughout the United States, all interested in telling him about themselves, and some even detailing thoughts of what they wanted to do to him if they ever got close enough to him to do it. Interestingly enough, Rusty was engaged to a young woman named Carolyn, so he could look but not touch. Nonetheless, lobbyists who came into the office with serious looks on their faces and political issues on their minds that needed to be discussed were always cracking up when they came out of his private office because Rusty had shown them some of the "hotter" letters he had received from his "babes."

In those days, the transiting planets smiled on the young politician. Girls adored him and flirted with him up and down the halls of the Capitol. Press cameras were always clicking wherever he went. An example of this popularity occurred when Rusty won second place in the Calaveras County Frog Jumping contest that took place in the park of the Capitol every year. What was so unusual about it was that Rusty's picture appeared in the newspaper, but the legislator who came in first place didn't.

I would talk to Rusty about his chart once in a while. He tried very hard to do what everyone expected of him. For example, I could see that the loss of his mother was devastating to him. He missed her so much that he confessed to me that he felt a lot of pressure to get married and have children to carry on the family name. As he talked, it reminded me of his cattle on the ranch. People buy them for the purpose of producing offspring to carry on the bloodlines. While he longed to comply with his family's wishes, deep down he feared that he wasn't ready to marry his fiancée` and hesitated to set an actual date. I am sure the letters from all the attractive single women across the country didn't help matters between them. Not surprisingly, they eventually broke up.

Rusty used to throw the most elaborate fundraisers I ever attended. I went to one in his district where tender slabs of beef that were from the Harris Ranch were grilled in enormous fire pits. I remember it was then that I met Rusty's father. While Rusty was good looking, I always thought that it was his father who was the handsome one in the family.

Most memorable for me, though, were the garlic galas Rusty would have at Sutter's Fort in Sacramento. It is an old fort that has been restored as a museum in Sacramento, complete with cannons, rooms that replicate the old west, and a lookout tower. Inside were tables and chairs, a band playing, and a place for people to dance. A bar of beer, wine, and soft drinks was set up for the guests. The highlight of the annual event were the chefs that came in from Rusty's district that also cooked for the famous Gilroy Garlic Festival that they have every year in Gilroy, California.

I remember the meal that was served consisted of calamari, tender slices of grilled beef, pasta, green salad, and French bread, all created with loads of garlic. For desert there was ice cream. It wasn't garlic ice cream, but it could have been for all the garlic flavors that were still in my mouth from the food I ate.

Rusty was good about giving complimentary tickets to staff and also to the Sergeants-at-Arms, so they could attend his functions. For the sergeants, it was a payback for all the personal things they had done for him. Sergeants were required to pick members up at the airport and take them back. They also took their laundry to the cleaners, deposited and cashed checks for them and ran errands. But often times, the sergeants shared with me how Rusty asked them to do things that they weren't required to do but since he was a member, they didn't make an issue of it. For example, they said he would ask them to stay in their cars and wait for him while he attended various dinners. He also asked them to drive his fiancée` to the beauty shop and pick her up and one Sergeant shared with me that he even asked him to drive his fiancée` back to the district which was several hours away.

Many celebrities attended Rusty's fundraisers. I loved taking pictures of them and was able to capture Jessie Unruh and Willie Brown, Jr., the former and present Speakers of the Assembly at the time. Betty Vasquez, was there from *KCRA Radio* along with numerous legislators from both the Assembly and Senate. Well-known lobbyists attended who had been targeted to buy several tickets in order to make the fund-raiser a success.

Eventually, term limits were enacted, which meant that Areias would be out of a job; as a result, he ran for State Controller in 1994. The bid was unsuccessful, however. On September 6, 1994, Pamela Podger reported in *The Fresno Bee* that Areias had lost the election for State Controller despite the fact that he had raised $2 million in the campaign.

Areias returned to his hometown of Los Banos to face the wrath of his fellow farmers who were up at arms against him for helping sell underground water to agriculture's urban foe: the Metropolitan Water District of Southern California. Rusty was also named in a sexual harassment suit that was filed against his former chief of staff.

Of the negative press, Areias said, "I've probably gotten more negative newsprint in the last six weeks than at any time in my career."

Then he went on to say, "This isn't what I expected, but sometimes you cannot control the timelines."

As an astrologer, I deal with timelines, so naturally those words would catch my attention. By looking at Rusty's chart to see where the planets were on September 6, when he talked to the reporter, I could see deep disappointment, a sense of betrayal of some sort, financial expenditures that would have shook up most, and enormous roadblocks he was feeling in life at the time.

A lot of what he went through was karmic. I am sure he felt as if he went into an art gallery that represented his life and saw that all the pictures were crooked, a few had fallen off the wall, and some were even stolen. Later, when Saturn moved away, Rusty would go on to serve as the Director of the State Parks Department.

As a committee secretary working for Rusty, I got to experience what it was like sitting at the dais in front of a room full of people while cameras rolled and the press took notes. Every time I called the roll and recorded votes through the microphone, I knew my job was on the line if a bill passed or failed passage by a vote I heard wrong. It was my job to know the rules of the House when the Chair asked me a question about proper procedure. This responsibility alone exerted a lot of pressure on me when members sometimes tried to bend the rules. I always made it known that I didn't care what rule they were breaking, but it was my job to tell them which one it was before they tried to do it. It was also my responsibility to keep an eye on which members were walking out of the room or coming back into it, so I knew whether or not we had a quorum present before trying to take a vote.

It was then that I learned how legislation was really handled in the Legislature. As tragic as it was, sometimes the fate of legislation was in the hands of an intern writing the analysis who had never written an analysis before. In Committee, the banging of the Chair's gavel and the words, "This meeting is adjourned," could also determine the fate of a piece of legislation. During the close of session it was the Speaker's gavel that decided when the House would adjourn and whether a bill would die because the hour was late, the members wanted to go home, and the legislation therefore wouldn't get a chance to be heard.

Over the years, I edited many analyses whose fate had already been determined because the Chair of one of the committees wanted the bill killed or passed. Worse yet, there were times when the Speaker gave word to the consultants that no bill that a certain member authored was to get out of a committee, and no member of the Speaker's political party was to vote in support of those bills if they somehow managed to get to the Floor of the House. When wars were waged between the parties the war was waged on legislation. Then the party controlling the House determined the fate of the bill. The games in the political arena were brutal and the instruction manuals non-existent. Survival of the fittest was always in play.

The support and opposition to the bill was typed on the committee analysis so members could see where the most clout was in it for them in their districts. It was hard getting all the support and opposition noted in time for the hearing because letters would straggle in at the last minute, and the clock said we had to go to print. It was so important to know who was in support or opposition of a bill that a supplemental list had to be created when additional positions came in late. A lot of times, members didn't even have to read the analysis, just the names of various lobbyist or grassroots organizations to decide whether or not they, as legislators, were in support of the legislation, which made me question all the work and late hours the staff invested in writing the analysis. Why bother? It would be easier to just make a list of organizations and their positions.

If one wanted to get the bill out of a committee, the consultant would emphasize the good points and use the argument of the people in support of it. If one wanted it killed, the consultant would write the analysis from the opponent's perspective.

I remember an attorney who was a consultant who was enthusiastic about his work and always got the analyses done on time. That person was fired. I went to the chief-of-staff and asked why. He said it was because the consultant couldn't "feel the pulse of the party" and write the analysis accordingly despite the fact that this person was otherwise good at his job. In other words, the consultant failed to know if the party wanted a bill to live and instead tried to be objective about legislation, letting it live or die on its own merits – something simply not allowed.

While consultants and secretaries were being driven by deadlines, I was being driven by fears over my son who was still locked up. One time when I went to visit him, my son complained about a tooth hurting him. His counselor wasn't going to let him go to the dentist, but when I intercepted, they let Jon go. The dentist said he had an impacted wisdom tooth that was severely infected, and he immediately pulled it. On another occasion Jon hurt his arm and I had to do battle with the ranch to get it looked at by a doctor. The doctor said it was broken and needed a cast on it. The counselor was so furious that Jon couldn't work that he demanded that my son spend sunup to sundown sitting on a picnic bench for three days in the sun as punishment.

Then something strange happened. Jon may have finally understood what I had been trying to teach him and sent a message out to the Universe, saying, "I have had enough."

His original sentence of only a few weeks had grown longer and longer due to his continued misbehavior while at the ranch. When one last petty offense resulted in an even longer sentence, that's when he decided to escape the ranch and run home. I came home only to find him lying in bed exhausted like a limp rag from walking so far. It tore my insides out to say, "Son, you have to go back."

When I took him back, he was transported from Boys Ranch to Juvenile Hall to wait for his hearing before a judge. We didn't know what was going to happen since he had so many months left to serve. On one visit I asked him what he was mentally visualizing as a potential sentence.

"I see myself being locked up for six months," he said waiting for my response to see if I approved of what he said.

"How strange," I told him. He watched my face closely as if wondering why I said that.

"I was only visualizing a lock up of one month," I smiled.

"You can do that?" he asked, his eyes lit up.

"You can visualize whatever you want to the Universe. I told you that we create our own realities with our thoughts," I laughed.

When Jon's case was heard, the judge sentenced him to six weeks in Juvenile Hall. Suddenly, the many months he would have served at Boys Ranch if he hadn't run away were gone. That particular lesson in life was over, and he graduated for the time being. He had told the Universe that he had enough of the Hall and then manifested a way to leave that experience and journey on to another one.

In the years that followed, Jon's drug issues would finally have to be dealt with and the only way they could be was by my learning not to interfere with the arrows the Universe was trying to shoot at him. Each one I tried to intercept was a lesson he didn't learn. Each time I tried to use my money to help him out, it took more money the next time to fix his problems.

One day I went looking for Jon because his boss had called from work saying he didn't show up that morning. William, Jon's older brother, moved to Sacramento when he got out of the Army after being stationed in Germany for several years. He decided to let my Jon stay with him for a short time until he got on his feet. Because I was concerned about the call from Jon's boss, I decided to go to their apartment to see what was wrong. William told me Jon was there. Just then he came out of the back room wearing only a pair of jeans. His shoulder muscles were flexed. I told him his boss called looking for him.

"I have done a lot of thinking," he blurted out with a mean look on his face.

"I want counseling," he shouted inches away from my face, standing six feet tall.

"Get it yourself," I answered.

"I want an education," he snapped. "And I want my dad to pay for it," he demanded.

That was a cheap shot and it hurt, especially since his dad hadn't done anything for us ever, let alone acknowledge my son as his. Right away the guilt over the pain I knew my son felt about never having known his father threatened to overwhelm me. As a mother, my guilt bothered me more than the verbal darts he was throwing at me.

"Get an education yourself. I've tried to help you with books in the past. This time you do it," I retorted, then took a step backwards, fearful he might haul off and hit me.

Then I turned and walked out the door, loudly slamming it shut. My son's remark about his dad hurt me. Worse yet, in a few days I knew William would be moving out of town, and Jon would be left homeless. I decided then and there that I wasn't going to help him, no matter what, even if he showed up on my doorstep with no place to live.

Two weeks later I heard someone knocking at the door of my lovely little home in Laguna Creek just South of Sacramento. It was the smallest house on the block, but it was all I could afford and I took great pride in it. I had planted the lawn in the backyard by hand, landscaped it with beautiful roses, and hauled in river rock that I put on the side for a stream that flowed when it rained.

When I opened the door and saw Jon standing there, it was my worst nightmare. My heart pounded as the Universe delivered another cosmic fist that sent a crushing blow to my gut.

"Mom, I have no place else to go. Can I come live with you?" he asked.

My mind quickly went into its memory bank to see what kind of data I could come up with on how to deal with the moment, but there was nothing there. This kid had stolen a diamond ring from me the last time I let him stay with me, and it couldn't be replaced. He had stolen my vehicle late one night to go joy riding even though that was my only means of transportation to get to and from work. Then there were the cop cars that were always parked in front of my house because my son had done something or another to break the law. This was a new neighborhood. I just wanted a new life. I didn't want it to be the way it had been anymore, yet woven into my thoughts was the fact that he was my son.

I had attended a couple sessions of Tough Love, an organization created to help parents having problems with children who have been on drugs. In my mind, I could hear them yelling at me, "You are not to give him a dime for a phone call, let alone anything else. He's on his own. Don't give in. DON'T GIVE IN!"

"Jon, you can't stay with me...." I began.

"Wait, mom, before you say anything! I got a job working at a pizza parlor around the corner. I am enrolled at the junior college a couple of miles away, and I am in counseling," he reasoned. I noticed how nice he looked with a haircut.

Against the advice of Tough Love, my heart kicked the door wide open.

"Come in, son," I said, stepping aside.

During the months that followed, I watched a healing take place. I had a nice car in the driveway, while his car, which he parked in front of my lovely home, was beat up. He had spent so much time at the river fishing and doing his drugs that the car's front window was broken and its paint was faded and chipped. But suddenly, I didn't care what the neighbors thought anymore. I didn't even care what the Tough Love members said. My inner voice whispered, "Take him in," and I had.

This time when my son said he needed some money to fix his car when it broke down, I said, "No." Instead, I watched him trade his car for a bicycle. The bike that he traded it for didn't need any money for upkeep. For the first time, I could see that he really could make it without me. Of course, he still tested me when he could, but for the most part his attitude had changed for the better.

One day he called me to pick him up at school because it was raining. I remember laughing and saying, "I didn't put a bicycle in my Universe." Since he had manifested that as a means to get around, I said, "Ride it." A few months later, he called to say he needed a piece of paper sitting on his bed because he was signing up for fall classes and had forgotten it. That I took to him.

In the end, the healing took place only when I stopped saving him and allowed him to empower himself. After six months passed, I told him it was time for him to move out because that was how long I said he could stay. He was doing really well, but I knew he needed to be on his own. Later, his counselor let me know how concerned he was. He said Jon was taking baby steps and needed to be encouraged to continue the good work and remain with me. Instead, I told Jon he had the power to manifest what he needed in the Universe by using positive thoughts.

It wasn't until after Jon moved out that he told me he had visualized a room that had a bed in it, a place that would be close to school and also to his work, and one that he could afford. As it turned out, he found a house across the street from his school that had been converted into a place for students. His room had a mattress on the floor to sleep on and a desk where he could do his homework. The rent was cheap enough for him to afford and his job was so close that he could ride his bike to it. Interestingly, one of his roommates was into meditation and Eastern philosophy. Amazingly enough, not only was Jon keeping his room neat now, but he also took it upon himself to plant a beautiful garden in the backyard. Seeing these changes let me know that a part of him was at peace.

Chapter 9

I eventually left Rusty's office and went back to work for the Secretarial Services Unit where I could go back into different member's offices, which I always enjoyed doing. My experience as a committee secretary added to my skills and put me in high demand by the members who needed to temporarily replace staff. But it was my astrology business that really took off at this time. Various members of the Legislature and their family members were regular customers, including Barbara Collier, the wife of former Senator Randolph Collier, who was born July 26, 1902 in Etna, California. Mrs. Collier frequently had me look at her husband's astrology chart. His Sun was in the sign of Leo, and he had numerous planets in Cancer. His chart told me that he was a proud man who loved his home and family. It was through his family that I first met him.

My files are full of letters from Senator Collier's wife Barbara. Barbara was the love of Randolph's life. Randolph's hair was snowy white against his fair skin, which gave him the reputation of being the "Silver Fox of the Siskiyous." Nothing pleased him more than to introduce to his colleagues to his wife Barbara, who was 35 years his junior, and later their baby, Natasha, who was born in 1973. His wife told me she was Russian although she was born in China and spoke French fluently. Her skin was milky white against her auburn brown hair, and she treated everyone she met as if he or she was the most important person she ever met, and to her they probably were at the moment.

I remember the childlike innocence of this beautiful woman who was a product of her times. Barbara Collier told me many stories about her life before she came to America and each one was interesting enough to be part of the book she wanted to one day write. Her first marriage ended in divorce, leaving her with two small girls that became Randolph's stepdaughters. She and Randolph had two daughters of their own. I knew the two young ones better than the two older ones who were fully grown by the time I met Randolph's wife.

On numerous occasions Randolph would find himself outside my two story apartment building, sitting in his car that had a state license plate acknowledging him as a member of the Senate, while he waited for his wife to get an astrology reading.

Randolph was the Dean of the Senate and was known as the "Father of the California Highways" because he chaired the Senate Transportation Committee for many years and presided over the massive expansion of the State's freeway system. He also co-authored the landmark 1947 legislation that triggered the onset of highway construction in the State.

Collier was a simple man and a proud one. On the other hand, his wife, Barbara, was a nightingale that attracted a lot of public attention wherever she went. Unfortunately, her past was heavily laden with difficulties, which she experienced as a child. Reading her chart was always interesting, and she was always grateful to me for doing so.

Another person in Randolph's family for whom I read was his sister, Ruth. She was working in the Assembly Secretarial Services Unit when I first went to work for the California State Legislature back in 1968. Ruth was in her sixties and had never been married. Ruth was proud of her brother Randolph and was always boasting about what he and his wife were doing, but the thing that makes me fondly smile now is the stories she would come to work everyday and tell about her neighbors.

Ruth lived in a small apartment building across from the Capital Park. It was an old building, but it was within walking distance to work, which made it nice for her. Every morning she would approach my desk when she came in with a look of despair in her eyes. Then she would proceed to tell me about all the sexual noises her neighbor was making all night long. It didn't take long to figure out that her neighbor was probably a prostitute. Although I would never have admitted it, every time Ruth told me the latest story, I would picture her holding a glass up to the wall, so she could better hear what was going on in order to have some excitement in her own life. It was through Ruth that I met Randolph's wife.

Randolph had a vision in 1970 of dividing California into two states: the western-urban coastal and the rural-interior. Several legislators thought California should be divided and some thought it should have a different name as well. After reapportionment of his Eureka-based district, Collier lost his seat in 1976 to Ray Johnson, a Republican who registered as an independent. Barbara was very upset that reapportionment had done this to her husband, who had contributed so much to the history of California. But it was many years later before I finally knew what kind of an impact reapportionment could have on a member's district and his ability to win a race.

Randolph Collier died in Mercy Hospital on August 2, of 1983 of chronic obstructive pulmonary disease. I attended his funeral services, which were held at St. Paul's Episcopal Church in Sacramento, but the memorial service was held in Eureka. He was 81 years old when he died.

While most people watched intently at what was going on politically within the Legislature, my astrological eyes were watchful as to what was happening to various members according to their astrology charts. I gathered their birth data from their public biographies and in some cases from the member himself that I kept over time.

The charts helped me to see them without their masks, which certainly helped me to get along with them better when I was called into their offices. It also helped to warn me if I was about to get my head chopped off from their anger when some transiting planet ignited their planets. As one friend of mine used to say, it got to the point where I could warn her months in advance of when she was going to have a fight with her boss the legislator, and inevitably she did. The fights would occur even if my friend were on vacation on those predicted dates and times; not surprisingly, her boss would simply end up calling her at home to provoke an argument.

Sometimes I was observant of the impact a planet had when it moved into a sign. For example, Saturn moved into Scorpio back in 1983. Scorpio rules the underworld, sex, and that which is unseen. Saturn is a planet that can suppress or restrain conditions according to what sign or house it transits. In 1984, Pluto moved into Scorpio. Pluto destroys in order to rebuild. With both of these planets in place, it was as if a time bomb had begun to tick. Since both of these planets are considered to be "malefics," their combined influence would be felt by all of us. Pluto's need to destroy in order to rebuild results in secrets being exposed, for it demands that our karmic lessons be learned. In fact, during the time span of 1985 to 1988, while Saturn transited Scorpio, revelations about sex and money scandals were running rampant in newspapers throughout the United States.

In July of 1985, for example, Anaheim fireworks manufacturer W. Patrick Moriarty testified in Los Angeles Federal court on the issue of whether or not he paid prostitutes to entertain political figures in the California State Legislature.

William Overend reported in the *Los Angeles Times* that Moriarty admitted in court to spending several thousand dollars for prostitutes to entertain state political figures but couldn't remember which politicians were supplied with the prostitutes, only that they possibly included state senators and assemblymen.

Overend went on to say that Moriarity's former associate, Richard Raymond Keith, told the *Los Angeles Times* that since 1978, Moriarty and his associates "had possibly spent over $750,000 on prostitutes for legislators." Keith also told the newspaper that those political figures that were supplied with prostitutes included Assemblyman Bruce Young, Assembly Democratic Leader Mike Roos, and Assemblyman Richard Robinson.

Then Assembly Speaker Willie Brown's name came up later in the testimony. A letter was produced on Assemblyman Young's stationary, saying that Brown wanted contributions given to several political figures, something Moriarty finally acknowledged. All told, there had been $634,000 given by Moriarty and his associates to 125 political figures, either currently holding office or running for one, the newspaper reported.

Another story involving prostitution was that of Assemblyman Jim Costa that appeared in the *Los Angeles Times* on February 6, 1994. Costa was charged with soliciting a prostitute in 1986 when he and a nineteen-year-old prostitute approached a woman they thought was also a prostitute for a sexual threesome, only to learn that she was an undercover cop. Assemblyman Costa later pleaded no contest. He was placed on three years' probation and fined $255.

What was so fascinating is that it wasn't just the Legislature that was having problems. Even greater scandals involving money and sex were being revealed in the churches across the country. Reverend Jim Bakker,

Chairman and founder of "Praise The Lord" (PTL) television ministry, based in South Carolina, and his wife, Tammy Bakker, known for the thick black mascara on her eye lashes and her endless tears, made headlines as auditors investigated the misappropriation of millions of dollars in charitable donations that had been made to the PTL ministry. Art Harris reported in the April 29, 1987 edition of *The Washington Post* that the IRS contended that Bakker and other officers spent lavishly on $8,000 dinner parties and $350 a night hotel rooms. Jim Bakker finally resigned from his position as Chairman with PTL ministries when he said he had been blackmailed about an alleged sexual encounter. Before it was all over, ministers, engaged in a "holy" war, were claiming that they had evidence that Bakker was involved in homosexual acts. There were also reports in newspapers that Tammy Faye Bakker had to be treated for drug dependency at a center in California.

Art Harris and Michael Isikoff later reported in *The Washington Post* that ministry sources said that on top of salaries and bonuses, the Bakkers had received what amounted to $4.8 million since 1984. Auditors later identified at least $620,000 in cash advances had been made to both Jim Bakker and a top aide during the previous two years without any records accounting for how that money was used.

Running on the coat tails of the Bakkers and the PTL scandal was none other than TV evangelist Jimmy Swaggart, who was under scrutiny for spreading rumors about Bakker to church leaders. The irony of that gossip showed its ugly head later when, in February of 1988, Swaggart himself was under investigation by his church over his alleged sexual misconduct with a prostitute. *The Toronto Star* reported at the time that Swaggart was president of a TV ministry worth approximately $140 million a year, that was televised into 143 different countries.

In *The Washington Post*, Art Harris stated that Jimmy Swaggart, weeping, confessed his own sins to a crowd of more than 6,000. He begged to be forgiven and said he would step down from the pulpit for an "indeterminate period of time."

Jerry Falwell, Moral Majority founder, replaced Jim Bakker as Chairman of the PTL television ministry in March of 1987. Falwell's first order of business was to announce a new board of directors. Slowly, he would try to pull an entirely new ministry together, one without all the corruption in its shadows.

As for the Legislature, every attempt was made to correct the damage the scandals caused, but it took time. In my own case, I kept quiet and never allowed a scandal to develop regarding my son and his father, especially since the legislator involved had grown even more powerful and influential and now chaired one of the post powerful committees in the State. By that time, I had finally broken up with him once and for all, but I still didn't dare to speak out about his relationship to my son. Too much was at stake.

After months and months of hearings and discussions amongst political leaders, Richard C. Paddock reported in the _Los Angeles Times_ on April of 1990 that the top state lawmakers had agreed on a landmark package of new ethical standards which also included the first conflict-of-interest penalties for legislators with the hope that it would boost the poor image they had before the public. It was supposed to be one of the toughest codes of ethics in the nation, one that set fees for legislators on speaking engagements and set $250 as the value limit for a gift given to a legislator. If nothing else, such standards looked good to the public and helped ease some of the tension.

People tried to stop the scandals and the other problems within the Legislature. Many were constituents who sensed something wasn't right but who looked like crackpots when they threw a stone at the Legislature. Even Jessie Unruh, former Speaker of the Assembly, known as "Big Daddy" knew there was a problem when he wrote the book, _Disorderly House_, a book full of examples of the problems inherent in the state's legislative system. When Senator Tom Hayden was ousted from the Legislature by term limits, he made several references in his speech on how dysfunctional the Legislature had become. No one knew how to fix it.

Nevertheless, a few great men inside the Legislature tried to offer suggestions as to how things could be improved. Those legislators were seen as troublemakers who had to be taken care of in-house. A leader of one of the political parties would issue the command, "No piece of legislation that this particular member presents is to pass out of this Legislature and make it to the Governor's desk." It didn't matter if that legislator was trying to get the bill out of a committee or off the floor of the Legislature. It was dead before it ever got there.

I would see that kind of control and a lot more by working for Assemblyman Dan Hauser, who was born June 18, 1942 in Riverside, California with his Sun in Gemini. I went to work for Hauser in 1987. Little did I know that my position with Hauser would uniquely position me to see the story behind the headlines of the "Gang of Five" and many other scandals that were occurring as a result of that particular Plutonian influence that was rocking the world.

As an astrologer, I always kept myself open to pearls of insight the Legislature put before me that further explained the impact the planets at birth had on an individual legislator's life. A perfect example was happening to Speaker Willie L. Brown, Jr. in January of 1988. The difficult aspect presented itself as the "Gang of Five," a group of members who created a massive political scandal within California's Legislature.

The members of the House elect the Speaker to the Assembly. The California Assembly has 80 members, whereas the Senate has 40. In order to be elected Speaker, one needs 41 votes; in other words, the party with the most votes controls who will be Speaker. Therefore, it is imperative that the Speaker keeps his party members happy and content. Keeping them happy isn't important just for the purpose of having him stay Speaker. It is also important so he can make sure legislation that will benefit his party is passing off the Floor when it is heard. It's difficult to get those 41 votes under normal circumstances, but in this case, it was even harder because half the members belonged to the Republican Party and the other half to the Democratic Party.

In 1987 transiting Saturn in Sagittarius, started to slowly move into a square aspect with Speaker Brown's natal Sun that was in Pisces and also to his Mars, which was in Aries when he was born. A square aspect to a person's Sun will happen approximately every seven years; the aspect lasts for about a year to a year and a half. It's a time when karma kicks in and sometimes it kicks us in the butts. That's exactly what happened to the Speaker.

In January of 1988, Saturn was within two degrees of being a perfect square to Brown's Sun sign. Brown had held the position of Speaker for seven years. Now, five Democrats – Assemblymen Rusty Areias, Gary Condit, Charles Calderon, Jerry Eaves, and Steve Peace – openly tried to thwart Speaker Willie Brown's authority by withdrawing three bills that had been defeated in a committee and forcing a vote on them by the full Assembly instead – an unheard of act. If a bill were defeated in a committee, typically only the Speaker had enough juice to resurrect it. In this case, two of the measures related to insurance reform legislation and one related to testing prostitutes for AIDS. While the bills may have been good ones, Speaker Brown wasn't about to let them live.

The actions of these five renegade members could only be interpreted one way – they were going to engage in a direct war with the power of the Speaker. The assault on the Speaker's leadership prompted an immediate Democratic Caucus. It is customary for the Speaker to bang the gavel and say, "Democratic Caucus in the Member's Lounge at the rear of the Chambers; Republican Caucus in the Assembly Rules Committee room," if there is a problem with a bill being heard on the Floor. This time there were three separate bills, and the stakes were much higher. The five Democratic rebels remained on the Assembly Floor and waited. Instantly, they became known throughout the Legislature as the notorious "Gang of Five." When the Members of both parties returned from their caucuses, the Speaker adjourned the session, leaving the gang of five members standing in the chambers alone.

Words flew back and forth as several news conferences were called. In the meantime, Republican legislators were pleased to see the in-house problems the Democrats were having with their own members. Strong party leadership usually controls the outcome of bills in committees; in this case, however, Republicans were now openly siding with the "Gang of Five" members to help get their bills out of committees, bills that Brown or the Democrats would have defeated, thereby tipping the entire balance of power.

During the year that followed the "gang" became vocal in trying to accomplish changes in the way the House was run by Speaker Brown. This attempt at change wasn't the first time it had happened in California's political history. In the past, many members tried to correct the dysfunctional House by writing about it, passing legislation, and by sharing their concerns with their colleagues, but nothing ever worked.

The Speaker wielded too much power. One wrong look and a person lost his or her committee assignments because he or she had upset the Speaker. One wrong move and a member could be crippled when he or she tried to get a piece of legislation passed off the Assembly Floor.

All of that changed, however, with the "Gang of Five," who became a solid group instead of individual members with individual concerns. One of the most radical things they did was to ban together and draft legislation to weaken the Speaker's power to punish members by removing them from committee assignments. They also proposed a constitutional amendment to make it illegal for a legislative leader to put pressure on a member to get him or her to vote a certain way.

These attempts at change really upset Brown. Eventually, all five Democratic members started being stripped of their committee assignments and were moved to smaller offices. The House was in upheaval. In the past lobbyists knew where to throw their financial backing. Suddenly, the Speaker wasn't sitting as solidly as he had been. Lobbyists weren't sure if Speaker Brown would be able to maintain his position or if one of the gang would become Speaker, which had been rumored. To make matters worse, the automatic 41-vote majority the Democrats once had was denied now and the fate of all Democratic legislation (both Assembly and Senate) was jeopardized.

One of the issues that upset the "gang" was the manner in which campaign funds were distributed. A constituent could contribute funds to a candidate or Member of the Legislature to help get him reelected because that person shared a similar political view. However, as it stood, a candidate could then take those same funds that were contributed to his campaign and give a portion of it to whichever candidate he wanted, perhaps in exchange for a favor. Of course, that is precisely what happened on a regular basis. The "Gang of Five" hated that situation. In 1988 the ***Los Angeles Times*** reported that approximately 1,000 of Assemblyman Areias' constituents showed up for a fund-raiser he had titled, "Live with the Gang of Five."

In March of 1988, while Saturn still squared the Speaker's Sun and Mars at birth, Brown really got upset when the gang opposed a $5.5 billion bond package. If any member of the gang still had a committee assignment it was stripped. The Speaker was doing the very thing the "gang" was trying to get corrected; he was exercising his muscle power as Speaker.

When April arrived, the Senate started getting concerned about how their House would be affected by the upheaval going on in the Assembly. Whenever the Assembly got caught up in political battles, it impacted the Senate because good legislation could be defeated, including legislation that Senators introduced because they had to be heard in the Assembly. While sometimes minor disputes just delayed the legislation traveling from one House to the other, the "gang" situation threatened legislation of both houses. The fate of legislation literally resided in the hands of the "gang" and their supporters.

Again, lobbyists didn't know where to put the money of their clients. Would Brown remain Speaker or be toppled by all the internal party problems? Jerry Gillam and Carl Ingram reported in *The Los Angeles Times* that two capital lobbyists jokingly wore paper sacks over their heads to conceal their identity when they went to a $500-per-ticket fund-raising event given by Gary Condit, one of the 'Gang of Five' members. Little did anyone know that Gary Condit would once again be at the center of a political firestorm years later with the disappearance of an intern with whom he was associated – Chandra Levy.

The press continued to question members to try to find out what was going on, especially when it was rumored a vote might take place on the Floor to topple the Speaker. In May, Assemblyman Calderon, a member of the gang, actually dared to made a motion that would force the Speaker to vacate his position, but that and any other attempts to oust the "Unsinkable" Willie Brown, Jr. always failed.

In December, Speaker Brown won a record fifth term as Speaker by securing the votes he needed on the Assembly Floor, something no one was quite sure how he managed to pull off. How did he get Republicans to vote for him when all along they had been supporting the "gang?" In January 1989 when the new session began, Brown saw to it that no Republicans or any member of the gang were named to any of the 24 committees.

Interestingly enough, however, Gary Condit was elected to Congress, reducing the "Gang of Five" to only four members. By late January plush assignments were given to the remaining gang members that were still in the Assembly, clearly a signal that some sort of peace treaty had been put in place, and with that the entire "gang" situation was resolved.

Astrologically, the whole uproar made sense to me. A planet that is within ten degrees to another planet is considered in aspect. Transiting Saturn stayed in aspect to Brown's natal Sun and then continued to stay in a difficult aspect to his natal Mars throughout the political battles. Mars rules Aries, the god of War, which is why there was a battle in the first place. The squared aspect stirs frustration, which causes aggression. When Saturn moved out of aspect, the whole war was over.

This political situation caused me to do a lot of research. I figured if Brown's Saturn could create this kind of a problem in his life during 1988, what in the world happened to him back in 1980 to early 1981? I knew something had happened, and that whatever it was it would have been significant.

Of course, I found that for which I had been looking in the stars. At the end of 1980, a battle was waged over Speaker of the Assembly. Willie Brown, Jr. was fighting the same battle he had just finished fighting. It wasn't the "Gang of Five" back then, but it was a similar kind of problem.

December of 1980 was the year that Brown was first elected the first black Speaker of the Assembly. One would think that was a good thing, so why was it similar? It was similar because it wasn't the Democrats that elected him to the position. It was the votes of the opposing party, the Republicans. The vote consisted of 28 Republicans and 23 Democrats, which gave Brown a total of 51 votes, 10 more than he needed. Then Saturn slowly moved away. What was the karma? Something Brown had done in a past lifetime kept cropping up to remind him to stand guard but also that he would always be rewarded eventually in his lifetime when Saturn's transit moved out of aspect.

I had come to know well the aspect that Saturn makes and how it affects us. The battles I dealt with weren't just because Saturn was going to make a squared aspect every seven years. I was born with Saturn squaring my Sun sign. My karma was to serve others and wonder what it would be like to be like other women and just live for "my man," feed him grapes, and have him adore me. But then again, I wouldn't have learned the spiritual pearls my path put before me. Like Brown, rising triumphantly out of adversity stronger than ever, there is almost always a silver lining if we look for it unless we really angered the gods in a previous past lifetime.

While the gang of five waged their war with Willie Brown, who is currently serving as Mayor to the City of San Francisco, I was being a proud mom. Life with my son had finally settled down. Through counseling and my unwillingness to rescue him, Jon went on to give the commencement address at the junior college from which he graduated.

Truthfully, even though I watched what was happening inside the Legislature, much of my attention was focused on doing my job for Assemblyman Dan Hauser who had become my new boss. This man really stood out in my mind because he seemed to be everything a constituent would want in a legislator. He was honest, an active scout master for the Boys Scouts of America, enjoyed the outdoors, and loved his wife Donna. He was one of few legislators who had his wife accompany him while he drove from his district to Sacramento and returned each week.

Dan wore a clean-cut beard and mustache. Most of the time he was smiling. I attended a couple of staff retreats in his district. Retreats took place when the Legislature was in recess. It was a time for members to connect with their staff and assess where they were and what they wanted to aim for in terms of legislative goals. Sadly, not enough legislators held them. One of Dan's retreats was in the form of a camp-out in the wilderness, complete with sizzling bacon and eggs in the morning.

I remember entertaining the staff by doing their astrology charts for them. At first it seemed like a simple thing to do, but I was dragging by the time I did about 19 of them, an unusually large number of staffers. How many people Hauser had working for him was a well-kept secret.

Another retreat we had was one in which we stayed at a place near the river and went canoeing down it for about four hours one afternoon after our work had been finished. Everyone was really sore from all the oar action they weren't used to doing. I remember doing a quartz crystal rock workshop that night on the second story of one of the buildings in which we were staying. I made a crystal vortex, by surrounding an individual with crystal stones, and then ran a long crystal wand counter clockwise around the person as if activating the energy of the stones. Nine out of eleven people noticed their pain leaving. The other two felt relief after I remembered to stop and cleanse the crystal wand that I had been using on everyone else.

It was interesting to see everyone feel healed but also disappointing to then watch several of the people return back to their painful conditions the next day. This kind of thing happens a lot in healing because in order for the condition to be permanent the person's mental state has to change from what it was prior to the condition. Otherwise, the health condition returns when their consciousness reverts back. In other words, unless the person was genuinely willing to be healed, they wouldn't stay that way.

Assemblyman Dan Hauser was forced to leave the Legislature after fourteen years in 1996 because of term limits. Prior to leaving he held a "debt retirement" fund-raiser to help offset some of his campaign expenses. The tickets to attend the fund-raiser were $750 a person. It was sad to see Assemblyman Hauser leave the Legislature. He went to great lengths to do what he could to protect fish and animals from poachers and other dangers. He held hearings with the committee he chaired, traveling to other states to meet with their advisers, and had one of the finest fish experts that I had ever known working on his staff.

Chapter 10

Healing workshops, studying planetary formations, counseling clients – all of these things taught me that our thoughts are energy. The energy that our thoughts affect resembles a nebula in outer space. It swirls around and attracts people and situations to us based on the signals our thoughts transmit. If the signal is strong enough and fed over a period of time, then it will be manifested into our reality and we will laughingly call it a coincidence. However, this thought energy isn't to be taken lightly at all because it is one of the many secrets of how our Universe works.

A perfect example of this was shown to me when one of my astrology clients came to me frightened by a stalker who had appeared in her world. She said she had been stalked many times during her lifetime. I had to explain to her that her strong fear of stalkers was actually sending out a signal into the Universe that attracted a passing stalker who fed on fear. I explained to her that if she could trust her guides to protect her, whether it was an angel, Jesus or her fairy godmother, the signal would stop and there wouldn't be any more stalkers. They wouldn't be attracted to her vibration. It's fear they want.

Another case demonstrating the power of our invisible thoughts can be seen in another astrology client who came to me. She said she was desperate to get her ex-husband out of her life. I looked at her and her husband's astrology charts and saw that the marriage was over; however, the aspects of Venus and Mars between the two charts told me there was a strong physical attraction between them.

I asked her how she treated her ex-husband when he came to her house to pick up their son for a visit. She said, "Cool and aloof." Then I asked what her thoughts regarding her ex-husband were when she wasn't around him. She said she pictured them still together. Sometimes late at night she imagined him making love to her the way he used to and she visualized her loving him back.

"You are sending him signals that you are still in love with him," I warned.

"No, I am not," she answered. "I treat him like we were never married when he sees me," she countered.

"You treat him like you are still in love and married in your thoughts. He reads that signal and probably doesn't understand the way you act when he sees you," I added.

She sat quietly staring at me for a moment. "You're right," she spoke up with a look of surprise on her face.

"You divorced him in what you consider to be your real world. Now all you have to do is divorce him in your thoughts and he will go," I reassured her.

She thanked me, gave me a big hug when it came time for her to go and bounced out of my office like a big weight had been lifted from her shoulders.

To this day, I am careful of what I allow myself to think. When negative thoughts come, I immediately cancel them and replace them with something positive. It is the only way to make sure that we don't attract unwanted negativity into our lives. It is important to understand how our thoughts work.

Science has proven that we have four levels of brain waves that can be measured – beta, alpha, theta, and delta. When we dream or are deep in mediation we are in an alpha state. It is here that the brain waves slow down tremendously. The alpha state produces psychic ability and increases our power to manifest things into our reality. All it takes is intent and a desired goal.

People believe hard, strained, concentration on their goals will bring a desired result into their life. But the method, much the same as constant prayer to remove something negative from our lives, which could relate to financial restrictions or ill health, can negatively reinforce the very thing we don't desire in our life. In other words when we say, "I hurt. Make it go away," or "If only we weren't so poor and could afford more," we send out a signal into our world that says we hurt or don't have money.

Our brains produce in our worlds whatever we repeatedly tell our Universe to produce. That's why ministers say, "Pray like your prayer has already been answered." When we do that kind of positive thinking, we attract positive results. We must see our goal and then listen and watch as the Universe brings messages to us that can lead us to our goal. It might come in the form of a song on the radio. It might appear as a stranger who talks to us while we are getting our car serviced, but no matter what, the answer always appears. Sooner or later, help comes. Help always comes if we are receptive to receiving it.

I was learning more and more on my spiritual journey and while I was, I still took time to notice the way politics had started changing. In the political arena, Pete Schabarum authored Proposition 140, which would radically change California's State Legislature. The voters passed the proposition into law in November 1990. This ballot measure placed a limit on the number of terms a legislator could serve; therefore, it was hotly challenged by the sitting members of the Legislature, who used funds from the private sector and campaign funds, rather than those of taxpayers, to fight against it. Their attempts to stop the measure failed, however, when the California Supreme Court announced its decision to validate the decision of the taxpayers almost one year after the measure had been voted into law.

On the soul level I knew what the taxpayers were trying to do, but they didn't have the necessary insight as to how to do it. To me, it was like a miscarriage that got botched, but it would take a long time before taxpayers would realize this fact – and many still don't realize it at all.

By the time this took place, I had worked for the Legislature long enough to become familiar with it and its problems. At various times I watched when golden handshakes were offered to employees wanting to retire. A golden hand shake is when an employee is offered a bonus of a couple of years of service credit, or even a couple years of age credit (adding two years to their existing age) to leave employment. Since the amount of one's retirement is based on both age credit and service credit, a golden handshake translated into thousands of dollars for the employee receiving it. When golden handshakes were offered, several top-ranking aids with historical legislative memory left the Legislature.

I watched and helped train consultants who were hired off the street who didn't have a clue as to what they were supposed to be doing. People can't even imagine what I saw. New members tended to hire

121

friends who had helped them to get elected, rather than hiring experienced staff. As a result, we suddenly had inexperienced members with inexperienced staff trying to do the job that only a seasoned veteran could reasonably be expected to do.

For example, I talked to two consultants, both of whom had been hired "off the street" to work in a Republican Committee office where I was assigned. One of them told me that the legislator who hired her said she wouldn't have to work late in the evenings. Quietly, I asked her to bring the other consultant into her office and behind closed doors I gave them the real picture.

I told them that when a committee bill appears on the Assembly Floor, that bill might need to be amended.

"If it is," I added, "you are going to have to be here to analyze those amendments so it can be rushed back to the Chambers where the bill will be voted on by the House. It won't wait until the next day when you don't have a date or aren't busy with your husband and children if you are married. Every time session is in, you will have to be in your office listening to it while you are working on the analyses for the next committee meeting."

I also warned that lobbyists would try to talk to them and give them their positions on a bill. The more time they spent listening to the lobbyists and enjoying a conversation with them, or perhaps visiting a friend that stopped by the office, the later they would have to stay to finish up their work in the evening because they were on a deadline to get their analyses done for the next hearing.

"In other words," I said, "count on basically living here most of the time."

Both consultants thanked me for the insight I afforded them. As I walked away I think they quietly wondered what they had got themselves into. Then I noticed a secretary, who for some reason wasn't that fond of me, walking towards me. She thanked me for taking the time to explain how it was with the Legislature. She had figured that because I had only worked in Democratic offices as committee secretary I wouldn't offer to help Republican staff, which couldn't have been more wrong because I wasn't partisan. I did my job and I did it well, but as an astrologer most of what other people considered politically important didn't move me at all. Mine was a parallel world in which I worked hard but was fascinated by what I was seeing on a deeper level.

As an example, I watched a chief consultant for whom I worked ignore all the incoming mail and just read the newspapers, all of them. He said that was the single most important tool there was for that job. I recall him also saying that things have a way of working out if we just let them work out. Later, a female consultant that took his place felt all mail should be answered and any incoming material processed immediately. Her inbox was always empty, whereas, her predecessor's had always been full. Don't ask me why, but both systems worked. Given that kind of reality, it was hard to get too emotional about a lot of things that happened.

In-house, it was always understood that it took about two years to season a consultant to do his or her job properly, and that happened only with good tutorship by a seasoned consultant already working for the Legislature. For a legislator, however, it took much more time for them to learn what they needed to know. Nothing in the Legislature was even remotely similar to what is taught in school. Senator Hayden made reference to this in his retirement speech when he addressed the Senate.

In school we learned a legislator introduces a bill on the Floor of the Assembly. That bill will be something that is in the best interest of his district. Perhaps he listens to a bill on the Floor that another member is presenting. He gets to vote on it as it best serves his constituency. Well, that's not the way it really was, and it certainly isn't different today.

As a legislator, one learned quickly that one had better stick with the party and vote the way the party wants one to vote. If one doesn't do that, then suddenly it would be impossible to chair a committee or even sit on a committee, and worse, it would be impossible for him to serve his constituency. Without power, that legislator is completely ineffective. To make matters worse, the party never left anything to chance. Party officials always passed out analyses of the legislation members would be hearing that recommended how members should vote. If one belonged to the other party, almost certainly one would receive an analysis showing that the vote should go the opposite way. Each party has its voting guidelines, and woe is the legislator who fails to pay attention to them.

Most of the time, while serving as committee secretary, a legislator who was absent from the room when a vote was taken would walk up to me when he returned. If he were a Democrat he would ask how the Chair voted, who generally took the lead on giving his vote as a clue to the party when roll call was taken. I was always instructed to put that same yes or no vote down for that member as well. If he were a Republican, he would be holding documents several pages long that analyzed the bills according to his party's perspective and recommended which vote was most in the party's interest. He would point to the vote of aye or nay and tell me to put that down for him.

House rule requires that the minority party be given the analyses of the bills from the committee that is going to hear the bills 24 hours in advance of the hearing, so they can prepare their version of the analyses for their party members.

One day, I recall a Democratic consultant sitting in my office when the Republican consultant working on the bills walked into our office and politely asked for the analyses. She looked at him and said they weren't done yet. I knew they had already gone to print and that we did have a set put aside for him in our office because I announced that fact to her when it was done.

When he left the room, I advised her to call the chief consultant who wasn't in the office at the time to tell him what she had done. She looked into my eyes and asked me why.

I looked straight into hers and said, "There is going to be trouble, and what you just said will be what triggers it," so she called him and confessed.

The next day in committee, a day that was late into the session when bills needed to be heard in order to meet their deadlines and when the agenda was full, the chair to the committee and his Democratic colleagues sat and waited to get a quorum (a majority present). Everyone waited and waited, but we didn't have a quorum to start the meeting because the Republican legislators were missing. Eventually, the Sergeant-at-Arms handed the chair a letter that had been handed to him by a Republican staff member who had come into the room. It was from the Republican members. None of them showed up to the committee meeting due to the dangerous game the consultant had played the day before. Many important bills were now at risk of dying – all because a consultant wanted to play a political game of cat and mouse because she weren't seasoned enough to know better.

When the hearing was adjourned for lack of a quorum, the consultant walked up to me in the hall as we walked back to our office and said, "You knew," with both fear and astonishment in her voice.

"Yeah," I responded, not feeling there was a need to say anything more.

Now if a legislator votes the way he is supposed to and still is able to maintain a balance with his decisions matching the needs of his constituents, there is one other problem with which he must deal. He needs money to get reelected. That simple fact can create some of the most difficult situations of all. For example, what if the lobbyist who financially supports him the most talks to him in the hall or slips him a note and asks him to vote one way, but his constituents want him to vote another? Now what does he do? These are just a few things they FORGET to mention in school when they teach political science, yet they are important enough to determine the outcome of any piece of legislation.

Of course, term limits voted on by the taxpayers didn't solve the problem and never could. In fact, quite the opposite happened because term limits made it all worse. Without seasoned veterans, there was no one left to teach the freshmen legislators and the untrained staff what would be required of them. Worse still, the only ones left with any real historical political memory were the lobbyists who knew exactly how to manipulate the unseasoned legislators – a problem that continues to this day. In reality, people the voters never elected – lobbyists who walk the halls of the State Capitol, disappearing in and out of member's offices, lobbying their own political agendas – largely control the Legislature.

While many people complain about legislators, their lives are not easy ones; in fact, quite the opposite is true – it is a grueling job. Their phones are always ringing from people demanding to talk to them; mail and published reports pile up in their in-baskets, and hundreds of letters and other documents need to be read and signed. Members must be in the legislative session almost every day and when there is no session, they need to report to daylong meetings for the committees on which they have been appointed to serve. If the Legislature is in recess, members need to attend interim hearings.

Despite the arguments to the contrary, the simple truth is that legislators have no real spare time. If members mistakenly think they have found some free time then they probably forgot about flying or driving to and from their district. When the legislators finally get to go home to their districts, their legislative secretaries have scheduled people for them to meet. They have dinners to go to and those endless fundraisers they are supposed to hold and attend along with the endless pasted on smiles they are required to wear, so they can generate funds to win the next election. They also have to make sure they are seen with their wives, husbands, and children because being good "family" men and women helps with their voter image.

While legislators dealt with their daily grind, and the voters thought they had found a solution, I saw a completely different solution. There was an entirely different way the voters might have changed what happened in Sacramento. No one ever mentioned it. They could remove the heart from both the Assembly and the Senate, which would put the people back in charge.

Forget about term limits. What is the heart of the California State Legislature? The heart is the Assembly Rules Committee and the Senate Rules Committee. Those two committees are the real cores of the Legislature – not money like someone would suspect. The Rules Committee is responsible for the laws of each house and how it will conduct its business. It also determines to which committee a bill will be assigned. The members of Rules Committee review appointments to departments and commissions. It is the accounting system of the taxpayer's money being spent by legislators. Rules Committee determines staff holidays, hires staff, disburses all supplies and furniture, and dictates enforcement of ethics or settlements of worker's compensation cases.

If we were to put the Rules Committee into the private sector and put professional overseers in place, we would take back control of the Legislature and also stop the flagrant and serious problem of nepotism in the employment practices of the Legislature. Currently, that committee has no outside oversight – only the members control it. As a result, the members of the Legislature have no boss. While the taxpayers are the figurehead bosses, the truth is that they are too far away and never see the books. Most don't read the newspapers, and if they do read the newspapers, they are only getting what is reported about their member in their district. The average voter never really sees the Legislature as a whole because they don't read the newspapers in other towns. I saw it because for some unknown reason I was chosen by the Universe to see everything that was going on in the place from a unique vantage point – not only was I able to see the place from a professional standpoint, but I was also able to see behind the scenes on a personal level.

As the sensitive observant astrologer and secretary that I was, I saw it all – from the members' private lives to how the place was really run. So much of it didn't make sense to me even after all those years.

A legislator once told her consultant in a firm voice, "You must always stand taller than the lobbyist to whom you are talking or sit up higher in your chair to show your importance. If you forget to do this, you will harm our position."

That didn't make sense to me. Why did we have to play such power games all of the time? I watched as interns off the street were asked to analyze a bill that meant a lot to the member that introduced it or the lobbyist that asked a member to carry it simply because the consultant that was being paid by the taxpayers who was supposed to do it didn't want to do it or was too busy. How could these completely inexperienced and typically inept people ever really do the job of a highly trained and well-paid consultant? Of course, one was never sure if the members would even read the bill or its analysis, which made even less sense to me considering how much work and money went into publishing them. Then if the members did read the bill would they be able to see beyond what was in front of them. For example, a "one word amendment," was and still is used to hide major amendments to legislation.

For example, if I made major changes in a bill, those changes, by law, had to show up in print with all of the stricken text still visible. Members didn't want all of those amendments showing, so they would change a single word of the bill because that would force the bill to be reprinted with only that new change showing which was one word – not all of the other amendments that were now a part of the bill. To kill a bill, a member would leave the amended version of the bill with all of its stricken text in print. Frankly, the bills that end up getting passed often have no resemblance to the original bills whatsoever – but most people never realize it because of those "one word amendments."

Everyone in the Legislature knew the game, so they learned to live with it and just be a part of the system. Yet there will always be those tiny little things that really didn't make any sense and as little as they were, they sometimes felt like a cat's claws running down my back. For example, if I called Senate Reprographics office and asked for a ream of paper, the office I worked for would be charged for one ream of paper. They would tell me to ask for an entire box that held numerous reams, and then I wouldn't be charged.

If I submitted a claim for the Commission members who were flying into town to attend a meeting where I worked and submitted a bill to Senate Rules Committee, they would pay for the taxi fees to and from the airport for each person attending the meeting. When I asked them if they would pay the twenty-some-odd cents a mile to reimburse me for numerous trips to the airport to pick up several of them and take them back with the hope of saving the Senate a lot of money, I was told "no." Accounting said they don't reimburse staff for mileage to go to and from the airport. I asked if they would cover individual taxi bills that I submitted, and they said yes.

"Let's see," I thought to myself, "it would have cost ten dollars for me to go get them form the airport verses as much as a hundred for a bunch of taxi cabs. That makes no sense!" But what was the point of trying to fight it? I just resigned myself to it and let it go.

It seems to me that if we put qualified professionals from outside the Legislature to serve on the Rules Committee, everything would change. There wouldn't be so many relatives working for the Legislature, and trust me, there are many people who are related to each other being paid to work there. Justification for expenditures would be different. We could even require performance measurements (currently there are none) and real accountability. Unfortunately, the power of the Rules Committee continues and the public doesn't realize that if they reformed it, they would probably reform the Legislature.

I am not alone in thinking term limits were an exercise in futility as far as making any sort of real change. William Endicott reported in _The Sacramento Bee_, February 25, 1997, that term limits didn't solve anything. He found no evidence, six years after its adoption, that limiting terms had produced a Legislature that was more effective. Instead there was more instability than ever and the Assembly was as dysfunctional as it was under the old system. Now there were a lot of new faces but several of the members that had been termed out in one House of the Legislature, simply ran for office in the other (i.e., members of the Assembly were running for the Senate and lawmakers of the Senate were running for the Assembly).

Interestingly enough, in 1966 Members' salaries were set at $16,000 per year and they were permitted to adjust their own salaries by a two-thirds vote of the House as long as it didn't exceed 5% over a designated period of time; otherwise, the Governor would have to approve it. In 1990, however, the voters passed Proposition 112, which amended the Constitution to establish and confer salary-setting authority on the California Citizens Compensation Commission. This seven-member commission was given the authority to set the salaries of legislators and elected officials. By March of 1998, Members' salaries had reached $99,000 per year.

Each member was also entitled to a per diem of $121 daily for expenses incurred while they were in session. When a holiday came up and there was a three-day weekend, members made sure the House was in session on Friday just so that they could get that extra money.

Jon Matthews and Steven A. Capps reported in _The Sacramento Bee_ that this type of session was one of the oldest rituals on the political scene. It is known as a "check-in session." The Legislature would report to the floor of their respective houses solely for the purpose of members signing in and they could do that at any point in the day before the House would adjourn, which it inevitably did shortly after all of the members leisurely signed that all important attendance form. The cost of a three-day weekend to taxpayers would be $43,560 although not all lawmakers accept per diem and it isn't given to legislators with unexcused absences. This per diem could mean as much as $25,000 to lawmakers each year and generally it is tax-free.

Over the years that I worked for the Legislature, many times I would hear a member tell his scheduling secretary to please call him early in the morning wherever he was staying to remind him to check-in for session. Once the member checked in, a Sergeant-at-Arms was immediately called to drive the member to the airport, so he could catch a plane for home.

Looking back on it now, I realize that Californians haven't really figured out where the real power of the Legislature lies. When they do, perhaps we will see changes and an end to abuses such as these. Spiritually, I know it is about our intent. When enough people really want change, it will happen. I saw it happen when crusaders like Howard Jarvis took a stand, and major tax cuts followed his efforts. The power of our collective thinking is what allows all major changes and is what carries us forward into the future. Unfortunately, many taxpayers have gotten discouraged which has caused them to adopt an attitude of, "I just don't care." Then nothing gets done.

Chapter 11

While I was contemplating the mysteries of life, I went to work for the Assembly Committee on Elections, Reapportionment and Constitutional Amendments, chaired by Assemblyman Peter Chacon in 1991. The Census Bureau had released its population figures for California in December of 1990. This was done every ten years. Once the figures were in, it was time to start redistricting. In theory, reapportionment is supposed to ensure that legislators properly represent the voters, so every ten years boundaries of political districts are redrawn. In practical application, it never quite works out that way.

My job was Committee Secretary. Assemblyman Chacon had a legislative secretary who had worked for the Legislature as long as I had or perhaps longer. She took care of Chacon's dictation, tracked his legislation, and scheduled his appointments. There was one secretary that served as her assistant and receptionist. My job was to work on the committee only. If I needed help with my workload, I needed to get the Legislative secretary's permission.

The problem was that my workload was crazy. Since it was time to reapportion the districts, the Speaker of the Assembly put more legislators on the Committee than the number that normally served on it. This "sleeper" of a committee was now high profile. Whenever we had a Committee meeting, I had to prepare twenty-one binders, one for each member who served on the Committee, and also one for each of the consultants. These binders could end up being many inches thick with documents. The consultants would type up the analyses of the bills that were assigned to the Committee; then I would edit, reformat them, and send them back for the consultant's approval. When all the analyses were finalized, I sent them to reproduction. After they were returned from reproduction, I put them in the committee binders that would be hand delivered to the office of each member of the committee. This way the member had a chance to read the analysis before the hearing.

Aside from preparing analyses, bills needed to be ordered on every piece of legislation that related to elections or reapportionment that was introduced in the Legislature. If the bill had an amendment, then copies of that amendment were needed for the main files and the consultant's binders in each consultant's office. Since it was reapportionment time, I made sure that the Speaker's team, who was overseeing our committee, always got a copy. I did this with publications that came into the office as well.

Interestingly enough, the team of consultants with whom I worked backed off getting involved with reapportionment and instead kept busy working on legislation that was traveling through the Assembly and Senate because that's where their expertise was needed. Therefore, I became involved with the Speaker's staff and flew to all the reapportionment hearings that were being held throughout the State. If a Democrat came into our office with a question on reapportionment, I referred them to the private office the Democrats had in back of one of the committee hearing rooms. One of the advantages of being the party in power is that one is given expensive equipment and therefore one could be more selective as to whom one would or would not assist. Our equipment was state of the art and a young woman was assigned to do nothing else but work on the redistricting maps.

If they walked into our office and were a registered Republican, we were instructed by the party leadership to deliberately not help them, especially if they were running for office and needed to know the boundaries of the district for which they wanted to run for office. If we had maps outlining an area, we would give them a copy, but they were only a vague outline rather than having details such as what cities or counties fell into that district. Unfortunately, that is standard operating procedure most of the time. Seldom do the two major parties really work well together.

Hearings were held throughout the State to make sure that everyone had a chance to testify. Major cities were selected, as well as cities where the population had changed drastically since the previous census had been taken ten years prior.

At the time, Lou Cannon reported in *The Seattle Post-Intelligencer* that Hispanics constituted 7.7 million of the 29.7 million Californians that appeared on the 1990 census. They were a quarter of the population, yet only 10 of the 105 legislators were Hispanic. The voter turnout was very sparse at the hearings, yet one organization always seemed to be there and that was the Mexican-American Legal Defense Fund (MALDF), which was trying to protect Hispanic voters. The League of Women Voters was also actively involved in the reapportionment process because the census showed women to be in the minority and they wanted to have representation on the level as well, which the redistricting could give them. One last group I recall was the gay community. This minority, too, wanted to be represented in Sacramento and voiced this at many of the hearings where I listened to them present their opinions about reapportionment and how they felt it should be done fairly. I can still remember seeing the maps one of their spokesmen presented at the hearing. It had different colors on the map indicating where the AIDS breakouts were most prevalent. I noticed that Sacramento had a large breakout of AIDS in the Oak Park area of town at that time. But many of the cities throughout the State were also marked by the outbreaks.

The other group watching reapportionment intently was of course the Republicans. The 1980-reapportionment experience for them left a lot to be desired. Everyone feared "gerrymandering." I never really knew what that word meant until I went to work with this Committee and got involved in the reapportionment process. Gerrymandering was a term used when one outlines the boundaries of a district. The end results look like a salamander with arms stretched here and there as it wiggles voters in and out of existence, voters who were carefully placed into its boundaries based on their party affiliation and how they are going to vote at election time.

The crazy thing that happened back then is that the Republicans presented two initiatives on the ballot. One was Proposition 118, which would allow the Legislature to remain in charge of reapportionment, as it had been in the past, but it called for a 2/3s vote of the members of the House in order for the plans to be passed. The second initiative that was presented before the voters was Proposition 119. This initiative would have a 12-member commission of retired judges decide on the redistricting of the Assembly, Senate, and Congressional seats.

Republicans spent a lot of money on television ads for these initiatives. They said in some states the people chose who would represent them, but in California the politicians chose. Nonetheless, when election time came, the voters voted down both propositions. Some speculated that it was because of voter confusion. From what I saw at the hearings that took place throughout the State, it was from voters not wanting to get involved. The price it would cost them later was expensive as huge political wars started breaking out in the Legislature.

One concern that kept cropping up was the suspicion that over 1.1 million people had been left out of the census data. This caused the Assembly and Senate to both file lawsuits requesting that the census data be released. U.S. district judges in Los Angeles and San Francisco ordered the government to turn over the information to the State of California, but the U. S. government appealed.

In September of 1991 three separate legislative proposals were given to Governor Pete Wilson (Republican), which had been approved almost along party lines. Democrats figured if the Governor vetoed the plans, they would override him. Naturally, he did veto them. In September of 1991, the Senate and Assembly tried to override the Governor's vetoes, but both Houses fell short of the votes needed. This failure threw reapportionment into the hands of the California Supreme Court. The Supreme Court appointed a panel to do the redistricting. In January of 1992, the panel appointed by the California Supreme Court presented the new legislative and congressional boundaries. The new lines would have to be accepted by the U.S. Justice Department and the federal courts, which happened in February of 1992.

While reapportionment was going on, my work for Chacon, who was born in June of 1925 in Phoenix, Arizona, was exciting. Chacon was a short, small-framed, soft-spoken Hispanic gentleman. I frequently went into his office to get his signature on bill jackets that needed to be taken to the Assembly Desk. A bill jacket was the report wrapped around an original bill that gave the outcome of the hearing in which the bill had been heard. The bill could have failed passage, passed out of the committee, or died because it failed to meet specific deadlines spelled out in the House rules.

Chacon had a big heart when it came to minority problems. I remember he introduced a piece of legislation that would allow a Native American to sit on the Assembly Floor during discussions on legislation so Native Americans could have a voice in the Legislature, but it wouldn't give them voting rights. However, the bill never passed.

One of the biggest controversies that kept plaguing Chacon was that he didn't travel down to San Diego enough to visit his constituents. Since legislators were paid a per diem to help cover the expenses of having to live in Sacramento and then commute back and forth to their districts where their primary residence was, voters expected him to show up in the district on a regular basis. In Chacon's case, he bought a place in Placerville where he lived with his wife, Jean, and made it his primary residence. This put his residence at the opposite end of the state from his district.

While doing what little traveling back and forth to his district in 1990 that he did do, Chacon used campaign funds, which caused criticism because he was traveling to San Diego for campaign purposes rather than on legislative business. When he was in San Diego, it was reported in the press that he stayed with his brother-in-law because he had no home there, yet that was the district which he represented and those were the constituents who had elected him.

As Michael Smolens reported in *The San Diego Union-Tribune*, Assemblyman Chacon also gained attention for putting relatives on state and campaign payrolls, accepting controversial honorariums and for having moved his home hundreds of miles away from the San Diegans he represented. When asked by a reporter why he spent so much time in Placerville rather than his district, Chacon replied that he had been married for 36 years and felt that one of the biggest challenges to a marriage is separation. Therefore, he lived with his wife in Placerville, rather than being away from her during the week.

The bad press that followed him may have been part of his karma. Assemblyman Chacon was also investigated by the attorney general's office. It was alleged that he accepted a bribe of $7,500 from the California Cash Checkers Association, $4,000 of which came on the same day that a bill, which would have capped the fees that check-cashing businesses can charge their customers was shelved.

In a *California Journal* article, Chacon was ranked next to last in effectiveness. In response to this, Barry M. Horstman reported in *The Los Angeles Times* that Assemblyman Chacon pointed out some of his legislative highlights which included establishing bilingual education, producing low-income housing, creating a toll-free hot line for runaway youths, the outlawing of mandatory retirement age, and developing a comprehensive prenatal care system.

One day Assemblyman Chacon called me into his office and said he wanted to talk to me. Seldom ever putting much importance on my interest in astrology, he asked me what his astrology chart looked like as far as whether or not he should run for office again. I advised him that he didn't have the strength that it would take to fight the battles that lay in front of him if he did run. I don't know for sure how much my reading influenced him, but amazingly enough, the next day he announced to the press that he was retiring. This meant I needed to find a new job.

Over the next couple of years, I would work for the Assembly Public Safety Committee and the Assembly Insurance Committee. Political wars would periodically break out, but Speaker Willie Brown, Jr. was able to put out most of the fires. By 1995, however, the power was beginning to shift. Suddenly, Republicans, who had been in the minority for many years were now in much better position to call some of the shots, having won a slim majority of seats in the Assembly. In fact, they had exactly one more seat than the Democrats did.

The Republicans were elated, confident that they could finally control things in Sacramento. Assemblyman Jim Brulte was especially happy. He was rumored to be the next Speaker. Helping the Republicans to hold onto their majority was Republican Assemblyman Dick Mountjoy, who would have been termed out in 1996 anyway. Winning a special election for the Senate seat vacated by Senator Frank Hill, who was removed from office in the summer of 1994 after his conviction on a bribery charge, Mountjoy delayed giving up his Assembly seat under a quirk in state law, so that he could cast his vote for a Republican speaker.

Tension was often so thick in the building that I felt as if something was sure to break at any moment. The Republicans were so paranoid about Willie Brown, Jr. that a former sheriff's deputy, Assemblyman Larry Bowler, cut the wires of the internal microphones in the

Republican caucus chamber where they met out of fear that Democrats might be listening in. Eventually, the Democrats ousted Senator/Assemblyman Mountjoy from the Assembly. Mountjoy's Assembly seat was later filled in yet another special election.

I quickly became a casualty of the shifting tide of power in that I was fired from my job as Committee Secretary for the Insurance Committee. The principal consultant at the time told me he would have let me keep my job but I was tagged as being a Democrat because I had served with Democratic members of the Legislature. What he didn't realize is that I wasn't like other employees. My views were never political. I was just a hard worker doing my job. My mind was only interested in trying to figure out why we are on Earth to begin with – not why Democrats and Republicans felt their political views were more important than their soul purpose here. To me that kind of focus took away from real truths, but real truths aren't what the Legislature was about

Since I didn't have a job, I put in an application in an office I had heard had a vacancy. Not being political, I never checked out why there was an opening, a mistake I would have to live with for quite some time to come, for the Universe sent me into a mine field where I would become even more mindful of life and its many lessons for all of us.

I went to work for Assemblyman Paul Horcher. After I was in his office a couple of days, he learned I was interested in astrology and asked me to tell him what I saw in his chart. I did his chart for him and explained it to him in his office where he confirmed my feelings that nothing went right for him since the day he was elected. He was facing some heavy karma there, and nothing would stop his lessons.

Assemblyman Horcher was born August 31, 1951 at 1:45 p.m. in Freeport, Texas. As an astrologer studying his birth chart, I noticed several planets in Leo, which made him the showman who wanted public attention, but there was a conflict because he had many planets in Virgo, which caused him to be fearful of whether or not he was being accepted.

This poor soul had his worst nightmares come to life when he went to work for the Assembly. He was a Republican who never quite fit in with his party. His frustrations over this situation grew, so when Speaker Willie Brown, Jr. propositioned him to change his party to Independent and vote for Brown as Speaker of the Assembly for one more term,

Horcher did. Since the Republicans were finally the majority party in the Assembly, Horcher's action caused a war to break out between the parties in the Assembly that lasted for months and had repercussions we still feel to this day.

It didn't take long to figure out what I had walked into when I took the job with him. Constituents elected Assemblyman Horcher to office in his district in Diamond Bar as a Republican. When he switched his party to Independent just to help Willie Brown, Jr. retain his remain as Speaker, his Republican constituents were furious. His Republican colleagues were just as furious. He was called "Judas," "maverick," and "traitor." His district cried out in long distance calls constituents made to his office protesting what he had done. Most of the calls were buried on an answering machine that I listened to one day. I had never heard such anger and frustration as people tried to relay to him the betrayal they felt. Others threatened to do something about it when election time came. Some said they thought they were friends, until he did what he did for Willie Brown, Jr., especially since it was the only real chance the Republicans had in years to oust the democratic Speaker. All the callers felt as if he had deliberately back-stabbed them and left them helpless as mere pawns in the hands of political warriors.

Death threats against Horcher became a constant concern. One day I even saw a Sergeant from the Assembly Sergeant-at-Arms Office deliver two lightweight black bulletproof vests for him to wear when he went to his district. The death threats were so common; in fact, that we staffers had to take security precautions just to answer the phone or to deal with people we didn't know who came into his office.

Although I was afraid for Horcher, knowing that police dogs like Maverick were around, was a comfort. Maverick was a black lab working for the California State Police. Whenever I saw him around the Capitol with his partner, Officer Koobs, he was either entertaining visiting schoolchildren or sniffing out bombs. According to Officer Koobs, there were then approximately 88 bomb threats a year and the figure goes up 10% a year.

When Horcher changed his party registration to Independent, it was very unsettling working there and not knowing if someone were going to walk in and lose control. The only other time that I recall such a threat to the Legislature was when the Black Panthers were making front-page news. Stories still fill the Capitol halls about the Black Panthers showing up in the gallery of the legislative chambers. Stephen Maganini reported in *The Sacramento Bee* that members of the Black Panthers wore black berets, black leather jackets, shades and bandoleers. Fists were clinched and they were carrying riffles. A couple dozen of them led by Bobby Seale and Huey Newton showed up.

Needless-to-say, legislation was immediately introduced and passed to ban firearms from the chambers. The law prohibits ordinary citizens from carrying guns under the dome, but it does allow enforcement officers to carry a gun. Assemblyman Bowler, a Republican from Elk Grove, took advantage of the legislation saying that enforcement officers were exempt from the law banning firearms under the dome. As a former lieutenant for the Sacramento County Sheriff's Department, Bowler carried a concealed firearm into the Capitol and Assembly chambers.

Over the years, I saw security systems put into place to try to make members and staff safer, such as silent alarms concealed under the desks, so that staff people could push it if they sensed danger. The buttons would send a signal down to the State Police, who would in turn dispatch an officer to check it out. Eventually, metal detectors were installed at the entrance of both the Senate and Assembly galleries.

An attempt was also made to secure the entrance to the basement of the Capitol Building where the members of the Legislature have a private parking. Emily Bazar and Stephen A. Capps reported in *The Sacramento Bee* about a mishap that occurred because of a Capitol Barricade Anti-Terrorist Device. The system was designed to trigger a steel barrier if an unauthorized vehicle attempted to enter the garage.

One day, an unprecedented accident occurred. Republican Leader Scott Baugh was driving into the Capitol garage when the Senate Republican leader, entered close behind him. The car driven by Senator Brulte triggered the anti-terrorism device, which caused a barrier to rise up under Baugh's state vehicle being driven by his deputy chief of staff. Baugh and the driver were taken by ambulance to a local hospital where the member learned that he had suffered a concussion. Apparently, Assemblyman Bill Leonard, a Republican from San Bernardino, asked the Assembly Rules Committee to investigate whether the security device should be disengaged or not. Not surprisingly, the Capitol now utilizes police kiosks at the driveway entrances to the basement. Closed-circuit television cameras monitor the building and park grounds and officers patrol the grounds on horseback.

While Horcher's staff members and I worried over his personal safety, two other events triggered a renewed interest in security by the Governor and Members of the Legislature in 1995. The first incident was the Oklahoma City bombing in a federal building that killed 168 people. The second incident was a mail bomb that killed a timber industry lobbyist, which was the work of the work of the Unibomber.

It took more than two years, but finally In 1997 Governor Pete Wilson asked the California Highway Patrol (CHP) to devise a plan that would thwart would be bombers. In 1998 the proposal was delivered. It called for a $5.1 million low concrete wall topped by a cast iron railing that would be erected around the Capitol building, and a portion of the park according to an editorial in *__The Sacramento Bee__*. The report the CHP delivered said the fence was a modern version of the fence surrounding the Capitol in 1880, but it was in the wrong place and used the wrong materials and would forever alter the beauty of the historic park.

The months that followed Horcher's announcement that he had changed parties left the Assembly dysfunctional, Democrats and Republicans were in an all-out war. The Democrats had promised to help Horcher because he had helped them, so Speaker Brown organized a fundraiser at the Sterling Hotel in Sacramento to help offset Horcher's expenses. It was a reception where wine and hors d'oeuvres were served and the cost was $1,000 a piece.

The Republicans were so angry about his party change that they gathered 1,000 people together and went down into Horcher's district to fight for his recall. Assemblyman Jim Brulte, the Republican who lost his chances at becoming Speaker by Horcher's actions, walked door-to-door soliciting votes from constituents in favor of the recall.

Ed Mendel reported in *__The San Diego Union-Tribune__*, on January 12, 1995, that Governor Pete Wilson jumped into the battle for Speaker that week by mailing 52,000 petitions to recall Horcher. Because Horcher had voted for Willie Brown, he created a 40-40 deadlock. The article went on to say that Governor Pete Wilson threatened Horcher. In fact, Horcher reportedly said that Wilson told him during a 50-minute telephone conversation that he should vote for Assembly GOP leader Jim Brulte... or else.

Sometimes Assemblyman Horcher would arrive at work happy and in a good mood. Other days he looked like it was the end of the world. That is the way he sounded when he called his Capitol office from his home the day after his recall. I answered the call. He sounded extremely depressed and as if he couldn't believe what had just happened.

I remember him asking me what they were saying in the halls of the Capitol about him. But I couldn't give a better response than *The Sacramento Bee*, on May 17, 1995, when it summed it up by saying that Assembly offices at the Capitol were deserted that Tuesday and the legislative calendar was blank, reflecting the fact that hundreds of staffers and dozens of lawmakers had gone to Southern California to campaign for or against Horcher. Republican Governor Pete Wilson sent a delegation of about 100 staffers, appointees and party activists. It went on to say that altogether bout 1,000 Republicans descended on Horcher's district to help get out the vote against him. A similar number of Democrats worked on his behalf. As for me, I stayed behind and covered the office.

Newspapers throughout California reported that Assemblyman Paul Horcher became the first state legislator to be recalled in 81 years with 100 percent of the vote counted. He lost 62.5 percent to 37.5 percent. Immediately, we all knew that the war to gain control of the House would again be waged by the Republicans. Eventually, Paul Horcher went to work as Director of the San Francisco Waste Management Program where he continues to earn a salary over $103,000 a year in the city where Willie Brown, Jr., is the Mayor, San Francisco.

But Californian voters paid for more than one recall election at the time. Interestingly enough, the Republicans also decided to organize a recall against Democrat Assemblyman Mike Machado because he had supposedly agreed not to vote for Willie Brown, Jr. as Speaker and failed to keep his promise. The recall effort failed, however, and Machado filed an $800,000 claim under a law allowing public reimbursement of expenses for those who survive recall elections. Machado, not surprisingly, carried a piece of legislation to address the problems he faced, AB 2782, which would have reimbursed counties for costs incurred by recall and special elections and would have reimbursed the campaign expenses incurred by state officers who have not been recalled. Unfortunately, the bill died on the Assembly Inactive File.

While Paul was battling his fellow Republicans, Latinos and Democrats were battling Proposition 187, a controversial ballot measure that denies educational, health, and social services to undocumented immigrants, and portended a national anti-immigrant mood. Chief among the proposition's supporters was Governor Pete Wilson, who was making a bid for the 1996 Presidential election and who used the issue of illegal immigration as a scapegoat for the majority of California's socio-economic problems at the time. Democrats, of course, screamed "foul" and produced a television ad that accused the Governor of flip-flopping on the issue. Wilson, who was determined to be President, introduced tough measures to halt illegal border crossings, but the Democratic ad argued that as an U.S. senator, Wilson wrote legislation that allowed for more than 1 million migrant laborers. One of the most controversial of Wilson's proposals was his attempt to deny citizenship to the U.S.-born children of illegal immigrants.

What was so sad about much of the anti-immigrant rhetoric flying around at the time was that the real facts of immigration simply weren't known. My friend, Linda Vasquez, a consultant to the California Assembly Select Committee on Statewide Immigration Impact, once told me over lunch in the Capitol park, that more than 60% of illegal immigration came from VISA over-stayers – not people madly dashing across the border from Mexico. Worse still was a little known loophole in the law that remains today. Birth certificates are known as "breeder documents" because if one has a birth certificate, one can obtain all other forms of identification, including social security cards, driver's licenses, and even credit. In California, birth certificates are considered public record, and anyone can go to any local registrar recorder's office and get a certified copy of anyone's birth certificate – even those belonging to complete strangers. In essence, one can get a document officially stamped and certified to be valid by the State of California as being a legal proof of identity.

Linda also said that because birth certificates "prove" identity, if someone wanted to change identities, he could then simply go to a local Social Security office, claim he lost his Social Security card, and receive a new one issued in the name of the person on that birth certificate. With those two documents in hand, he could then go to the Department of Motor Vehicles, claim that too had been lost or stolen, and receive a new driver's license, also not in his own name. From that point on, the person would effectively be someone else. He could go to any bank in the country, say that he was someone else, and become that other person, taking over that person's credit and checking accounts. Because birth certificates list a person's mother's maiden name, something that banks typically use as proof of identity, he would have no trouble verifying who he claimed to be. What my friend had said really alarmed me.

In 1995 and 1996, legislation was introduced to attempt to fix this loophole in the law. Unfortunately, it never made it to the governor's desk. One thing that became clear in the various committee hearings on the bill, however, was the fact that "breeder documents" were – and still are – big business, a white collar crime that helps both illegal aliens and criminals to change identities by using a document certified by the State of California as one of the only ways to prove one's identity.

Anti-immigrant bashing just kept escalating. In a May 21, 1995 article entitled, "Immigration Mockery," in ***The Los Angeles Times***, Ron K. Unz remarked on the ironies of the whole illegal immigration issue. As he noted, "The revelation that Gov. Pete Wilson, leading scourge of the undocumented, had himself employed an illegal immigrant housekeeper will certainly deepen our political cynicism. Wilson joins the sorry band of hypocrites Dianne Feinstein and Michael Huffington, both of whom made the crusade against illegal immigration the centerpiece of their senatorial campaigns and were then revealed as having entrusted the sanctity of their homes to undocumented employees."

One thing I wanted to know as an astrologer is what role Governor Pete Wilson played in it all. Of course, I looked at his chart. Governor Pete Wilson was born August 23, 1933 in Lake Forest, IL at 4:10 p.m. He was born with the Sun, Neptune and Jupiter in Virgo, which shows that he has an analytical mind and a critical eye towards others, often times being very judgmental. With his Venus and Moon in Libra, I am sure he feels as though he is a fair person, but as we have seen in other political charts, he has a tendency to see life idealistically.

Harsh squared aspects between Uranus, Pluto and Mars show forceful energy that could manifest in his own anger. However, Pluto, the greater planet of the three in the sign of Cancer would say he could turn the energy inward which could create stomach problems. To look at Saturn in his 2nd house, his karma would be money in this lifetime. Nonetheless, Uranus, Pluto and Mars would be enough to bring him to his knees under certain transits.

This situation brings up an interesting observation I made over the years and especially from 1989 through 1991. Those years stood out in my mind because Uranus and Saturn had entered Capricorn where Neptune already resided. Right from the beginning, I thought we would see imbalances on Earth that would match what was going on in the heavens. While the planets affect our lives, they also affect weather, national disasters, etc.

On October 17, 1989 a devastating earthquake hit San Francisco, unexpectedly collapsing freeways, buildings, and causing fires and numerous casualties. When the earthquake occurred, the transiting Mercury and Mars was in aspect. On October 21, 1991 we had a devastating fire whip through Oakland, one of the worst in U.S. History. This time the Moon was in Aries, a fire sign that squared into the hovering malefic planets in Capricorn. On March 3, 1991, the Moon squared into these transiting planets and so did Venus. On that day, Rodney King attracted national attention when he was beaten up by several Los Angeles police officers.

While some incidences similar to this one would have just moved out of the news, the public became alarmed when a taped video of the incident was rebroadcast over and over again into their living rooms. Added to this mixture during this timeframe was a drought that happened when the rainfall fell below 75% of normal, and farmers feared it would mean the death of their livelihood as they tried everything they could to keep their crops, which were obviously dependent on water, alive. Another thing that was happening in California at this time was the fact that we were in a serious financial crisis.

Since the planets affect us as humans, anyone born under the sign of Cancer, Libra, Capricorn, or Aries or a person that had lots of planets in these signs was affected as well. Governor Pete Wilson, for example, took office in early January of 1991. The transiting planets squared into his birth planets causing difficult aspects. One of those transiting planets was Saturn, which brings heavy lessons or karmic experiences full force. In Wilson's case, Saturn brought the new Governor face to face with his worst nightmares when he had to declare more than one state of emergency over fires, earthquakes, and drought and try to do damage control over the budget shortfall he inherited. Then the planet slipped into his 2nd house. For two or three years money would be his main focus. The only question was, "Where was he going to get it and what budget cuts would he make?"

In time, Saturn moved out of the difficult formation. But also in time it moved back in. Wilson wanted to be President of the United States. As the transiting Saturn started forming difficult aspects to his natal planets, affirmative action issues started bringing down his popularity. Perhaps directly as a result of his stance on illegal immigration, where he once had 40 percent of the Hispanic vote, now polls were saying he only had 25%. The fact that he himself had employed an illegal worker couldn't have helped his political standings, and when Saturn moved into place in 1996, his chances of becoming president went down hill. Eventually, term limits booted him out of office altogether.

Chapter 12

Of course, I didn't spend too much time caught up in the political difficulties of our former governor because I had my own planetary aspects and squares to worry about. Once again I found myself confronting deep-seated emotions about my son and his father. The issue between my son and his father didn't resolve itself. Looking back now I am not sure why I always thought it would just go away. Maybe I just hoped it would. However, when my planets formed difficult aspects again, I got a call from Jon saying that he decided to confront his father himself by writing the legislator a letter. I found myself speechless, grappling with a disparate array of emotions.

All Jon wanted to do is tell his father how he had finally made something of himself and to have his father respond favorably to that. He wanted, in other words, to try and make friends with a man whom he had never really known and to try and resolve some of his questions about his heritage, which included learning about his family's health history.

As was to be expected, Mark again denied that he was Jon's father. Over twenty-five years had passed since Jon's birth. The sleeping snake kept waking up and showing its fangs ready to strike at any moment, only this time, only the truth would satisfy my son. Determined to put a stop to it all, Jon called Mark's secretary and demanded that a DNA blood test be done to prove once and for all that Mark was his father.

"Of course he is Mark's child!" I thought as my heart sank. "After all Mark flew to Washington, D. C. to see me when I moved there, wrote me all the time and called me every time he went to a political function he was attending. "What did he THINK happened?" I thought. Since Mark never knew about my one-night stand, I am sure that deep down we both always knew my son's father was Mark.

Suddenly, I really resented that I had to play the role of mother and father while keeping my mouth shut when it all should have been properly settled legally over 20 years ago when I tried to see an attorney to exercise my son's legal rights. But I let the political giants prey on my emotions like they did with their convincing speeches to their constituents that were full of ulterior motives like winning their votes.

In my mind, I reviewed my entire relationship with Mark. Despite the fact that he was married, I recalled this legislator being so possessive of me that once he scolded a lobbyist for flirting with me while I took them both a cup of coffee, causing us both to be embarrassed by the member's outrage. I even caught him listening in on my phone conversations when I was assigned to work in his office. If I were sitting in a committee room waiting for the committee on which he served to adjourn so we could go to dinner, I had to sit alone. No other man was allowed to come near me. He really made that clear one evening when I was laughing and talking to a reporter in the audience while I waited for the committee to adjourn. Mark came flying down from the podium and scared the daylights out of the reporter as he reprimanded him for sitting next to me. The reporter, once a good friend, never spoke to me again. On another occasion when I went out to dinner with someone, I recognized Mark's car outside my apartment when I got home. It infuriated me yet flattered me as well that he cared that much.

Yet, when confronted with paternity it was as if Mark didn't know me. What's worse, my silence had been bought with threats and a relatively tiny sum of money. In short, members of the Legislature took care of their own and allowed a legislator to become a deadbeat dad. Ironically, the political hot button of making "deadbeat dads" pay was a big issue in the State Legislature with members desperate to appear tough on the issue, but apparently the laws they were so pleased to tell the news reporters they passed didn't exist when it related to one of them.

Mentally, I reviewed my life in the Legislature and my involvement with Mark. My emotions were complicated. On the one hand, I deeply cared about him and didn't want to hurt him. On the other hand, I knew that had I tried to speak out earlier, I would have lost everything that mattered, including my job. Mixed with all of those tumultuous feelings was the realization that I was my son's mother and needed what was best for him to happen. In the end, silence was the path of least resistance.

A few days later, Mark's secretary told my son that the legislator would not agree to a DNA test.

147

Angrily, my son snapped back, "Fine, we can order it done at his grave site in front of hundreds of people when he dies. "

When that message got back to Mark, the DNA tests were done immediately. Even though I knew Mark was the father, fear grabbed hold of me and never let go until the results came back. "What if the tests are done incorrectly and say he isn't the father? What if they can't tell? What if he really is so powerful that he can have the results modified?" Numerous frightening scenarios played out in my mind, especially in the middle of the night when I lay awake thinking about it like I had so many times before.

Ultimately, the DNA test came back saying it was 99.99 percent positive that Mark was the father. I was both relieved and concerned. The secret I had kept for so long was finally out in the open among the three of us. Eventually, things worked out as best as they could. In time, my son and his father did in fact develop a relationship. After graduation from junior college, Jon enrolled in Sacramento State College. He spent many years working while he went to school until one day he finally achieved his dream of going into private practice counseling teenagers who faced many of the same problems he did growing up.

What was so remarkable, however, is that the planets I had which marked my karma in this lifetime and that related to a child also had my son's Saturn in aspect to them, which told me he was the child with whom I had the most karma. In fact, our karma with each other was set into motion every seven years at the same time. Eventually, he would have his own issues about children with which he would have to deal, but because his Saturn was in Taurus in his 11th house at birth, his karmic lessons in this lifetime related to friendships and also to money. Would Jon handle his karmic lessons better than his parent's had? Only time would tell. Then again, perhaps this experience we all shared was nothing more than to give him his chance at bat to prove that he could be a better parent.

Shadows in the back of the chambers of the Legislature – there were many. Mine that was silenced many years ago was small in comparison to other shadows that still hover back there, shadows that perhaps included a member telling another member about the outright dirty election race going on in his district. Perhaps a wife was telling her husband, who was a member of the Legislature, that she wanted a divorce because she knew he was secretly having an affair with his secretary. Maybe a gay member was telling another gay member to meet him or her across the street, so they could have dinner and later make love to escape that day's monotony when session ended. These and hundreds of other scenarios are played out in the State Capitol daily. Interestingly enough, California is not unique, and these dramas occur in every state in the nation, including Washington, D.C.

Shortly after Jon confronted me with his father and Horcher was recalled, the Assembly, which had been hopelessly locked in political gridlock, was once again changing. With Horcher out of office, the Democrats made another play for control over who would be Speaker. Just as they had convinced Paul Horcher to become an Independent, they knew that if they could find a sympathetic Republican, one who was unhappy with the party, they could retain control of the Assembly. That put their next plan into action – courting Assemblywoman Doris Allen, a Republican. They succeeded. On June 6, 1995, Speaker Willie Brown, Jr., a Democrat who had been elected to that position 14 ½ years prior by the Republicans, handed his gavel to Assemblywoman Doris Allen, a Republican from Cypress who was the first woman to be elected to that position. The votes that put her into that role were those of the Democrats. Of course, the Republicans cried "foul" and many called her Willie Brown's "puppet" and "a turncoat."

Since Horcher was recalled, I was out of a job once again, something that depressed me no end. I, who had always been a valuable employee, was a victim of the shifting tides of power. It was then that I was asked if I would help out for a while in Assemblywoman Doris Allen's Health Committee and I said I would. Most of her staff had quit during one of the busiest times of the Legislature. The primary reason her staff had walked out on her was because she supported the Democrats. However, deadlines for bills had to be met, and she needed reliable staff members. When I got there all I found was one female consultant, who hadn't worked there very long single-handedly and bravely holding down the fort.

Many events transpired that led up to Doris Allen becoming the Speaker of the Assembly. Naturally, I wanted to see her chart. Doris

Allen was born May 26, 1936 in Kansas City, Missouri. She came to work for the California Assembly in 1982, never once realizing the role she would play in California's political history. Her astrology chart revealed that she had the Sun in Gemini along with a couple of other planets, which showed me that she liked to talk and always had something to say. Her Moon in Leo revealed her interest in politics and being before the public, but what stood out in her chart was the fact that four of her planets formed a rare CROSS. Based on her planets, I also felt as though she may have had problems with depression. The position of her Mars and Mercury indicated that she could get in trouble for things she verbally blurted out – something that would become quite evident as her time with the Legislature progressed.

Allen had become disenfranchised from her party for several reasons, including the fact that she lost a Senate special primary election to fellow Assembly Republican Ross Johnson, primarily because her fellow Republicans failed to support her candidacy. As the March 22, 1995 morning edition of **_The Orange County Register_** noted in a report by Marc Lifter, "Allen made her displeasure known to fellow Republicans during an angry speech in a closed-door caucus luncheon meeting." It further quoted her as saying, "I told them I don't think you should eat your own." Rumors among staff were rampant after that caucus meeting, most saying that her anger was aroused when the Republicans supported Assemblyman Ross Johnson's move to Irvine just so he could run for the Senate seat. Although he was a "carpetbagger," he secured the support Allen couldn't get.

Allen also expressed her dissatisfaction with her own party when she failed to support former Assembly Republican Leader Pat Nolan when he ran for Speaker. Interestingly enough, Nolan was later convicted on corruption charges and was sent to federal prison. Worse still was the bi-partisan spirit with which Allen worked in the Assembly. While most Republicans stayed strictly within party politics, Allen worked with Democrats to get laws passed on education, the environment, and the budget. It was that work on the budget that got her into the most trouble. Rumors about her defection to either the Democrats or an Independent party stance flew for days. Republicans and Democrats both courted her in near desperation for her support. In a thinly veiled move, the

Assembly Women's Caucus, which was made up solely of Democrats, named her "Woman of the Year." Governor Pete Wilson met with her privately and supported the title.

No one knows what was really said behind that closed-door session except those who were there, but the never-ending gossip mill worked at full tilt. Some staff claimed that he threatened her, while others said he simply tried to win her over with soothing reassurances about passage of her legislation and good political future.

After that meeting, Allen continued to be dissatisfied with the Republican leadership – and Assemblyman Jim Brulte in particular. According to Daniel Weintraub 's story in *The Orange County Register* on May 11, 1995, Allen said that Brulte was "...only the last in a long line of Republican leaders who have put loyalty over civility and politics over policy." At the time, Allen was her party's senior member, something that normally would command the ultimate respect from her peers, but as that newspaper article later noted, she "chafed at what she said was the abusive, insular leadership of a small circle of Republicans who ostracized anyone who broke ranks."

By the time she was elected Speaker by the Democrats, her Republican colleagues called her a "sell out." Matt Coker in the October 1-7, 1999 edition of *The Orange County Weekly* noted, "One Republican leader said of Allen, 'The first thing she ought to do is her hair.'"

Allen did not just accept her treatment, however. As Steve Wiegand reported in *The Sacramento Bee*, when the bad jokes circulated about her, she complained that she was being forced out of her post by "a group of power-mongering men with short penises." But maybe she got the last laugh: When some male Republicans entered their offices Friday, they were greeted by little cans of Vienna sausages and a note saying, "Compliments of Doris Allen."

Her take-over of the Assembly was well crafted. House rules were rewritten and adopted, which shifted the power to make Republican committee assignments from the caucus to the speaker. The rules also created a position and a title of "Speaker Emeritus" for Willie Brown, Jr. and he ended up with a nice office in the historic restored section of the Capitol.

Allen was a gentle woman fighting to survive in a man's world. I can still remember what the transits in her chart looked like the day she took over as Speaker. What most people didn't know was how frightened she was. The day she was elected to Speaker, a friend of mine, Linda Vasquez, who was a consultant also working at the Capitol and a gifted intuitive, was asked by a member to do a psychic reading for Allen. Linda wouldn't tell me the details of that reading, but from the look in her eyes I knew she was worried about Allen and whether she would collapse under the pressure of it all.

Ultimately, the Republicans didn't take kindly to Allen becoming Speaker and decided to recall her. In the months that followed she became more and more frustrated knowing she couldn't fill the shoes of her predecessor and that a recall election was ominously approaching. She got so frightened about what was happening to her that a member of the Legislature again asked Linda, who frequently was called upon to meet with members including dignitaries from Washington, D.C. and foreign countries, to see Allen. Linda later told me over lunch that Allen seemed to calm down after she spoke with her but again would not reveal the details of the reading, a silent agreement we had about all of our many clients. Our spirituality required confidentiality.

One constant supporter of Allen's was Republican Assemblyman Brian Setencich. As a matter of fact, he was her only ally from her own party and often attempted to lighten the mood. There was a price to be paid for supporting her, however. On June 28, 1995 Setencich presided over the Assembly session and joked about a voodoo doll he had received as a gift, threatening to use it if his colleagues didn't stop challenging him. Since he was the only Republican to consistently stand by the Speaker, he faced non-stop problems with his peers.

On November 28th, 1995, with her worst fears confirmed, voters replaced Allen with an ardent conservative Republican, Scott Baugh. The recall vote had an overwhelming majority against Assembly Speaker Doris Allen. Around the capitol, Baugh was secretly referred to as Scott "Slime" Baugh because, as Matt Coker, in ***The Orange County Weekly***'s October 1-7, 1999 edition, noted, "Four associates of Baugh and Assemblyman Curt Pringle, who wound up Speaker once the smoke cleared, were later convicted of falsifying election documents."

While those around me mourned the loss of her seat, I wondered, "Was her karma fulfilled? Had she learned what she had come here to learn?" Four years later, Doris Allen died of cancer at her daughter's home in Boulder, Colorado. The September 1999 services were held at the Crystal Cathedral in Garden Grove, California. She was 63 years old.

Throughout this time, I paid close attention to Assemblyman Jim Brulte, who had been consistently out to get even with Horcher for supporting Willie Brown, Jr. He was one of the driving forces behind Horcher's recall. As an astrologer, I realized early on that Assemblyman Brulte was like a karmic Santa Claus. He had karmic presents for more members of the Legislature than any man or woman I had ever met or observed in all the years I worked there, but most of his presents were not pleasant ones.

Assemblyman Jim Brulte was born April 13, 1956 in Glen Cover, New York. Although I never worked for Assemblyman Brulte, I did run into him in the halls of the Capitol on an almost daily basis. He was a tall, very overweight man who wore the innocent face of a young boy. His face, however, was deceptive – he was anything but innocent. As time went on, I watched him take his karmic fist and politically hit several legislators with it in his attempt to become Speaker of the California Assembly, especially when he tried to oust Willie Brown, Jr.

Like Doris Allen, Brulte was born with a CROSS in his chart, which is created when four planets aspect each other at 90 degree angles. His Sun in Aries squared his Mars in Capricorn, which squared his Neptune in Libra, and that squared his Uranus in Cancer. This cross let me know that he had a temper that was born out of heavy frustrations, which could flare at the drop of a hat. Since Neptune was one of the planets involved, it told me that he had felt betrayed more than once. Then I remembered Assemblyman Paul Horcher's vote. Brulte must have felt deeply betrayed by Horcher, but it certainly wouldn't have been the first time in his life. Betrayals were part of Brulte's karma in this lifetime.

He also had Saturn opposing his Venus, which told me his love life was disappointing to him, and all of his relationships had a karmic quality to them. The chart also told me that he liked his freedom, but I believe the career path that he chose in this life never afforded him the freedom he desired and needed.

Months later, some of what I saw in his astrology chart was panned out by a memo I found in the trash can next to the Xerox machine when I went to retrieve something I had accidentally thrown away. The trashed memo gave me political insight that left me speechless. I never showed it to any of the members for fear they would have a field day with it. It was dated March 4, 1994 and it was from Assemblyman Gil Ferguson. Not only had Gil Ferguson gone after Assemblyman Tom Hayden, a Democrat, but also he apparently took bites out of his own Republican colleagues who were in leadership positions. Suddenly, I was seeing my suspicions of Ferguson's planets and those of Brulte confirmed and I realized that both political leaders were archetypal warriors.

The memo addressed an article that appeared in ***The California Journal***, which regularly rated legislators in the California State Legislature on how effective they were. This story was just updating the past rankings of former legislators and comparing them to the current members. Clearly Brulte had taken some pride in his high ranking but failed to be concerned about the low rankings of his colleagues.

Ferguson's memo stated that "scum bag liberals" had written the article. Ferguson further claimed that liberal lawmakers were at the top of the rankings and conservatives ones were ranked at the bottom. He went on to say:

"Jim, I have never seen you as a tower of strength or integrity, but I did think that you would understand the basic principle of leadership: protect and look out for your people. Your self-serving and stupid words are going to be reprinted and used against each of our members this year. You have given legitimacy to the fraud. You have validated their lies.

"In the future, swallow your first impulse to respond. It's obviously going to be self-centered and wrong. Then, use your brain. All of our leaders are always ranked high! If they were not, it would on the surface, invalidate their poll. After all, over 40% of the legislators (our caucus) voted our leaders #1 when they elected them. Wake up!

He closed the memo by saying, "When Doris Allen asked you what you intended to do about this, you should have answered her directly with a simple, straightforward and total denunciation of the magazine, the poll and Democratic politicians in general. You should also have deflated any fool among us who took any pride in a "'good ranking.'"

Having his own party members against him couldn't have been something that Brulte would handle well. Democratic legislators would have had a field day if they had seen the memo, but I quietly tucked it away as a piece of insight I was afforded into what was going on at the time that was meant for me and me alone. I am sure the memo disappointed Brulte or maybe even infuriated him.

Interestingly enough, Brulte took a particularly big hit during that time. An example of it appeared in a story Mary Lynne Vellinga reported in *The Sacramento Bee* on June 7, 1995, in which she notes, "The morning after his party ostensibly won the Assembly Speakership for the first time in a quarter-century, Assembly Republican leader Jim Brulte was forced to vacate his ornate office." Whether the memo had anything to do with his "punishment" remains to be seen, but one thing was certain: Brulte didn't get to move down one Floor to the Speaker's quarters as he had once dreamed. Instead, Speaker Doris Allen slapped Brulte in the face by giving him the almost closet-sized, substandard office that was previously occupied by the very man he had succeeded in ousting – Assemblyman Paul Horcher of Whittier. One can only imagine what went through his mind as he put his things into Paul Horcher's desk.

Suddenly, the karma had gone full circle. What was Jim Brulte supposed to learn from his challenges and what had Paul Horcher learned? Eventually, Assemblyman Brulte moved on. With Allen and Setencich out of the way, he was elected to the Senate where he became the Republican Floor Leader. Both Brulte and Horcher had survived in different ways. Their lesson together in this lifetime was finished and they went on with their lives.

Although Allen was recalled, the power of Willie Brown, Jr. seemed unstoppable. His nickname, "Slick Willie," was well earned when he managed to convince another Republican to become Speaker, Allen's former political ally, Assemblyman Brian Setencich. Naturally, as an astrologer and employee now caught in the middle of everything heated going on, I had to see the chart of the new Speaker, Assemblyman Brian Setencich.

Brian Setencich was a nice-looking 6-foot-5-inch tall former professional basketball player who held the position of forward. Running with the ball is something the Republican legislator from Fresno had to do when he found himself elected to the position of the Assembly Speaker on September 14, 1995. Once again, as had happened with several previous Speakers of the California Assembly, it was the Democrats who elected him to the position. Who was this young man who appeared out of nowhere and rose to such power in such a short period of time? The night he was elected, I went home and calculated his chart and stayed up half the night studying it.

Assemblyman Brian Setencich was born March 29, 1962 in Fresno, California. Brian Setencich's astrology chart reminded me of a lotus flower that opens and closes. He was born with his Sun in Aries squaring his Moon in Capricorn, Saturn in Aquarius squaring Neptune in Pisces, and Mars in Pisces opposing Pluto in Virgo. Squares and oppositions in astrology are hurdles that need to be climbed. On the historic day in his life when he finally was able to grasp the golden ring of Assembly Speaker, he must have felt like he was on top of the world, but I could see that he was also frustrated. Since transiting Saturn would slowly move forward and hit his Sun and square his Moon, it was only a matter of time before the planetary support he received from the heavens would turn on him and the public support that had once been there for him wouldn't be.

The biggest problem, however, was the fact that his closest Republican supporter was Doris Allen, so it took his own vote and hers just before she left office for him to be elected as the Assembly leader. Unfortunately, Willie Brown, Jr. was running for Mayor of San Francisco and Allen was nearing a special recall election, so neither would be there to protect him when he came into power.

Brian Setencich's election to Speaker gave the Assembly its third Speaker in less than four months, an unprecedented occurrence. I distinctly recall walking through the hallway that led to the Assembly chambers and looking at the portraits of all of the Speakers that are hung there. I noted the names and the dates of the person who was Speaker. Years would go by with the same person being in that position as if there were an unbroken line. Suddenly, however, the Speakers were changing faster than any one could have imagined.

Since the Republicans had more seats in the Assembly, they could decide whether a member's bill would or would not pass. Many enemies were born out of the political war games that had thus transpired, so the mounting tension reeked throughout the Capitol, and the lower House was completely dysfunctional. Once Allen was recalled and Brown was elected Mayor, the Republicans decided to change the balance of power to their favor. On January 4, 1996, the Republicans were able to pass new rules that removed power from the Speaker and gave it to the Assembly Rules Committee.

Then on January 5th the Republicans ousted Setencich and elected Republican Curt Pringle of Orange County as the newest Speaker of the Assembly. In the meantime, the planet Saturn continued its course until it was finally conjunct with Setencich's Sun and squared his Moon in his natal birth chart. In November of 1996, Setencich lost his seat in the Assembly. Suddenly, the window of opportunity that had opened up for him slammed shut.

Interestingly enough, the U.S. District Court later found Brian Setencich guilty of tax evasion in September of 2000 because he had looted his campaign account and failed to report $19,301 on his 1996 income taxes. He was ordered to spend seven months at a halfway house and would no longer be allowed to vote, the ultimate comedown for the formerly second most powerful man in the State.

Ultimately, the Republicans were determined to take out their revenge on the Democrats for all the abuse they had taken from them when the Democrats were in power. Getting Doris Allen recalled didn't satisfy them either. They wanted more.

Assemblyman Curt Pringle was perhaps the most anti-Democratic member of all, and it was he who became the next Speaker. Pringle was surrounded by scandal from the moment he first ran for the Legislature. In 1988, to make sure non-citizens wouldn't vote in Orange County, Pringle posted uniformed poll guards outside voting booths. The Orange County GOP was sued, and the lawsuit was settled out of court for $400,000, money that was mostly paid by his insurance company. His rise to Speaker was also tainted when several aides, one of whom worked for him, pleaded guilty to a scheme to recruit a Democrat as a decoy to split the Democratic vote and ensure a Republican victory.

Things in the Capitol changed dramatically with Pringle's election to the office of Speaker. One afternoon in January of 1996 I was returning to work in the Legislative office Building, a six-story tall structure that houses legislative staff that work for the Senate and the Assembly. Along the side of the building I noticed a garbage truck that was surrounded by staff, a couple of legislators, and some people walking by who had stopped to see what all the commotion was about. Apparently, newly elected Speaker Pringle had state agents seize the garbage truck that he suspected was carrying Democratic documents in it that had been tossed when the Republicans had taken control of the Assembly.

While the State Capitol housed the legislators, the Republican and Democratic caucuses were housed in the Legislative Office Building. So, when the Republicans really did take over, it would seem natural to assume documents would be destroyed, but if there were any wrong doing going on, both parties would have been guilty of it. In this case, however, the Republicans were so determined to have their revenge that going to extremes such as poking through entire garbage trucks was considered politically expedient.

One of the most unsettling things I noticed was the fact that during the years I had worked as Committee Secretary, I had tried to preserve a history of each Committee for which I worked along with all books that pertained to it. Now I was actually required to go into various offices and throw out the very documents I had previously thought were important simply because they belonged to the Democrats. Now that the Republicans were in power, they decided they didn't need any "Democratic leftovers." Worse still was the fact that what the Republicans didn't toss, the Democratic staff did before they left the Committee – just to ensure that the Republicans wouldn't have anything of value.

The Secretarial Unit for which I had worked for so many years in the Assembly was also destroyed. Suddenly, dozens of people were unemployed. A lot of the secretaries were asked to go to work in members' offices, while many went to work with the caucuses, but for many months all of them lived in fear of what was going to happen to them. It was a new day and a new era, but it didn't last. Democrats had held the power positions for so long, that the Republicans were not experienced in such positions. It wasn't that they were incapable of doing the job – they had just never done it. That lack of experience would cost them.

I went to work for a short time in one of the Republican Committees. It never mattered to me whether they were Democrats or Republicans. In my mind, staff had to stick together – all staff. At one point when I first came to work for the Legislature and was seated with some people at a dinner table, I was asked what the difference was between working for a Democratic or a Republican member. I answered, "In a Democrat's office, if you make a mistake on an envelope, you throw it away. In a Republican's office, if you make a mistake, you correct it." That answer never changed in the years that followed.

Apparently, the Legislature needed another house cleaning because no sooner had support staffs been fired and documents and materials thrown out when the Republicans lost their control of the Assembly to the Democrats. Once again, a Democrat was Speaker.

While all of the political wars over who would be Speaker were going on, I remember quietly looking at Jackie Speier's astrology chart. How karma worked was always on my mind, and nowhere was it more visible, in my way of thinking, than in the life of this articulate and beautiful woman about whom everyone always spoke so highly and that everyone always admired. Leo Wolinsky, quoting Speier, in _The Los Angeles Times_ on Dec. 14, 1986, reported that Speier, looking back on her life's "triumphs and tragedies," went on to say, "She is convinced that they are all bound together by a single thread that she calls fate."

When I looked at Speier's astrology chart, I realized that she herself had identified the situation correctly. It was indeed fate that bound Congressman Ryan to both her and to Jim Jones. It was fate that she, a mere legislative staff person, later became a California State Senator. It is fate that determines all of our lives.

Speier was born May 14, 1950 in San Francisco, California. When I first looked at her chart, my reaction was that it was betraying me because I couldn't see the tragedies that this woman has had to survive. Then after awhile the chart started unraveling and showing me significant aspects that were being made between the planets under which she was born. Her Sun was in the sign of Taurus at birth in

159

favorable aspect to two malefic planets, Saturn and Mars, both of which were in the sign of Virgo. Then I noticed that her Venus in Aries was squared to Uranus in Cancer, which made 90-degree aspects to Mars and Saturn in Virgo. This configuration showed me that we should expect her to face the unexpected tragedies that had affected her so deeply emotionally and which I felt were part of her karma. At the same time, however, several planets in her chart make favorable aspects to one another, which let me know that she had a lot of support with which to face her pain.

On the day she was shot, Speier's chart, which also had Mars squared into the natal Uranus at birth, was devastating. Most of the transiting planets were in aspect to planets in her birth chart, which is extremely unusual. Her aspects during the Guyana experience would be compared to the magnitude of the "Shaman's Death" in the Native American culture. When people experience it, their entire belief structure is challenged as the very foundation they have built their life upon is ripped out from beneath them and they have to crawl back to life. I believe that is exactly what Speier did. The eighteen months to two years that followed Guyana were extremely difficult for her.

Speier underwent ten operations in two months before she was able to leave Arlington Hospital after being shot in Guyana. Doctors were not able to restore the full use of her shattered right arm and decided not to remove two bullets that were in her chest and her pelvis. But even with all of the difficulty, she left the hospital determined to continue the work of her late boss, Congressman Ryan.

As noted earlier in the Uzelac article, Speier herself said that the thread of fate connected the tragedies in her life because voters elected her to serve as Assemblywoman to the same district Ryan had represented. As soon as she sworn into office, reporters told her that Larry Layton had been convicted in the Jonestown massacre in which her former boss was killed. She broke down in tears on the spot.

Speier's tragedies didn't end there, however. She married Dr. Steven Kent Sierra and had a little boy. About five years after his birth, her husband, who was chief of emergency services at San Mateo County Hospital, was tragically killed in an auto accident when his car was hit broadside by a driver who ran a red light.

This woman not only had to go through the emotional ordeal of losing her husband, but she also had to once again witness a trial related to a tragedy, a trial which ended in the perpetrator only serving a one-year jail sentence because he pleaded no contest.

To add to her difficulties, she was once again bedridden for two months because of complications in a second pregnancy. She had discovered she was pregnant only a few weeks before her husband was killed. In August of 1994 she gave birth to a healthy little girl she named Stephanie Katelin Elizabeth Sierra, six and a half months after the death of her husband.

As an astrologer looking at Speier's chart, I can truly say she had her heart broken more than once, yet from each incident there was always a golden thread that she herself was insightful enough to appreciate. Her life happens in cycles. Whenever this is the case, we can go back in time and see what set the pattern in motion. It appears as though something probably happened to her when she was approximately eighteen months to two years old. Perhaps it was something as simple as the loss of a pet at that time or maybe she was hospitalized and separated from her mother while she was getting well. Something that simple sets a pattern of events into motion that will affect a person for a lifetime as situations unfold that are tied to a karmic lesson we've come here to learn. Furthermore, who knows, maybe one of her children was none other than Leo Ryan himself coming back to finish what he hadn't before.

I have spent a lifetime studying people and watching the merry-go-round turn in their lives, even in my own. Incredible books like the ones written about Edgar Cayce, a man who could see past lives under hypnosis, were all that made sense to me. How could I see karma in an astrology chart unless it had all been predetermined? Clients that came to me were strangers, but I could see their divorces, illnesses, frustrations and multi-million dollar financial rewards or losses. Sometimes I could even see what happened in a past life.

"Lessons," I would think to myself. "It is all about lessons we've come here to learn."

Chapter 13

I never knew what cosmic lesson would come my way next or who would be the teacher delivering it to me. A former Senator, who was chair of the State Democratic Party at the time, delivered a valuable insight into the mysteries of life to me. It happened when my friend Linda called me to say the Senator's father's was dying. She asked if I would look at the Senator's father's astrology chart.

Not only did I look at it and see that the father was facing a difficult time, but I also said I would burn a candle for the man who was so sick that he had surgery facing him. It was then that I learned to make my own candles. I melted wax and added various herbs and scents when I poured the hot wax into a glass holder. The only intent I ever put into the candle is that any discomfort be removed from the sick man no matter what the destined outcome would be.

That evening I lit the candle, and then I checked it from time to time. Several hours later I gasped when I looked at it. The herbs had formed what looked like a large clump of blood at the base of the burning wick and what I was sensing sent chills down my body. Then I left the room, and I didn't think anymore of it.

A few days passed when I got a call from the same Senator trying to reach someone for whom I worked. While I was on the phone, he said our mutual friend had said I burned the candle for his father. He thanked me and said the operation was a success. He laughed when he shared with me that his father was flirting with the nurse in his hospital room when he visited him earlier that day. Some people would have been content with that answer.

As an astrologer who had seen his father's chart and the ominous candle, I quietly said his father needed two or three days for his difficult aspects to pass before everything would be fine. In fact, I said, I was still really worried about the man. He still thanked me for my concern but the tone in his voice let me know he didn't believe me. Quietly, I put him on hold and buzzed my boss on the intercom to let him know who was holding on the line.

Forty-eight hours had barely gone by before my friend called me and told me that the Senator's father had died while he was still in the hospital. I remember feeling so devastated at the Senator's great loss, but humbled by an aspect that I had seen many times before in the charts of people who never got beyond the difficult aspects that I called a "wall" whenever planets formed it in a chart. Once again, it made me freeze in my tracks and question how vividly our birth chart resembles a "star map" we are born with that charts our souls' journey, even though I had seen such things so many times before.

At this stage in my spiritual journey I was a good astrologer and a good secretary, but my world had become plastic. I understood the spiritual laws of life and studied various philosophical teachings a lot, but my life was lacking luster. Well, the Universe must have realized just how stagnant my existence had become because that is when my friend, Linda Vasquez and I started meeting almost everyday for lunch. Linda was an oversized whirlwind of psychic energy with long red hair that also worked for the Assembly. Linda later introduced to me to a beautiful blonde Dutch friend of hers named Louise Pastor. Louise worked for the Senate. They both knew each other from Palmdale, California where they once lived and taught metaphysical classes together.

Together the three of us would meet for lunch and delight in sharing the metaphysical experiences each day brought us on our spiritual path. Some were joyful and at other times challenging.

Occasionally, Linda would reach into her pants pocket and pull out a tarot deck.

"Pick a card," she would chuckle with a gleam in her eye.

Then she would start reading what the card was telling her about me. Whether she was reading a card from the deck or just looking at me, she said she got visions like one would see on a picture screen but instead of watching a movie, she was viewing some aspect of my life. Sometimes she would giggle and I would have to pry out of her what she was seeing about me. She was like this with everyone for whom she read. Many times I watched people be moved to tears by her psychic readings, which were based on the picture her guides showed her. One example was when I walked out of a metaphysical store in Old Sacramento one dark evening after work looking for Linda who said she wanted to wait outside the store for me while she smoked a cigarette. There was Linda in front of me, talking to a stranger on the wooden planked walkway.

"Don't go there," I heard her shout at a nice looking young man, who was sewing a small leather pouch she was buying from him.

His eyes were glued on hers, listening intently to what she was saying.

"You know what I mean. I see you. I know what you were going to do," she insisted.

A friend of his came up to me when he noticed me waiting for her, and whispered, "Your friend is really something else. I am glad she nailed him in that reading," he smiled walking away.

When Linda and I away from them and out of their sight, I asked her what in the world she was talking about with the stranger.

"He was thinking about committing suicide. He tried to do so a few nights ago and was gonna try it again tonight. Just told the dude not to go there. That's all," she said calmly as if thinking nothing of it.

Louise was quiet in comparison to Linda, and she could see things in shapes that I never noticed before such as fairies, elementals, etc. Louise would delightfully go around teaching me to see medicine wheels, gnomes, and faces in trees, such as the shroud of a biblical character that we once saw etched in the bark of a tree along a path leading to the Capitol building.

Sometimes Spirit talked to Louise on the way to work when she passed fields of cranes and other birds developers hadn't displaced yet. I remember when she told Linda and I there would be a mass exodus of people soon. Not too long after that there was an earthquake in Turkey and then another in Mexico; Mother Nature just kept at it removing as many as 30,000 an incident for several months.

When we talked about the natural disasters that were happening throughout the world, Louise would just calmly say, "Everyone is living longer nowadays."

Linda would nod and say, "These occurrences are the only way Mother Earth can get the extra fleas off her back."

164

Together, they would both laugh and tease me about my astrology, saying they could see me using more gifts in my toolbox then just astrology when I talked to a client. I would just debunk what they were saying because already my astrology business had grown beyond the Capitol, Sacramento, and the State. "Do these two so-called psychics have the nerve to think they can see something about me that I can't?" I silently chuckled smugly to myself. "I really do know all I need to know."

No sooner had I said that then I found myself in an auto accident that was a near death experience. At the same time, two other events occurred which would change my mind in a hurry – my salary in the Legislature had been reduced about a thousand dollars a month because of political wars. I also broke up with someone I had dated for about eight years when I learned he was seeing another woman.

As the reality with which I was familiar was stripped out from under me, I crawled back to life studying the wisdom of the mystic masters of Egypt, Tibet, and the Middle East. I read about famous Native American medicine men and even read about Wicca after reading something on the Internet that caught my interest.

After all this happened, my eyes began to see things differently in the Capitol Park. In Wicca they say, "So Above, So Below." It took years of studying to figure out that simple message. I added the words, "So In, So Out." In essence it meant that our outside world reflects that which is inside us. If we consciously think in terms of abundance, our lives will be filled with abundance. If we think in terms of restriction, restrictions will manifest in our world, such as financial lack or even health problems. In order to make changes in our lives, we have to see it differently, which changes the vibrations we are attracting from the Universe, which has a lot to do with the reality we are co-creating.

I learned the importance of being nonjudgmental about what the Universe is showing us and to be open to its messages when I had been reading a book about a Native American Medicine man. I vividly remember walking back to work on N Street, along the sidewalk I had walked for over 32 years, when suddenly I turned to my right as if something were trying to get my attention. I thought I saw a huge coiled snake on the green grass. Right away logic stepped in and said, "Ignore it. You don't want to be late getting back to work." Then I remembered the book in my hand that I had been reading about the Native Americans, who probably wouldn't question such a vision and I decided to follow where spirit was guiding me.

As I got closer to my huge snake, it turned out to be a large rock under a small oak tree. In the shade of the tree was a little sign that said, Indian Grinding Rocks. They had been put there in 1968, the same year I started working at the Capitol. I was thrilled at what I had found hidden in the park all these years. Then deep sadness came over me as I looked around at the Vietnam Memorials we had built and other monuments tourist stood before admiring. I wondered if the grinding rocks were crying out to be noticed.

I tried writing Governor Gray Davis, explaining that none of the staff that worked for the Legislature knew about the rocks and suggested that maybe we should put a bench there. All I got was a letter from the Department of General Services (DGS) saying, "The general evolution of memorials in the park is that each memorial in the park is requested by an individual special interest group. Their request would be sent to the Legislature for approval by resolution. The individual special interest group then does fund raising for the memorial and submits final construction drawings to the DGS for review before construction. Once the memorial is completed, DGS maintains the memorial in its original form. Should the special interest group desire further changes-improvements to the memorial, it is their responsibility to obtain further legislative approval and fund raising. DGS does not have budget funds for improvements to individual memorials."

It was the first time I had ever written a political official.

"No wonder people don't get involved in government with all of this mumbo jumbo," I thought to myself, laughing at my having the audacity to think I could make a difference. After all, hadn't I worked there and opened enough mail from constituents over 30 years to know nothing I was going to say would matter unless it personally affected the political official reading it? The bureaucracy was too complicated, so I put it back in the hands of Great Spirit.

One thing was for sure my experiences were different in the Capitol Park now that I had diligently read and studied so many books. Linda and Louise also played a major part in making me the new person I became. They showed me what forces of energy great psychics, spiritualists, and Native American tribes people touched into when they walked in other worlds.

Linda used to say, "Everything – and I mean everything – is alive, awake, aware." I used to shake my head at her, not really understanding what she meant. But as my own awareness grew, I began to get glimpses. Linda would point to a hawk flying above us, an ant crawling on the ground at our feet, or a squirrel climbing a tree next to us and tell us what the animals were trying to teach us.

"The hawk is telling us that we are to pay attention to the messages we will receive today," she would explain. Or, "That ant is reminding us to be patient and to serve the whole of our community today." She would grin from ear to ear and smile, "The Native Americans were wise. They knew that the animals have messages for us. That was the real point of the totems. Totem animals were lessons and reminders of certain qualities or things we need to work on in our lives."

As time passed I remember looking at Linda in wonder one day as we sat together, saying, " Your whole world talks to you, doesn't it?"

Linda smiled and whispered, "Even the rocks can speak to those who have ears."

I finally understood why that was true for her. The more I came to understand how our thoughts become our realities, and that what we say is what we create in our worlds, the more I could see examples of how it all worked. As I looked around the park now, my mind's eye could see that several trees had lost limbs. One showed me its clubfoot, another had a gouge in its side, and many of the trees were braced with metal crutches that had been pounded into their sides for added support. It was then that I wondered if the trees in the park were starting to deteriorate and fall apart because they had heard the negative gossip of members and staff passing by; their negative words were literally affecting the environment.

As I contemplated the power of our spoken words, I realized that Spirit had positioned me uniquely to think about such things in a political context. The Legislature had many people under its dome that made my spiritual journey an interesting one. One came forward just in the nick of time when I was working for a committee in a position that was about to come to an end. I received a call from a secretary working for one of the members named Jill. She asked me if I would talk to a man named John about working with him as Committee Secretary on a committee that the Speaker of the Assembly had just created for her boss to chair.

Jill became familiar with my work when I was the Committee Secretary to the Assembly Public Safety Committee. She used to call me when she needed to set bills in committee for the legislator for whom she worked. Back then I was tracking 450 bills that were swiftly moving through the Legislature. It wasn't an easy job, but I always tried to be polite and considerate with the various members' staff people with whom I worked, and Jill was one of them. I told her I would meet with John in her boss' office. I walked over to the office where she worked, which was just around the corner from me.

John was different than any staff person I had ever met. His energy was electric and so were his dark brown eyes that pierced my soul when he looked at me. When I spoke, he listened to every syllable I was saying as if searching for some deeply significant but hidden meaning.

John hired me and promised to try and protect me if I got caught in the political wars that were currently being waged. I learned he was an Aries with his Moon in Cancer with several planets in Pisces, which showed me that he was a warrior who loved his family and a cause, one that usually involved the underdog in some way.

It seemed as though history was repeating itself. He was a very religious man with a strong Catholic background. I enjoying talking to John about life and its mysteries every bit as much as I did back in the days when I worked for the Economic Opportunity Center with Victor, who taught me about the priesthood and the voodoo he saw when he was growing up.

Family values were something I seldom witnessed working for the Legislature the way I did with John. This man could chew up a political opponent and walk away with a feather sticking out of the side of his mouth over the victory. Then he would turn right around and smile as he recalled something one of his children had said or done the day before. John could meet with officials in the back room, which he frequently did, and then suddenly disappear and go take care of one of his kids or pick up the loaf of bread that his lovely wife Anne would ask him to get on his way home from work.

Since Speaker Setencich destroyed the committee for which I went to work, John helped me get a job working with him in the Senate. While I was grateful for the new job, this period of time in my life contained both my greatest challenges and my greatest opportunity for learning. By being on the path I now found myself walking, I was blessed with my most enlightening experiences out of the entire time I worked for the Legislature.

The challenges were huge. For example, my salary was reduced $1,000 a month. To make matters worse, I had recently contractually committed to making huge monthly payments on my retirement plan to catch up back-money I owed. Although I had been with the Legislature for years, I never joined the retirement system because I needed the money I made to take care of my sons. If I wanted a decent retirement, I had to pay back thousands of dollars to make up for those missing years plus pay the current amount due each month. The total of my current monthly retirement bill, the back retirement money owed, plus the pay cut added up to $1,525 monthly that I wasn't seeing in my paycheck.

Under the circumstances, I had no choice but to breathe life back into my astrology business that had fallen by the wayside as legislative deadlines took precedence. Within three months I was seeing clients statewide during the evenings, and in the years that followed I had clients throughout the United States. It was then that I also created my own astrology website at *www.JaniceStork.com* which is still active today.

From comparisons from John's astrology chart and my own I could see a karmic connection between us which might have had something to do with him rescuing me from a job that was coming to an end. Our Saturn's and Pluto's were conjunct in Leo in our overlaid charts. This suggested to me that we might have known each other in a past life and our association probably had something to do with politics, romance, or children. These were major malefic planets and their lessons are always heavy. The fact that we had them where we did told me that we might just as easily have done battle together or against each other at one time. On the plus side, the planets we shared in Sagittarius showed the enjoyable discussions we often had on philosophy and religion that I dearly loved.

I can still remember John standing with me on the steps of the Legislative Office Building where we worked one morning. We were both looking at the State Capitol building, across the street, which was quite a sight. The Sun's rays were bouncing off the brass dome mounted on rows and rows of snowy white pillars.

John perused the park with its lovely trees and towering California Redwoods, and then said, "When you served on the police force like I did during the Los Angeles riots, you develop an extra sense that enables you to look around at a scene and know when something isn't quite right with it."

Looking back, I cannot help but wonder what triggered John to tell me that while his eyes scanned the State Capitol building and the Capitol Park. Did his soul know that something wasn't quite right in the enormous building beneath the dome, or was he sensing things that had happened in the park about which few are even aware, such as the young girl who was raped in the restroom by a male predator many years ago after work when she was walking to the parking lot. "Did that energy still exist?" I wondered

John never said it, but somehow I think we both knew that there were many things wrong inside that building. Many individuals from both parties sought out this man because of his political insights. However, for me, it was John's spiritual depths that really drew me to him. Just as the Archangel Michael could slay an adversary and never question it, so could John – and both could quote scriptures from the Bible sanctioning what they had done.

I learned a lot about the spirit world from John without his ever knowing it. How strange it seemed that a person could enter our lives and prove to be a monumental teacher without ever realizing it and without a hidden agenda. In that sense, it always made John nervous to hear me talking about burning candles and studying Native American shamanism because he once studied to be a Catholic Priest. While I did not seek to become a shaman or study Native American ways on a big scale, I did enjoy an occasional ceremony.

For example, nothing fascinated me more than writing a wish on a piece of parchment paper, in charcoal pencil, then adding some herbs as an offering before burning it under a full moon. It always amazed me when the black writing was still visible on the burnt gray ashes because the pencil was a charcoal pencil. I would tell John about my joyful experiences while walking between both worlds. If hearing my stories made him nervous, he still never failed to be interested in what I was learning. But he firmly cautioned me that there was the light side and the dark side of life and eventually we all must choose which side from which we are going to function.

One day, I was determined to correct my pathetic salary that I had been led to believe would be restored although it hadn't been. John hadn't mentioned it in months, and things were becoming perilous financially. Therefore, I walked over to the Wishing Well, a local store that sold unusual items, and bought six yards of neon blue beads, several candles in different colors, and a package of fragrant opium incense. As I walked back to work, I mentally laid out the ceremony I was going to do to stir up subtle energies in the Universe to help me get my salary restored.

That night when I got home I made myself a cup of hot apple cider. I didn't go around drinking hot apple cider, but I was still very much into appearances back then and thought it added to the ambiance. Then I went to my library and found a book entitled, *Earth Medicine: Revealing Hidden Teachings of the Native American Medicine Wheel*, by Kenneth Meadows. I thumbed through the book watching the pages fall open on Wolf. When I read further in the book I learned that, "the Wolf's outer aim is to break free from entanglements and restrictions and to become detached from limitations imposed in the past."

Loving ceremony as much as I did, one day I decided to perform one. Long ago I had learned that we must make rituals our own unique expressions. My ceremony preparation was laborious because it entailed placing the beads I had purchased earlier that day in a circle like an astrology chart. Then I took ancient astrology symbols for the planets and moved them about the chart I was creating in the center of my living room floor. More planets were needed to represent transits outside the chart. When everything was in place, the ceremony began. Inside a very small iron pot was a piece of parchment paper with my name and birth date on it and the words, "Correct salary."

Then I lit some incense, burned some candles, and sat on the floor in the center of my living room and call in the Wolf animal totem to help me break free from the restrictions my salary reduction had imposed on me. I smudged the room with sage, and then I lit a block of charcoal in small cast iron pot. To the burning charcoal, I added bits of rosemary, lavender, and some corn meal to offer to the Great Spirit. Then I closed my eyes, releasing my prayer to the Universe for processing.

Some would have thought I had gone mad. I didn't know if what I was doing would help, but it was all I could do. I figured if people were lighting candles in churches for what they wanted and mailing prayers in letters to ministers throughout the world, what I was doing wasn't much different, and maybe it would help restore my salary. I needed to do something tangible in the physical realm to ignite the ethereal world into helping me make a change for the better. It was about energy. Since what we think we make happen, I was taking a nebulous, intangible thought and making it real on the physical realm. The energy of the thought would then become even stronger and attract to me that which I needed. This ceremony was terribly important because I was quickly sinking deeper and deeper in debt. Everything for which I had worked so hard, including my retirement and condo, was now being threatened.

I called in the Archangels Gabriel, Michael, Rafael and Urial who are the guardians of the North, East, South and West. Then I asked for their support from the spiritual realm. Afterwards, I burned the parchment paper that had my intent and wishes written on it and watched the smoke rise into the air, setting off every smoke alarm in my condo. Suddenly, my innocent ceremony had me running from room to room to dismantle blaring smoke alarms that were suddenly threatening to wake-up my neighbors.

The following morning I felt peaceful and full of joy at what I had done until I got a call from John at work. He told me he hadn't slept well the night before. Then I heard him coughing. I cringed when I thought about the smoke from the iron pot and the parchment paper. Then he told me he would be in shortly. Before hanging up he suddenly added that he would talk to someone about my salary, which surprised me even though I had done a ceremony for that very thing.

When John walked into the office that morning, he was carrying a picture under each arm.

"This is my Guardian Angel," he said looking down at one of the pictures.

"The wolf is my Native American totem animal," he said looking at the other picture.

Then he put the pictures on the round wooden conference table in his office until he could find a hammer and nails to mount them on his wall.

My heart pounded as I walked back to my desk. "John didn't know what I did last night," I thought to myself. "But his guides did. By having him bring those two pictures to his office, especially the one with the lone wolf looking back at me, was his guides' way of telling me that they knew what I did last night because they were there even though he was asleep. They saw me and wanted to make it clear that they don't want me doing anything to control another person and especially not John."

I stood there amazed. "Wow, I have just gotten busted by spirits from another dimension," I concluded in amazement.

It was awesome what the Universe had let me see. Although I thought what I had done was an innocent act that wouldn't bother anyone, the spirit guides were showing me I had no right to do it. Guilt set in for what I had done until finally, a few days later, I coughed up the fur ball of guilt in my throat and told John about the ceremony and what I had done. He just laughed with a twinkle in his eyes. Of course, he didn't really understand anything I said or believe me, but I felt better.

What had happened was monumental for me even though I had gotten my hands slapped by the spirit guides. It showed me that we all have protectors that don't have to be nearby in order for them to look out for us. Although I didn't see my salary restored right away, in time the raise I did get was higher than expected and eventually my salary was almost completely restored. What was more important to me was the fact that my job that was supposed to last for only three months instead lasted for several years until I finally retired. From the moment I saw those two pictures John brought to work that day, however, I couldn't help but to remember Victor and his story about the witch doctor. I realized in that moment that although there were consequences for the witch doctor's patient, the witch doctor would not go unscathed. From that day, I never again sought to manipulate the actions of others through a ceremony.

Chapter 14

I felt misplaced in the political world working for a Commission in the Senate whose demands were never the same as the high-pressured ones which had been placed on me by the various committees for which I had worked while I was in the Assembly side of the Legislature. However, my spiritual journey was becoming more intense as I tried desperately to make sense out of my job and tried to physically recuperate from the auto accident that I had been in a few years prior.

One morning, feeling kind of down, I called my friend Louise Pastor to see if she would have lunch with me in the Capitol Park, and she cheerfully agreed to. I remember her bubbly energy cheered me up the minute I saw her. We stopped and bought sack lunches at a small Asian grocery store nearby. Laughing and munching on chips from our bags, we walked into the park, and sat down in an alcove hidden by gigantic California Redwood trees, blooming camellias, and shrubs.

In the distance, beneath an ancient Gingko tree I spotted an old Asian man doing his Tai Chi exercises. On a walkway nearby, I noticed a scrounge-looking unshaven man in his thirties wearing baggy dirty jeans, dragging his feet from one round concrete trash bin to the next. He reached into the hole on top of the container and pulled out a soda can that he threw into the silver metal shopping cart he was pushing. He walked away with his head facing the ground. It was a typical day in the Capitol Park.

"Look over there!" Louise suddenly whispered as she pointed to the gigantic Redwood tree in front of us.

"Oh, no!" I gasped.

My heart raced at the site of a quivering gray squirrel that was hanging on for dear life about five feet up the red barked tree. A bulging gray fur ball was lumped close to its mouth. On the ground below was a large mangy white cat at which the squirrel was looking. The cat's coat had black, orange and brown patches all over it. It looked devilish as it sat upright, wearing the oddest black mustache. The cat tilted its head back and forth with both of his beady eyes fixed upward on every move the squirrel was making.

I quickly got up from the bench. "Get out of here!" I yelled at the cat as I raced towards it with both my arms waving.

The cat turned with a shocked look in his wide eyes. Suddenly, he ran out of the park into the street. My heart sank when I heard a loud screeching sound. I turned just in time to see the cat's body slam up against the front rim of a red sports car, causing the sound of a loud thud. There was another screech from a blue Chevy behind the sports car as the driver of it slammed on his brakes to keep from rear-ending the car in front of him. Several people stood frozen on the sidewalk nearby as they witnessed what was happening. In a flash of a second the cat sprang up on its feet, from the paved road where it had fallen and ran off into an alley across the street. Then it disappeared out of sight.

In the meantime the squirrel, seeing the cat flee from the tree, heaved the fur ball she carried under her neck into the air until it landed in the bushes down below. Suddenly, the ball unfolded out into a little baby squirrel she had been protecting. The mother squirrel was chattering with her teeth as she looked straight into my eyes, but I didn't know if she was thanking me or warning me to stay away from her. I sat back down on the bench and finished my sandwich.

Louise and I were silent as we watched the mother squirrel slowly climb down from the tree. When she got to the ground, she sniffed all around, gingerly taking a few steps at a time until her nose led her to a large green fern where the small baby was cowering. Once reunited with its mother, the baby squirrel looked around and then carefully started climbing the tree trunk without its mother's help. Its mother trailed behind as if to coax her baby into doing it for itself. Then the baby squirrel's body started to quiver as it looked high up into the tree. Soon the mother squirrel climbed up behind her baby and took his foot into her mouth. In midair the baby squirrel rolled up into a tight ball and tucked itself back under the mother's neck.

The mother squirrel looked both ways. After she knew it was safe, she edged back down the tree. When she got to the ground at the bottom, she cautiously looked around and then started leaping across the wet green lawn of the park towards a huge tree in the distance that had a hollow hole in its trunk just beneath some branches. She would go a little ways, stop and look, and then quickly go some more, never once dropping her baby that was tucked under her neck.

Louise and I were speechless as we walked back to work. The Universe was showing me lesson after lesson at warp speed these days. This lesson was one I never had thought about. The Animal Kingdom shares space in our world but has laws of its own. As a human being, I thought I was being a hero when I had tried to save the squirrel's life from the cat, but maybe the cat was hungry and would die if it didn't eat the squirrel or its baby. When my world collided with theirs, I almost killed the cat. Worse still was how I had almost caused a major traffic accident. This incident alone taught me the laws of cause and effect that are always in place in our world.

For years I had read books, meditated, listened to workshops and hungered for the meaning of life. No matter how difficult my own life got, I seemed to be comforted in knowing that there was so much more to life than what appears to be before us. With time what I was learning is that it wasn't the study or the struggle that revealed the inner mysteries of life; instead, it is relaxing and not fearing or judging what is being shown. The more I relaxed, the more they showed me.

One evening when I came home tired after work, the thought of television seemed boring, so I turned on the stereo to some soft music and had a salad for dinner. Then I decided to take a bath, but something came over me, and I no longer wanted only the relaxing bubble bath I was accustomed to at such times. I wanted something with atmosphere that would soothe the soul.

There was a small candle, no more than two inches high on the ledge beneath my five-foot wide mirror behind my bathroom sink. I lit it. Then I stood before the tub full of warm water I had drawn. Taking both hands and rubbing them together in prayer formation I closed my eyes and started visualizing an energy ball that I was rolling. As I separated my hands the ball of energy grew bigger and more powerful. Then I released it from my hands into the water while visualizing it exploding into a rainbow of colors.

I dropped the towel covering my body and slipped down into the water that immediately felt soothing against my bare skin. All the lights and the stereo music had been turned off. As I looked into the flame of the candle across from me I relaxed my body so much it felt like I had become part of the water, no longer conscious of my physical self.

In quiet awe I watched the flame of the candle grow from half an inch to three inches, which meant it was towering above its own size. Then I saw two cobalt blue circles resembling cigarette smoke flowing through the air from me to the candle.

Suddenly, in my mind's eye, I saw myself seated on a stone bench near water, which I often went to in my meditation. A voice inside me was asking what I was wearing. I thought that strange and laughed to myself for a moment.

"Since when do you have to be wearing a certain wardrobe when you meditate," I wondered. I had no idea what I was wearing.

Then I saw myself attired in a white gown with braided cording laced at the front of it beneath my breasts, similar to what I had worn when I was in the Job's Daughters as a teenager. It was an order that branched off Eastern Star in which my mother was a member.

As I once again entered the meditative state, a woman appeared on the side of me handing me a scroll. In the sky above I saw a cloud with a man's arm come down from it. A piece of the loose-fit maroon velvet sleeve draped it. It was handing me a ring. Then it disappeared into the cloud for a moment and then returned handing me a stick. Animals that were not of this world came running out of the forest from behind me. They were all happy and almost translucent with vibrating energetic colors. It was as if a celebration was going on, and I was what was being celebrated. Suddenly, I saw my mother sitting up in a bed that was about six feet above the water in front of me. Seeing her must have shocked me because suddenly I was back in the tub wondering what had happened and what it all meant.

The next day I remember wandering through an antique store and finding a section with ancient medieval items. A silver ring caught my eye. I asked the middle-aged woman who owned the store what it was. She explained that it was a magi's ring. The stone set in the center of it was labrodorite, and it was large enough to cover the first digit of one's finger. The magi used it for divination just as one would with a crystal ball. I fell in love with the ring instantly and asked if I could try it on. It fit perfectly, and I bought it not thinking about the ring I saw the night before until I got in the car and was admiring it. Then I remembered the arm from the cloud handing me a ring.

The overwhelming coincidences, which I know deep in my heart are actually synchronicities, didn't stop there. I was fearful that the vision I had in the tub of my mother meant she might die. Just then I received a call from my mother's board and care home saying the state was shutting them down, and my mother needed to move elsewhere immediately. Normally, that is a horrible request since someone with Alzheimer's disease isn't easy to place, but I immediately found a place for her close to where I lived.

The day after my vision, my friend Linda called me.

"Hello, Stargazer," she giggled. "I'm free Sunday. Want to do a Native American ritual over here at my house?"

I smiled and said yes. With wand in hand, I gathered up everything I wanted and went over her house in Greenhaven Sunday evening. Together we formed a big circle in her living room with sacred blue cornmeal we poured onto the carpet. At each of the four major compass points, North, East, South, and West, we placed a stone to mark it. Always eclectic, we put ceramic fairies we both had around it and her Grecian "Three Sisters of Fate" statute. Then she put her life-sized ceramic dog statue in the direction of the South. Although it wasn't exactly pure in terms of Native American traditions, the items we used were things that had symbolic meaning for us both, and no ceremony for us would be complete without that personal touch.

With everything in place, we went around the indoor medicine wheel, lighting the candles in the North, East, South, and West portions with another candle I was carrying. Something strange happened when I went past the ceramic dog, which was an exact likeness of Fonsworth, the golden retriever dog Linda had so loved but which had recently died. The bond between Linda and Fonsworth was so strong that he would get desperately ill every time she had to travel and leave him behind. She, too, would suffer in his absence. That night, their bond revealed itself to me fully. The candle started sparking or spitting but stopped when I moved passed it. In my heart I knew down deep that Fonsworth's spirit was present from the other side, or the candle wouldn't have reacted the way it had when we came close to the statue.

When I pointed it out to Linda, however, she just smiled and softly whispered, "Isn't that a lovely thought?"

When midnight came, I entered the medicine wheel from the East. Linda followed, carrying some sage she had set on fire and placed into a large abalone seashell. The smoke from the sage would purify our auras and the room. It was a ritual known as smudging, which Native Americans did at special gatherings and most rituals.

Then Linda offered up an invocation. "Winged ones, rock people, four legged ones, standing people, all my ancestors, hear my prayer. We ask that you join us tonight as we celebrate this night."

To make the energy present stronger, I stepped forward and said, "We are connecting with everyone in the world who is also doing a ritual tonight. Let this be a time of endings and new beginnings."

Together we bid farewell to things that we were glad had come to an end. When we ran out of things to say, we then gave thanks for the good things in our lives and thanked all that had helped us during the year.

Then we silently meditated upon our lives. Smiling, we broke the medicine wheel, put out the candles, and put everything away before hurrying off to Linda's patio to have a cigarette, since we both smoked in those days. We rejoiced about the high we were feeling from the ceremony we did.

"That was cool," Linda grinned. "Way cool."

I nodded in agreement. It was then that I looked through the trees near her patio at the right sky above her house. For a moment I was frightened, yet I was almost speechless at what I saw.

"Linda?" I whispered in a shaken voice. "Do you see what I see?"

"Oh, my, I see it, Jan," she said looking up.

In the sky above an enormous cloud formation towered over her house – one that looked like a crystal cathedral with three towers or perhaps it was the three sisters of fate, which was the statue we had used in the ceremony.

"Linda, quick! What do the three sisters of fate mean?" I anxiously asked while watching the formation.

"The three sisters of fate," she whispered, "are from Greek mythology and represent our lives, the connectedness of it all. One sister, the maiden, spins the thread of life. One sister, the woman, weaves the cloth. And the last sister, the old crone, cuts the thread. We all must face life and death. No matter who we think we are, we are all connected by this simple fact. Native Americans say, 'Mitakuye oyasin,' which means, 'We are all related.'"

We both stood silently staring up at it for the longest time. I knew connecting with the energy of the other ceremonies had given ours a lot of power. It was the kind of thing we couldn't talk about in public or people would think we were nuts, but with each other we didn't need words. As I gazed up, I remembered my visions in the tub, the ceremony with the fairies that night, my mother, the ring, and the wand – it had all come true within forty-eight hours.

All the way home from Linda's house that evening watched the sky. There wasn't a single cloud in the sky. Nothing could explain what we saw on top of her house. Looking back now, I know what I experienced in the tub that night, and which foretold all that was going to happen, came from a pure consciousness beyond the ego and that consciousness was all knowing. Call it God, Great Spirit, Creator, Higher Power, the Universe, it didn't matter, it was all the same. More and more my guides were showing me the spiritual forces with which they were familiar, things most of us never even dream of existing. Peace came over me as I realized we weren't born then abandoned in this world after all.

One of the greatest teachers on my spiritual journey in this life was my mother, especially since it was her library that introduced me to astrology. From watching planetary formations in different charts, I learned a lot about karma in this lifetime. While Karma is tied to everything we do, including a simple phone call we make during the day, it is the challenging lessons we face in our life that bring us to our knees which always stood out in my mind. I had learned that during such times, transiting planets in our astrology charts make difficult aspects. Inevitably, when the planets moved out of the way, so did the condition and our day-to-day lives were suddenly easier.

Sometimes the karmic issue I saw someone face was about his or her spiritual beliefs. It was as if the Universe were saying, "You are here to learn about your own spirituality. You passed the last test that you thought was about relationships, so let's give you an even bigger test." People for whom I was reading would think it was about finances or something else, but in truth it was still about their spirituality. In other instances it might be about money and the means by which a person accumulates it or uses money energy.

Watching astrology at work in my mother's life as the planets moved in and out of aspect was more dramatic than watching a movie on a picture screen, and it taught me a lot. Two planets, Pluto and Mars (both malefic), opposed each other in the second and 8th house in her natal astrology chart. The 2nd house related to money and the 8th house related to credit or money from the partner.

Born of poverty, her life would rise to social success, only to fall to ruin and scandal from her failed marriages to socially prominent men.

When she was a child, her home caught fire causing her to fear red fire engines whenever she saw them. Nonetheless, one of her marriages ended in scandal when her husband, my wicked stepfather, saturated their lovely mobile home with gasoline and caught it on fire. However, it didn't stop there, she screamed and ran every time she saw a fire engine when the only board and care home I could find for her to live in was across the street from a fire station. All the rises to social success and falls to economic ruin could be traced back to transiting planets affecting the same placements in her birth chart since childhood.

These planetary patterns formed highs and lows in many charts I studied, including my own. It almost seemed like the only way I could escape experiencing the aspects when they were difficult was by releasing it all and letting it run its course until it became favorable later, which it always did.

The same was true about how I had to cope with my mother. I had to just stand back and let the aspects pass. As my mother's Alzheimer's disease progressed, people almost cried to hear the music that was coming from the violin as my mother played, but in reality her personality had already abandoned her. I don't think she even knew she was playing. Once in awhile when I went to visit her I would softly sing part of a song, and she would hum the rest of it. But in time, my mother couldn't speak anymore, and eventually she didn't know who I was anymore. Knowing that I was a stranger to her hurt the most.

Despite the fact that my mother couldn't speak, however, she was still teaching me. One time I came to her board and care home to check on her after a fall. I found her in bed in a lot of pain with a cast on her arm. Her eyes were filled with fear. As I placed my hand on her forehead, I recalled the day Linda Vasquez and I journeyed to Mt. Shasta to get away from the Legislature during a Thanksgiving Holiday. It was in the Shasta Caverns that I came to realize what Linda and Louise Pastor had been trying to tell me about letting go of judgements and releasing our minds to other worlds. Inside the damp caves of stalagmites and stalactites images, which our tour guide was quick to point out, had been etched into the cavern walls. As our guide did so, he said, "Look at Snow White over here and the mountain climber over there."

It was that kind of trust in seeing that allowed me to work with my mother now and calm her down. That evening, after visiting the caves, Linda initiated me into my first level of Reiki, a healing system using Universal life force energy an ancient form of healing. Reiki (pronounced ray key) is a Japanese word. "Ki" means "Chi, prana or individual life force energy." It is Ki that one uses when breaking boards in a karate demonstration, for example. "Rei" means "Universal energy." Together the word means Universal Life Force Energy. Because Reiki deals with energy, it can be done either by placing one's hands on oneself or on others or by performing it from a distance. Reiki is thought to have been a Tibetan Buddhist practice that was removed from secret schools and made available to the general public in the late 1800s by Dr. Mikao Usui, a Japanese Buddhist.

By the time I stood before my mother, I had continued my studies and became an Usui Shiki Ryoho Reiki Master III, which means that I had been initiated into three levels of Reiki and could work with universal energies to do healing work. I put my hands in various positions on her body and then talked to her spirit mentally as if she could hear every word I said. Within four minutes she was fast asleep and totally at peace without pain. Her spirit talked to me as well. Knowing I could talk so freely with other people's spirits, or Higher Selves, came in handy when I met with clients.

The last lesson my mother ever taught me almost made me fly spiritually. One time when I went to Oregon to visit my father, I got an uneasy feeling that something could happen to my mother but I wouldn't know it because I had left town without telling her board and care home where I was. The nagging feeling that something was wrong wouldn't leave me. I had only been there for two days when I decided to turn around and head for home. When I got home there was a message on my answering machine from a dear friend of mine, Vinaya Battaglia, who unbeknownst to me had purchased a ticket for me to go listen to Dannion Brinkley at the Learning Exchange. The ticket was thirty-five dollars, and the lecture was going to be on death and dying. It would take place the next day.

There was no way that I wanted to go attend a workshop on death and dying, especially since I was very tired from the ten hour drive from my dad's house back to my home in Sacramento. But since Vinaya had gone to the trouble of getting the ticket for me and wanted me to meet some of her new friends who would also be there, I agreed to go.

It wasn't just the price of the ticket that made me go to the workshop. By now I had learned to acknowledge whatever appeared in front of me in my window in life. I knew it wouldn't have appeared before me unless there was a reason but attending a death and dying workshop really had me baffled.

Everyone applauded when Dannion walked into the room. He had a nice build, golden blonde hair, a mustache, and glasses. I knew he had written a book called, *"__Saved by the Light__,"* but I didn't know he had attracted attention worldwide or that he had been on the *Oprah* and *Larry King* shows – let alone why all the attention or why so many peopled had showed up that night to listen to him.

"What's so big about death and dying?" I wondered. "I know what I need to know. I deal with spirit guides and spiritual stuff all the time."

I continued to question why I needed to be there until he started speaking. He kept me and the entire audience spellbound as he talked with humor and force telling his story. He had been struck by lightening three different times in his life, one of them while he was quietly talking on the telephone. At one point, medical professionals pronounced Dannion dead, a state which lasted for twenty-eight minutes. Typically, a person is declared legally dead after only five minutes. That's when he started talking about what it was like on the other side when we die. He said the words "near death experience" should be called a "near life experience" instead. As had most people who have experienced "near death experiences," Dannion spoke about seeing a white light at the end of a tunnel. What he saw on the other side of that tunnel changed his life forever.

It was that experience and the knowingness of what he would again experience when he really did die that caused him to start up "Compassion in Action." It's an organization that has over 6,000 members in the United States that are trained to go out and assist people who are dying and share the good news of what is waiting for them on the other side. He also told us the statistics of the number of people in the audience that night who would discover that someone they knew was dying and who would want help with making the transition. If one were over fifty, the statistic was something like two people in the next year or two.

During the intermission I introduced myself to Dannion, who had people gathered all around him. I said I was an astrologer and that I was fascinated with the number of years between the lightening strikes he had experienced. Then I asked him if he would give me his birth date and time. He smiled and graciously gave it to me. Then he gave me a big hug, saying he knew who I was without my saying it because he could read the energy of my aura as I was talking to him. Later I did look at his chart and found the malefic that was hit by Saturn's transit that must have accounted for the lightening hits. I also saw Jupiter sitting in his 10th house of career and high honors at birth, which brought him fame because of these bizarre incidents. However, fame could never compensate for the horror stories I heard that night on how the lightening bolts had affected his life.

I dropped Vinaya off at her house after it was over and quietly drove home in the dark constantly thinking about Dannion. I would never forget his words and the importance of the little things we do in life like hugging a child or being there for someone when they need us when they are getting ready to cross over.

It was close to midnight when I got home and I was really exhausted. I almost didn't play the message waiting for me on my answering machine but decided I had better listen to it. My mom's board and care had called while I was attending the meeting. They had called "911" and an ambulance had taken my mother to Mercy Hospital because she had turned very pale and wasn't breathing properly.

I didn't know what to do. My body was so tired, and I had just come from down town. Deciding I didn't have the strength to go to the hospital, I put my gown on and went to bed, thinking I would check on my mother in the morning. But I couldn't go to sleep. The voice of my guide, or maybe it was the voice of God Himself, firmly said, "If it appears in your 'window of life' that you were supposed to go to this meeting and hear Dannion Brinkley talk about death and dying and helping people, since it is your mother, shouldn't you get your butt out of bed and GO?'"

With that I jumped up, got dressed, and headed straight for the hospital. I found my mother sitting up and looking frightened. Tubes were connected to her arm and other tubes to her nose for oxygen. She was also hooked up to a catheter. The nurse said she was very dehydrated. It turned out she had septicemia, which is a form of blood poisoning.

When the nurse left the room, I talked to my mom and whispered into her ear some of what I had heard at Dannion's meeting that night. I told her what it was like when we pass away. She completely relaxed and the fear left her eyes; a peaceful glow came over her.

Later that night the paramedics came to take her back to the board and care home. The driver smiled and asked me what kind of music my mother liked. I told him she was a violinist, so he put on classical music that had a lot of violins in it. I raced ahead of them with my car and was waiting for them when they arrived at her facility.

The paramedic hooking my mother up to her oxygen tank and making her comfortable knew I was very concerned yet realistic. I said I knew she was dying or the Universe wouldn't have sent me to listen to Dannion talk about death and dying that night where I learned what should be said to my mother to put her at peace.

Then the paramedic, somewhat reluctantly, asked, "Do you have power of attorney on your mother's health?"

I said I did.

"Your mother's lungs are full of the infection. You could just sign papers, so that they have to keep her comfortable instead of having them call the ambulance and going to extraordinary lengths to keep her alive. Instead of having her rushed to the hospital and poked full of tubes and X-rays taken each time something happens to her, you could just make sure she doesn't suffer."

He again emphasized that I should make it clear that I didn't want them to do anything heroically to save her. "Just make sure they keep her on the oxygen and gets whatever pain medicine she needs, but that's it."

That night, which was now the early morning after a sleepless night, I searched through several papers until I found the "power of attorney" form my mother and I had filled out years prior, naming me as the person in charge of her health. Then I went to bed only to wake up shortly afterwards, so that I could call her doctor and the administrator of the hospital.

"Look," I boldly told the doctor's nurse, "I know that my mother is dying. Illness is the vehicle that will take her away, but we have to stop interfering every time the vehicle comes for her by trying to fix it. My mother has had a full life. There is no reason to prolong it unnecessarily."

The nurse talked to me on the phone for about an hour. She was fascinated with my outlook on life as I told her about my trip to Oregon and how, when I came back, I found myself attending a class on death and dying only to get a message about my mother being taken to the hospital the same night. We also shared our thoughts on the miraculous ways we've seen life work in our lives. Then she said she would go interrupt the doctor and tell him about my decision to only keep my mother comfortable and not intervene medically anymore. She came back to say the doctor totally agreed and never fully understood why we were trying to save her all the time because she had been little more than a "vegetable" for years.

It never had dawned on me what the words "being a vegetable" meant. "How can my mother be a vegetable? She's my mom," I thought, suddenly realizing it had been many years since she uttered a word or even known what was happening around her.

It was then that I made the decision to take action. Not only was I required to talk to the doctor, but I would also have to call the administrator of the board and care home to discuss it. Once we got to talking, I learned that he too was a Usui Shiki Ryoho Reiki Master III. After listening to my story, he agreed that I needed to fill out some paperwork and bring him the legal documents he would need.

In the days that followed I became obsessed with visiting my mother. I was always fearful she would die the minute I left her, so one day I sat by her bedside for six hours until the staff finally said I should go home. The following day I was visiting someone in Fair Oaks when suddenly I knew I had to leave. I raced over to the board and care home only to learn that her nurse, Michael, had called me and had left a message on my machine at home to say he thought my mother was getting ready to pass over. I told him I got the message even though I had never gone home.

I remember Vinaya calling me to see if I was okay. She said she wanted to take me to lunch and to a movie to get away from all that I was going through with my mom. I asked her if she would go with me to visit my mom. She said she would.

When we got to the board and care home I remember Vinaya reaching into her purse and pulling out a bottle that contained fragrant biblical oil. She put it on her fingers and then rubbed it through my mother's hair. Then she did something I would never have thought of doing. She dabbed some of the nice smelling oil under my mother's nose, so that she could smell it despite the fact that oxygen tubes were shoved in it. After that Vinaya straightened out my mother's shrunken body and neatly draped a hand towel around her neck. Then she sat down and quietly sang a song into her ear. My mother looked like an angel, totally at peace. I was very grateful for the love and concern my dear friend had shown my mother. My mother, although sick, was not a vegetable in Vinaya's eyes. She was a real person with real feelings, deserving of our respect.

When we both grew tired, we went to lunch and a movie to try to get my mind off of the pain of knowing my mom would soon make her transition. Vinaya asked if I wanted to go back and visit my mom after the show since she was only five minutes away. I said I did if she didn't mind. Once again, she put oils on my mother, sang to her, and made her comfortable in her hospital bed. Then I took Vinaya home.

"I will go see your mom tomorrow," she said.

I told her it wouldn't be necessary. "Mom is ready to go," I explained. "The Universe doesn't do things by accident. You came to take me to the movies and to lunch to get me out of the way. That's all," I said holding back the tears starting to form in my eyes.

I also told her how I had thought of Jesus that morning and the herbs they used on his body. "I wished I could do something like that for my mom but I didn't know what to do. And then you appeared with oils without my saying anything and anointed her body, preparing her to transition over to the other side."

"All people matter," she smiled.

On the way to Vinaya's house, she commented on how dark a used car lot was. California was in the middle of a huge energy crisis and everyone was being affected by it. Then we both saw a small boy with a tricycle that was too close to the curb who looked like he was unattended. For a moment we both became alarmed until his father appeared behind him in the dark and pulled him back. I looked at the sky and I saw a strange formation like a fan spreading out in the sky that was quickly growing darker in the early evening hours.

"How eerie and creepy this all feels, I said to Vinaya. "Kind of like a London mystery."

I dropped her off at her house and tiredly made my way home while thinking about everything that had happened throughout the day. When I walked into my condo I played the message flashing on my answering machine. It was from my mother's nursing home asking that I call immediately. So, I did.

"I'm so sorry, hon," the nurse quietly said. "Your mother has passed away. Do you want to come view her body?"

I said no because I knew there was nothing more for me to do, but I did ask what time she died. It was the same time Vinaya and I were traveling down Folsom Boulevard to her home and the eerie feeling had come over me. I smiled knowing I got to see her go and wondered if she found me before she left.

Two of my sons and my daughter-in-law went with me to Bodega Bay where my mother's ashes were spread at sea in a ceremony that included tossing out popcorn for the sea gulls, which my mother loved. Dozens and dozens of those sea birds gathered. A couple drops of oil were put in the water to perfume her journey home, and flower petals followed her out to sea.

Chapter 15

Though many people came forward to bring me knowledge and new tools to use in my life's work, I would undergo even more massive changes when I met a man named Gabe. The fax machine in my Senate office kept jamming whenever I tried to send something to another person. Several people had been dispatched to try and fix it. As a last resort Gabe was called in to see if he could figure out the problem.

Gabe looked very polished with his jet-black hair, dark brown eyes, and tailored dark suit. Since I needed to test the fax machine from time to time while he worked, I stopped what I was doing and struck up conversation with him.

"What's your Sun sign?" I asked.

"Scorpio," he answered with a quick smile as he kept working with data flashing before him on the tiny window of the machine.

"I was born under the same sign, but I think it is harder to be a male born under the sign than a female," I said.

"Really. Why is that?"

"The Scorpio's motto in life is 'everything in moderation'. People who have Scorpio as their Sun sign have to learn not to go to the extreme with their emotions when it comes to love, hate, jealousy, and anger," I explained.

"You seem to know a lot about it," he looked over to me with his piercing eyes for which Scorpios are known.

"I am a professional astrologer. Many clients come to me in the evenings to have me interpret their astrology charts," I boasted with pride.

"That must be fascinating. I've never had my astrology chart read before. Do you also meditate?" he asked.

"Yes I do," I spoke up surprised that he asked.

Time seemed to pass by quickly while we talked and laughed, sharing some of the things we learned along our separate paths in life. There was an air of calmness about him as I watched his eyes scanning various programs while he listened and talked with me, undisturbed from what he was doing.

When Gabe was finished fixing the fax machine, he left the office, but before he did he gave me his business card with his phone number and email address on it. Then he surprised me by saying he would call me and ask me to lunch sometime, which showed me he enjoyed our conversation as much as I did. It wasn't much, just a conversation with a stranger, but somehow it was like lighting a match under dry straw and my life changed. He made me feel like I was alive, which the man I had been dating for sometime no longer did.

Gabe did call me a few weeks later, and we went to lunch. He asked me some questions about astrology, and I offered to do his chart. That seemed to please him.

"Come on over for dinner so I can interpret the chart for you," I offered.

He graciously accepted. That evening over dinner, I told him many things that his horoscope revealed to me, including some fears that might sometimes haunt him in this lifetime, fears related to something he may have done in a past one. This fascinated him because he believed in reincarnation and karma and seemed to know what I was talking about.

Fate would have it that as I started going to lunch with Gave from time to time, I noticed that I enjoyed being with him more than the man I had been dating. We always laughed and had fun while talking about life and its mysteries. Then one day he told me he was married.

Since I was starting to have a crush on him, it caught me off guard, but it wasn't a big deal because I was going with someone else. After a while, though, I would catch myself daydreaming about him. My mind wasn't on the person I was dating – it was on Gabe. Mentally, I would replay our conversations, delighting in some profound thing he said that related to an insight he had about life.

One day he called me from his home to ask if I knew of any vacancies in the condominium complex where I lived that might be for rent because he was getting a divorce. My heart pounded happily. Eagerly, I made a couple of phone calls. When he called me back, I gave him the phone number of the office manager who said they had a few for rent.

My mind had a field day. Suddenly, he was sharing something intimate with me. He was telling me what was going on in his personal life, and he was also calling me from home. A part of me hoped that might mean something significant could happen between us. That evening I pondered the phone call from Gabe and before the night was over I broke up with the man I had been dating for almost eight years.

As fate would have it, Gabe called a few days later saying he and his wife had made up and he wouldn't be getting a divorce after all. His voice sounded like he had given in rather than joyful or excited about the reconciliation.

As for me, I was suddenly alone, more than I had been since I started dating when I was 13 years old. It was almost Christmas. Word had gotten to me that my now ex-boyfriend was having his family and friends over for a lavish Christmas dinner party. I recalled how I used to help him go grocery shopping and decorate, only this time I wasn't going to be there. That night I lay in bed thinking about the Frankenstein movie I once saw. When the monster looked inside the window at a family eating and having fun, tears came to his eyes because he was the outcast. For me, it seemed my whole life had been reaching for something normal people had that I didn't or wasn't allowed to have – a loving and lasting relationship. But I also knew that I couldn't have stayed with my boyfriend whether Gabe was there or not.

The next day I decided it was time to go back to Beer's bookstore across from the State Capitol to see what my guides had in store for me next. I hungered for more books on Native American traditions. From studying their ways, I began to get in touch with my own emotions. I learned how intent played a large part in their beliefs and how they envisioned an animal and called upon its strength and special powers when they needed those qualities in their own lives.

Hummingbirds represent joy, owls represent deception, and wolves represent the greatest teachers of all, I read with great eagerness. It was the wolf that captured my imagination. Wolves are the pathfinders in some Native American traditions. They are also known for their loyalty because they choose a mate that will remain for a lifetime. It was that kind of bonding I most wanted. I longed for my soulmate like the one I once had in another lifetime, which I knew from transits I watched in my chart over the years that my soul still remembered.

But not even studying totem animals or clinging to my pocket full of stars erased what was troubling me. I felt not only alone but lost. By now Gabe was checking on me from time to time at work. He seemed to know when I was down and always had the charm and words to lift my spirits, which didn't help matters. Instead, it made everything worse. Before long, I noticed that every time the Moon traveled through my 5th house, which means issues or encounters with children or loved ones, I would see or talk to Gabe. To me, this meant there was a love connection, especially since his chart also showed him talking to me at such times when the Moon transited his 5th house.

At one point I remember going to lunch and laughing with him.

"My astrology chart shows great turmoil coming up and a lot of changes, but I don't know what it means," I grinned impishly. "A year and-a-half-later, the aspects hit you my fellow Scorpion, and you will find yourself doing battle with the same issues."

A few weeks later Gabe asked me out to lunch. I remember him asking me what I was doing in the sixties and if drugs or alcohol ever affected my life. I said I was married at that time, and no there hadn't been any drug or alcohol issues.

"Why do you ask?" I questioned.

"Because it was the sixties. It was a time of drugs, alcohol, rock bands, and free sex. It affected a lot of peoples lives, Jan," he said looking deeply into my eyes.

Then I sat quietly as he shared his story and how those years had affected him. From his words I saw a man of great strength and courage who loved his family and had solid values of his own that I hadn't seen in other men I had ever known. He also showed me his pain and disappointments. As he talked further, he then revealed his pride in accomplishment when he had slain his dragons. Suddenly, I felt intimately closer to him than ever.

Gabe was quiet for a minute. Then he looked at his watch and said, "My the time has flown. I've got to get back to work."

Together we climbed up the mahogany stairs that took us from the basement to the first floor of the Capitol building. Then he turned to me, put his arms around me, and gave me a hug. For a brief moment I felt safe, like I didn't have to be "on guard."

That night when I went home, my world started crashing in when I recalled my conversation with Gabe. He had shared so much of himself with me that day. Now, a part of me longed to let him know who I was. I remember logging onto my computer and emailing him about my past. Whereas his story to me had been straight forward, mine was more like a confession full of remorse and shame.

In the e-mail, the guilt over my failed marriage came out and so did the mistakes I felt I had made with my children. I remember crying uncontrollably as I typed on my computer. To make matters worse, I mentally scanned my astrology chart that had been burnt in my mind over the years to see if it would reveal anything about my life now that I had met Gabe. The position of the transiting planets said I was going to fall in love with someone, but he wasn't going to be available. Then I remembered Gabe's chart. He had so many changes ahead of him that even if he got a divorce, and we got together it wouldn't work because his heart would be frozen from his failed marriage. Then he would need to be alone later, like I was now, while he healed.

It was more than I could handle, and suddenly I felt more alone than ever. I couldn't be with the man with whom I was falling in love. To make matters worse, he wouldn't be available even if I waited until he got a divorce. That night I remember surrendering my life to God, Creator, the Universe or the Big Kahuna, while hoping under my breath that the Divine knew what it was doing cause surely I didn't.

Each day became a struggle. I got so depressed that I cried over nothing. My mother was gone. I was in love with someone who wasn't there for me. Not even my spirituality or the planets was saving me from the pain.

That's when my son, Jon, now a counselor, told me I had better seek help. The irony of that suggestion hit hard. After all those years of struggle with him, he was suddenly in the role of my advisor. He suggested that I go see a female counselor he knew named Nancy, who had a good reputation for helping "middle-aged" women who were having a "mid-life crisis."

"A mid-life crisis???" I muttered. "Is THAT what this is called?"

The tears and depression were so imbedded in my soul that I figured I had nothing to lose, so I called Nancy. It seemed awkward going to a counselor when so many people had come to me for astrological counseling. Despite my silent doubts, I went.

When I met the counselor, I warned her, "Here are the rules. I am an astrologer. I am depressed. This depression will leave on such and such a date. I like Gabe. He is not available. He will get a divorce in eighteen months. I believe in karma. Now having said all that, and without wanting to change, can you help me? Oh, and by the way, what's your sign?"

To give Nancy credit, she didn't suggest that I be immediately locked up. Instead, she just laughed and told me her birth date, probably just to shut me up. I learned she was born two weeks before Gabe in the same year.

This surprised me. "The Universe has pulled a fast one. If Gabe can't help me, they are sending me someone with the counseling credentials who was born with all the same planets as his except the Moon in her chart. I am going to face the lesson – only with her instead of Gabe!" I moaned.

But help me she did. She did get to see my depression leave at precisely the time when I said it would and Gabe did indeed get a divorce the following year exactly when I said he would. My insight into the astrology fascinated her, and she never discouraged my interest in it.

I continued to e-mail Gabe all the time. He neither responded to the e-mails anymore, nor did he speak to me. He knew I had fallen in love with him somewhere along the line, so he was silent. I knew his silence meant that on some level he cared enough to try not to hurt me. He also knew enough to understand there was karma between us. It would be almost a year before we spoke to each other again, but when he went through his painful divorce I was there for him the way he had been for me minus one thing. I dumped a lot on him, but he never dumped anything on me. I was always grateful that he came into my life and showed me that not all men were bad.

During the short time I saw Nancy something else happened. I went to Oregon to see my dad and my stepmother, Margie. One evening we were sitting on the porch talking about unusual psychic experiences I had in my life and some of the awesome truths about life the Universe had revealed to me. She and I started talking about my Uncle Lee Roy, my dad's brother who had committed suicide the night I dreamed someone in the family died many years ago. I asked her about the gun I remembered my dad carrying when he chased his brother off the property, when he found him in my bedroom one night.

"Don't you remember what happened?" she asked.

"Just the dog barking and seeing Dad with the shotgun," I edged.

She told me what happened that night which explained why my Dad had a gun in his hand. Knowing that my Uncle had written a suicide note to my dad, I asked Margie if she ever knew what was it in. Then she said, "You father never told anyone. He just cleaned up the bloody mess and came home. Then he didn't speak to anyone for days."

My body was numb and I was speechless. I watched as my stepmother waited for a reaction. When I didn't respond she looked nervous, as if having second thoughts for telling me about the great secret – I had been molested.

I remember going to bed that night, fifty-three years old, and feeling my inner child trying to pat me on the arm and comfort me as I cried uncontrollably; the blonde-haired child within me whispered, "It's ok. It's going to be ok. I am here." Then I fell asleep wondering, "Who am I and who is this little girl comforting me? Are we one or are we separate pieces of the same?" To this day, I do not understand how the molestation got erased from my mind.

Apparently, Gabe and Nancy had come into my life as part of the spiritual path I was walking on that would take me closer and closer to my own enlightenment. By sharing so much with them, I was cleaning out the skeletons in my closet by facing issues I had tuned out. I was learning how to release my guilt. Since the molestation issue came up at the same time after all those years of secrecy and silence, the Universe must have wanted it released too. While in the past I had always felt guilty for things I thought I was doing wrong, now I realized that as a child seeing my father come into my room with a gun might have triggered some kind of guilt on my part, which made me feel as if I had done something wrong. All I know is that suddenly I didn't feel guilty about anything in my life anymore, not even for how I raised my sons.

Soon afterwards, I stopped seeing Nancy because there was no longer a need to do so.

In looking back over the last few years and how difficult they had been for me, I could also see the gifts the Universe had given me. My past, the guilt I carried for so many years, was being dealt with and released like butterflies towards the heavens. My sons and I were growing closer now with healthy relationships based on honesty rather than need. I was also finally free of fear and shadows in the night.

However, the Universe decided to spiritually test me when it threw a fireball my way that I wasn't planning on. I remember going to a thrift store to look for unusual glass containers I could use for Christmas candles I wanted to make for gifts.

"Quit your job with the Senate," I heard a voice inside me say as I happily walked into the store.

I ignored it. "We all want to quit our jobs at one time or another. That's just my imagination," I reasoned.

"Don't make me go back," the voice deep within me cried out.

This voice was different than any voice I ever heard; it was not one that had guided me throughout my life. I could sense pain, and it felt like it was coming from the core of my being. That made me wonder what damage my job with the Legislature had done to my soul. Then it all started racing through my mind. It had all been about secrets.

When a child lives in a dysfunctional family, one of the parents can look straight in the child's face and tell her not to say anything to the neighbors about what happened in their home no matter what. It might be that the father had gotten drunk the night before. Perhaps the parents were just fighting and had gotten verbally abusive. Nonetheless, the common agreement would be to keep the dysfunction a secret and keep it home. "Don't tell anyone no matter how bad it was or what you saw," would be the message the child heard. Then child would live in fear that the secret might slip, someone might find out what was going on, and be blamed for it.

When a dishonest person goes to work for a boss in the Legislature, they will try to do things that aren't ethical when the boss isn't looking. I worked for a lot of consultants who tried to get away with things. I noticed that the more money they made, the more they felt deserving of the extra perks they etched out of their jobs for themselves. Some would leave the office early to go work out in the gym, go golfing, or visit friends and family out of town. Sometimes, the reason for leaving the office would be to meet a boyfriend or someone about a campaign they weren't authorized to run. No matter what the reason, they made it clear before they left that the boss wasn't supposed to know anything. When the staff person was away from the office, we secretaries covered for them and lived in fear that the boss might call and that we would get blamed if they found out the consultant wasn't there.

It was the same with the legislators. It didn't matter what proposition the voters passed; the constituents still didn't know what went on inside the Legislature. The Legislature created the Joint Legislative Ethics Committee in 1967 in response to a ballot proposition the voters passed. The State Constitution contains a prohibition against conflicts of interest among lawmakers. The Speaker of the Assembly always had problems finding members willing to fill the six allotted slots to that Committee. So did the President Pro Tempore of the Senate when he tried to assign his three members. No member wanted to sit in judgment of another member or to cast a stone at one of his or her colleagues. They also didn't want to tell the voters what had happened let alone that someone was guilty of a wrong-doing inside their Houses of the Legislature. After all, the voters were the ones who elected them, paid their salaries, and were their bosses. This was why the voters always sensed something was wrong but never knew how to pin point it.

Over the years I saw bad things happen to good people because of power plays by a member or perhaps by a chief of staff. I also saw good things happen to bad people when they were holding something over the heads of members of the Legislature and were rewarded with a nice position and a good salary for keeping quiet. Sometimes it was the work the person did outside the Legislature on campaigns or in contributions they had other people make to a member that afforded them their positions and salaries.

I remembered an example of being forced to live in fear of the secrets happened one day many years ago. I came to work and gossip was whipping around the Capitol about a member who got caught the night before having sex with a staff member on his couch. The Sergeant-at-

Arms who innocently walked in on the pair during an office security check was immediately fired, according to the rumor. A few days passed, and then staff from the entire Assembly was called into Room 4202 to get a tongue-whipping filled with threats about what would happen if anyone were to be caught gossiping in the halls about something they had heard.

"Gossip is vicious and it has to stop. If you are caught doing it, you can be fired," a spokesman scolded the audience. However, the member who had called the meeting was also the one who was rumored to have been caught sleeping with the staff person.

The hidden rules of the House that everyone abided by were tied to the secrets. These rules also applied to both parties. Two rules were extremely important. The first rule was, "Keep the voters happy." The second rule was, "Keep the press happy." Unfortunately, abiding by both rules often meant keeping terrible secrets.

Despite the propositions voters passed, the Joint Legislative Ethics Committee, the Fair Political Practices Commission, and the countless other safeguards that have been put in place, staff still lives in fear today that someone might find out what they have seen or what they know that really does go on inside their offices or in the Legislature itself. They are taught that it is their duty to be the keeper of Pandora's box. Strangely enough, they will keep the secrets no matter how little their salary is or how high their position is because it is so ingrained into the Legislature.

As an astrologer, I learned to let things flow past me and tried not to sit in judgment or throw stones while I worked there because I believed in karma. I also had the ability to look at my **_Ephemeris_** and see my planets and know when things would be better or when I was in harm's way. But it was a strange place to become spiritually enlightened within the walls of the Legislature because if one lost one's soul in it, several lifetimes might have to pass before one could get it back.

One thing I learned is that the karma gods were always watching, and they would settle the score if something happened behind closed doors. For example, I knew a legislator who sexually harassed a female consultant on his staff, who was a friend of mine. She didn't share this with anyone else. When election time came around, the member was voted out of office. If a chief consultant boasted his importance to his support staff and didn't look out for them, he, too, would eventually be brought down from his position and play havoc trying to get another job. Not all of the injustices have been corrected yet, but they will be – eventually. It is the way karma works. A price must be paid for injustice. It's just a matter of time. Whether it is in this lifetime or the next, retribution will be made.

My soul had been damaged by working for the Legislature so long, but what I learned while I was there would always be cherished. I always told my astrology clients to listen to their inner voices when their guides spoke up. Now I couldn't ignore my soul crying out. The next day I shocked many people when I announced that I had put in my letter of resignation. My soul seemed to rejoice that I finally stood up for myself, and that is when a new journey started. A couple of weeks later, I walked into the Senate Sergeant-at-Arm's Office and turned in my photo identification card and keys. Thirty-two years had passed since I was the naive young girl wondering what fate the Legislature held for me.

As I pushed open the Capitol's enormous mahogany doors, it felt like I was saying goodbye to an old friend. Memories raced through my mind as if a part of me were dying and trying to get one last gasp before letting go. I recalled the end of session barbecues we used to have in the Capitol Park while Willie Brown, Jr. was Speaker. It was his way of saying thank you to all the staff for a job well done. There was the time Bob Hope entertained staff in the park. I remembered when Mohammad Ali spoke to us in the Governor's office, and I got to ride the elevator with Arnold Schwartznegger. Once I raced to the back of the chambers with a member's lunch and almost spilled it on George Bush, Sr., before he became President of the United States.

I remembered standing near Governor Reagan and his wife Nancy as we watched the Christmas tree lights being turned on that were lit each year in front of the Capitol. But I also remembered the hundreds of protest marches, the people troubled by the times, and the broken promises. I remembered protecting members at my own expense, and the countless staff that worked into the wee hours of the morning to help make the system work at the expense of their spouses, children, and loved ones.

Sometimes the issues were hard for me to stamp my personal aye or nay on. For example, when the loggers circled the Capitol building protesting the spotted owl, I wasn't sure where I stood on the issue. If the endangered bird lived, it would be at the expense of loggers and their families when they couldn't harvest the trees and put food on their tables. The abortion issue was always a tough one and so was the death penalty. One thing was sure, though; no matter how a member voted, someone would always believe the member didn't vote the way he should have.

Although I had made the same walk out of the Capitol building for thirty-two years, this time when I left the domed building with its beautiful white pillars I saw it differently. It was all illusions, inside the building as well as out. No one ever knew for sure who would win the political battles or what price a member would pay for a moment in the Sun, let alone which star was guiding them all the way. But many wagered all they owned for a chance to just play in the game.

As I stepped into my car parked across the street, I looked back at the State Capitol building for one last time and said my farewells. Then I drove away. Suddenly, it felt like I had never worked there at all.

Epilogue

Retirement was a shock at first. I wasn't quite sure what to do with myself. Finally, I decided to improve my health. Every day I tried to walk two or three miles, get a little Sun and stop doing battle over food. Debilitating health problems such as serious bouts with allergies, asthma, three degenerative disks, fibromyalgia syndrome, and an autoimmune disorder all became less of a problem when they no longer served as a shield to the blows of stress I had once been taking on a daily basis in the Legislature.

One of the first things I did was visit my sons, William, in Southern California with my three delightful grandchildren and Jeff in Oregon who was part mountain man, part compassionate friend to everyone he met. I also went to see my dad in Oregon. It was my way of trying to make up for lost time that gets away from us when we are busy with our jobs. My life with the Legislature was over, but I was still traveling down the spiritual path and savoring each new lesson. I think I was finally on Enlightenment 101 (a figure ironically representing the number of times I thought I finally had the ANSWER to the mysteries of life but realized I didn't when a better answer came along).

Monumental things still happened along my spiritual path that brought me to my knees in amazement. For example, during the first trip I made to my dad's after retirement, he lost a gas cap to a two gallon red plastic container. My father needed to get some gas in town for his tractor. Together, we looked everywhere for about fifteen minutes. Finally, getting frustrated, I mentally said, "Okay guides. You know where it is – show me." I heard a voice within my head say it was under the wheel of the tractor. I looked. It wasn't. The voice laughed and said, "The other wheel." I walked over to the other side of the tractor and bent over to look. There it was.

Before going back to Sacramento, I wanted to stop and visit my son, Jeff, in Klamath Falls, Oregon. My father warned me about the snow storm expected the following day. He said I should leave early in the morning to avoid it, so I did.

I saw a sign that said snow chains required when I was leaving one of the towns on my way. At first I was concerned. But the Sun was shining and there was no snow on the road. Since I was in a hurry and didn't want to pay the extra money chains would cost, I ignored it.

Two hours later, I started getting frightened when there was so much ice on the road that you couldn't see the divider line. All I could see were the tips of enormous pine trees covered with snow that grew on the sides of the mountain along the road on which I was traveling. I realized the snow I was trying to get ahead of had already fallen.

I started chanting a chant I had learned and I called in every sacred saint, being, deity, and guru, and GOD to help me get through it. To make matters worse, no other cars were on the road, no houses, and no gas stations. An hour later I found a town, but so much snow was on the sides of the road I feared trying to pull off the road. My gas gauge, however, was on empty. Finally I saw a gas station and stopped to fill my tank. When I left the station, I noticed the car pulling all over the place. I figured it was the ice. A sign said 72 miles to Klamath Falls. I knew would take longer than usual to get there because a truck in front of me was only going 40 miles an hour and it was too dangerous to pass him.

When I finally arrived in Klamath Falls I pulled into a service station to call my son so he could come and guide me to his place. However, someone was in the telephone booth and snowflakes were falling which caused me to get impatient, momentarily forgetting all the spiritual beings I had asked for help from earlier. The man in the booth pointed to my back tire. I looked. It was flat and I knew I had traveled with it for 72 miles, when I first felt myself losing control of the car. Then I felt stupid for getting upset and thankful for being alive and having the chance to see one more time that we are not alone.

Several months after I retired, I decided to go downtown to meet an old friend for lunch. Looking over to the clock next to the Governor's office I realized I had just enough time to say hi to a former coworker I hadn't seen in a long time. As I opened the office door, I recognized the familiar voice of a consultant with whom I used to work talking on the phone. She was repeating dates to someone. When she saw me appear around the bookshelf that blocked her view of the door, her eyes lit up and she gestured with her fingers that she would only be a minute. Then she pointed to an empty blue upholstered chair in front of her desk, where she wanted me to sit.

"I really have to go," I heard her say. "Someone has just come into my office that I need to talk to."

"How strange," I thought to myself, "She wasn't expecting me."

"It's good to see you. You look fantastic," she smiled hanging up the phone.

"I am meeting a friend for lunch and only have a couple of minutes, but I did want to see you," I answered. She stepped away from her desk and came around the corner to give me a hug before relaxing on the white couch a few feet away.

"That was the press on the phone," she said nervously crossing her legs. "Your timing was perfect. I needed an excuse to get rid of them."

"I wouldn't want you to hang up on the press," I teased with a smile remembering the political consequences a staff person can have if they did.

"Yeah right. You know how it is around here. Sometimes we forget we aren't supposed to talk to them," she sighed. "This Congressman Condit thing is the talk of the Capitol. What do you think happened to Chandra? Do you think Condit...?"

"Chandra? Condit?" I asked puzzled.

"Girl, where have you been?" she chided.

"Laying by the pool," I boasted. "You know I don't listen to the news anymore. It's too much of a soap opera for me. The suds build as the story line gets bigger."

I watched her give out a hearty chuckle.

"But, Jan, this is big news," she offered trying to regain composure. "They claim Condit was seeing an intern that has disappeared. If you get a chance, look at his horoscope. Let me know if you see something interesting."

I thought back to the days of the 'Gang of Five'. I still had Condit's chart at home. My heart tightened; it was another intern story. For a moment I remembered Monica and President Clinton and how the public was so shocked when they learned what had happened.

"I really have to run or I will be late for lunch. I just came by to say hi."

"Next time stay awhile," she smiled as I walked out the door.

"If only she knew my story," I grinned to myself.

As an astrologer, when I first glance at an astrology chart, it feels like I am going into an abyss. Something happens. The planets call me to them as if they are trying to show me something or talk to me. Ever since I talked to my former coworker, Condit's planets called to me loudly.

As I drove home, I listened to an all-talk radio show host say that over 23 million people watched Connie Chung of *ABC* interview Condit the night before. When I got home I turned on the news. As I did, I saw Condit's picture, which I recognized from the days when he was a member of the Assembly walking down the halls of the State Capitol and going in and out of member's office in which I was working. Now, Condit was once again in the news, and it reminded me of all the press coverage he got when he was a member of the "Gang of Five."

According to the television news anchor, Chandra Levy had been an intern. On April 30, 2001, Levy disappeared. Levy's family claimed that she had been romantically involved with Condit, and law enforcement officials later said that Condit admitted having an affair with her to Washington police. In public, however, Condit said that Levy was only a friend.

On that night in August of 2001 as I watched the television news, I learned that Levy still had not been found, and reports that Condit had an affair with another woman had surfaced, but Condit denied having a relationship with her. Before the broadcast was over, I turned off the TV and went to my computer to look at his chart to see what the planets would tell me.

Gary Condit was born April 21, 1948. I had the same sense of uneasiness I had the first time I saw the planetary placements when he was born. The combination of Mars, Saturn, and Pluto in Leo told me as an astrologer that this man was power hungry and that he probably carried these issues over from a past life. The conjunction of Venus and Uranus in Gemini told me he probably liked verbal exchanges when he made love and that he also enjoyed reading. Since Venus was in a dual sign, it wouldn't be unusual for him to intimately love two people at once or to sexually enjoy twosomes. Clearly, he needed emotional excitement in his life.

Chandra Levy was born April 14, 1977 in Cleveland, OH. The aspects her planets made to Condit's told me she really did care about him but also that their karma was connected, and they may have known each other in a past life, one in which Condit may have been the one who disappeared. When I looked at her astrology chart to see what was happening the last day she was seen by anyone, I didn't see violence but I did see heavy aspects to Neptune that showed deception or betrayal and perhaps poisoning. If she did indeed die at that time, what I was seeing suggested she just slipped away peacefully without knowing whatever happened.

As I sat staring at Condit and Levy's charts, I knew the public was left with many unanswered questions just as I knew they were unanswered about what really went on between President Clinton and Monica Lewinsky.

I walked away from the computer and went out to my patio, looking up at the stars. I thought about President Clinton and Monica and realized that theirs was a karmic relationship, something quite evident in their natal charts. William Clinton was born August 19, 1946 in Hope, Arkansas at 8:41 a.m. This man had four planets in Libra, which was also his rising sign. This made him an incurable romantic and a real charmer – one who would change his accent and posture according to the personality and status of whomever he was talking to. He also has the Sun, Pluto, Mercury, and Saturn in Leo, which points out his pride and involvement in politics. He lives in an idealistic world filled with secrets.

In order to see what the karma was between Monica, the California girl born in San Francisco on July 23, 1973 12:21 p.m., and the President, all I had to do was put her planets on top of Clinton's. I shouldn't have been surprised at all when I saw her Sun in Leo on top of his Saturn in Leo, which astrologically showed me there was a karmic connection between them. I laughed when I saw her Venus in Leo on Clinton's Sun. They fanned each other's egos. Monica's Saturn was on top of Clinton's Uranus in Gemini. Her karma in this lifetime related to education and the media which Gemini rules. Both their karmic lessons were satisfied when Clinton had to feel the wrath of a love affair, and Monica had to feel the wrath of the media and other people's words.

By 1998, at the height of the Monica Lewinsky scandal and impeachment hearings, Neptune moved into Aquarius and opposed all Clinton's natal planets in Leo and Monica's Sun in Leo. His karmic issues came forward to haunt him, and Monica was pulled into it because of her own karma. Saturn nailed them both to a wall where they couldn't do anything except watch and wait until the planet moved away, which it eventually did. Since Clinton was born two years earlier than Condit, a few years would pass before Condit would find himself facing a similar scandal because of his planets in Leo at birth and a transiting planet igniting karmic problems with a loved one.

The sign, Leo, frequently stands out in political charts because of the need for one to be before the public. As an example, President George W. Bush, who was born on July 6, 1946, in New Haven, CT., has Leo ascending with Pluto and Venus in Leo. Ego and pride pull him along in life the same way it does with most politicians. Since these placements are in his 1st house, he is well received by others and himself. However, Mars his in Virgo squaring Uranus in Gemini that tells me he likes to use words as his weapon. The danger we face with Bush, as President is that he has the Moon conjunct Neptune in Libra along with Jupiter. He's very idealistic and might act on his vision through rose-colored glasses rather than what is before him.

One thing became clear as I stood thinking about these three powerful men and how the transiting planets had affected them. I realized that transiting Saturn would conjunct President Bush's natal Sun and square his Neptune, Moon and Jupiter by the end of 2003.

On September 11th, 2001 terrorists assaulted the United States when they hijacked several planes from commercial airlines and crashed two of them into the twin buildings of the World Trade Center and one into the Pentagon killing over 5,000 people. This event had a major impact on the world. As an astrologer, I knew the planets in the zodiac in the heavens when this event occurred now appeared in the charts of many babies that were born at the time this occurred and would be born for a few months afterwards. It made me wonder what issues relating to religion and communications would these babies take a stand on in their lives and how different would our world be then than it is now. Were these infants going to pilot spacecraft in the future? Would they find themselves blowing up a spaceship in the future that crossed territorial lines in outer space in order to protect our country? Were these infants feeling a need to defend the rights of clones that we might be abusing? It was hard to say but I knew the issue would be similar.

Nine days after this horrible event that became known as "nine-eleven," President Bush addressed the nation before congressional leaders, his cabinet, and advisors. The country appeared to be united while he talked of war and revenge. However, these circumstances do not sway an astrologer even though that is what the public sees. Planets change and conditions change. I already knew that by the end of 2003, President Bush would start experiencing public dissatisfaction over money matters, or perhaps he would have health problems as a result of the stress he encounters now. Only time will tell. It's not the end of the world for him, nor is it some great wall that he can't climb at that time, just another lesson he must pass, or a karmic coin he needs to toss into the collection plate, from a past life, to pay his debt, before the planets move back in harmony a little later. That is the way it is with all of us, ebb and flow, lessons learned, a karmic coin being tossed into a collection plate, then harmony restored if the amount we give, is enough to cover the debt we owe that we came here to experience.

As an astrologer, I know New York has a birth chart and its own destiny, one that impacts everyone who lives there, or is drawn to it. The same is true for California with all its earthquakes. It has its own birth chart and destiny as well, one that impacts everyone who lives there or who is drawn to it. All states, countries, pets, Presidents, businesses, lovers, enemies and spouses have a birth chart that will have an impact on anyone drawn to them. For some it will be favorable, for others challenging. It all depends on what planets are in aspect and the karmic coin waiting to be tossed.

I pushed aside my thoughts about politicians and future life in outer space and went back inside my warm condo. Slowly, I pulled out my paintbrush and began a new watercolor. Gone were my past romances, secret fears, and the cold mornings when I used to crawl out of bed and get ready for work. Now, with a few lessons from my gifted art teacher,

Stan Stevenson, the Universe delivered a new passion into my life, painting.

Dabbing the brush into some brown paint, I began painting footprints in the sand that would lead up to the Capitol building. I thought about my life as I painted and about all of the lives that had walked with me along my path or briefly crossed it. I also thought about everything I read when I thumbed through my diary.

#   #   #

Glossary

ADJOURN: This is what each house of the Legislature does when they have finished their business.

ASCENDANT: This is the zodiac degree on the eastern horizon of the chart when we are born. It is also popularly known as our rising sign.

ASPECT: Relationship between planets measured by degrees. The difficulty or ease of an aspect varies by the number of degrees involved.

ASTROLOGER: One who studies astrology.

ASTROLOGY: The study of how celestial bodies influence man.

BENEFIC: Planets considered favorable.

CHAIR: This person who heads a committee in the Legislature.

CHAMBERS: This is the room where the Legislature meets. The Assembly and Senate have their own chambers.

CONJUNCTION: When one planet is within 10 degrees of another.

DESK: Where daily business of the Legislature is conducted.

DIRECT MOTION: When a planet is moving on course through zodiac.

EPHEMERIS: Astronomical table listing planetary positions by date.

FLOOR: Members of the legislature are said to be on the floor when they are in session.

HOROSCOPE: Map of planetary positions within houses of a chart for a given date and time on Earth.

HOUSE – There are twelve houses in zodiac that have the following meanings:

First - Appearance, how you present yourself to others and see yourself.

Second - Finances, resources, how you make and spend money.

Third - Education, siblings, neighbors, short trips.

Fourth - Home, family ties, the mother.

Fifth - Children, loved ones, pets, speculation, sports.

Sixth - Health, working with others, being of service.

Seventh - Marriage, partnerships, legal matters.

Eighth - Sex, inheritances, taxes, other people's money, credit.

Ninth - Long distance travel, higher education, philosophy, religion.

Tenth - Career, public recognition.

Eleventh - Friendships, homes and wishes.

Twelfth - Hospitals, secrecy, seclusion, imprisonment.

KARMA: Law of cause and effect a soul experiences from one lifetime to another.

MALEFIC: Planets thought to have a negative or unfortunate influence.

ORB: Range of influence inside which a planet or aspect operates.

RETROGRADE: When a planet moves out of its range of motion.

RISING SIGN: Zodiac sign appearing on the Eastern horizon at birth. See Ascendant.

SESSION: When the house is called to order it is in session.

SIGNS: The zodiac has 12 signs. Each one is comprised of 30 degrees.

SQUARE: This is when one planet is with 10 degrees of being 90 degrees from another planet. Considered a difficult aspect.

TRANSIT: Movement of the heavenly bodies around the zodiac.

TRINE: A favorable aspect is when one planet is within 10 degrees of being 120 degrees from another planet.

SIGNS - Twelve signs in zodiac as follows:

ARIES - (March 21-April 20)
Born leaders that like a challenge, forceful if needed.

TAURUS (April 21-May21)
They are contemplative, cautious, slow, and materialistic.

GEMINI (May 22-June 21)
This sign produces individuals that are intellectual, communicative, restless, born teachers and reporters.

CANCER (June 22-July 23)

This is a nurturing sign that is emotional, sensitive, and natural mothers.

LEO (July 24-August 23)
This sign is proud, boastful, protective, leaders, politicians and entertainers.

VIRGO (August 24-September 23)
Is into good nutrition, serves mankind, analytical, and love detail.

LIBRA (September 24-October 23)
Loves partnership, peace, artwork, poetry and music.

SCORPIO (October 24-November 23)
They love to be mysterious, focused, emotional, and sexy.

SAGITTARIUS (November 23-December 21)
Philosophers and ministers of the zodiac that love their freedom

CAPRICORN (December 22-January 20)
Goal oriented, serious, hard workers, like math.

AQUARIUS (January 21-February 19)
Independent, ahead of their time, likes people.

PISCES (February 20-March 20)
These people are sensitive, intuitive, have psychic ability, and are the caregivers.

ZODIAC: Twelve divisions of the heavens as measured along the band of the ecliptic.

Works Cited

Associated Press. "Costa Fined on Soliciting Charge." *The Los Angeles Times*, Sept. 16, 1986: 1.

Arner, Mark. "There Are Many Hurdles Before Flying Train' Gets Off The Ground." *The San Diego Union-Tribune*, May 16, 1994: B4.

Bazar, Emily and Capps, Stephen A. "Legislator Asks Probe of Capitol Barricade Anti-Terrorist Device Injured Assemblyman." *The Sacramento Bee*, June 13, 2000: A4.

Bunting, Kenneth. "Veterans Mount New Effort To Oust Hayden; Ferguson Vows To Introduce Resolution To Expel Former Anti-War Activist From Assembly." Metro Section, Part 2, *The Los Angeles Times*, Sept. 5, 1985: 3.

Cannon, Lou. "Hispanics: Drawing New Lines." *The Seattle Post-Intelligencer*, Apr. 15, 1991: A11.

Carson, Daniel C. "Goggin Said To Forfeit Audit Funds." *The San Diego Union Tribune*, Jan. 10, 1987: A3.

Carson. Daniel C. "Lobbyist Pays for Donations Inside Capitol." *The San Diego Union-Tribune*, February 3, 1988: A3.

Coker, Matt. "Party Pooper." *The Orange County Weekly*, Oct. 1, 1999: 10.

Crewdson, John M. "The New York Times Company: Abstracts." *The New York Times*, Dec. 17, 1978: 42.

Editorial. "Capitol Fence." *The Sacramento Bee*, Feb. 9, 1998: B6.

Gillam, Jerry and Ingram, Carl. "Rebel 'Gang' Gives Capitol Taste of Legislative Anarchy." *The Los Angeles Times*, Apr. 17, 1988: 3.

Harris, Art. "Falwell Takes Control, Bars Bakker From PTL; Board Cuts Off All Payments to Evangelist." *The Washington Post*, Apr. 29, 1987: A1.

Harris, Art and Isikoff, Michael. "Bakkers Said to Divert Millions; PTL Office Assails 'Fiscal Sin'; U.S. Investigating." *The Washington Post*, Final Edition, May 16, 1987: A1.

Horstman, Barry M. "California Elections 79th Assembly District; Challengers Fight to Block Chacon's Well-Worn Path to Assembly." *The Los Angeles Times*, May 31, 1990: B1.

Jacobs, Paul. "Political Gifts Reflect His Influence; Treasurer Unruh: The Game Is Called Power." *The Los Angeles Times*, July 13, 1986: 1.

Jacobs, Paul. "Feinstein Agrees To Pay $190,000 For Violations; Campaign: Fine Is For Failing To Comply With Finance Disclosure Rules In 1990 Governor's Race. State Watchdog Agency Says Errors Were Unintentional." *The Los Angeles Times*, Dec. 22, 1992: A2.

Lifsher, Marc. "Irked Allen May Abandon GOP; Cypress Lawmaker, Smarting From Senate Primary Loss, Considers Becoming An Independent." *The Orange County Register*, Morning Edition, March 22, 1995: B2.

Magagnini, Stephen. "Black Panthers' Capitol Arrest Made Headlines." *The Sacramento Bee*, Dec. 31, 1999: OC33.

Marelius, John. "Deddeh's Case Points Out How The Legislature Takes

Care Of Its Own." *The San Diego Union-Tribune*, Aug. 15, 1993: A3.

Matthews, Jon and Capps, Steven A. "Check-In' Keeps Legislators Paid." *The Sacramento Bee*, July 3, 1999: A1.

Meadows, Kenneth. *Earth Medicine: Revealing Hidden Teachings of the Native-American Medicine Wheel.* MA: Element Books, Inc., 1999.

Mendel, Ed. "Wilson Joins Speaker Fray, Mails 52,000 Recall Petitions." *The San Diego Union-Tribune*, Jan. 12, 1995: A4.

Overend, William. "Supplied Lawmakers With Prostitutes, Moriarty Testifies." Metro; Part 2, *The Los Angeles Times*, July 11, 1985: 1.

Paddock, Richard C. "Legislators Back Tough Ethics Bill; State Government: Conflict-of-Interest Penalties Are Part Of The Landmark Package." *The Los Angeles Times*, April 6, 1990: A1.

Podger, Pamela. "Areias Exits the Capitol Amid Allegations, Defeats." *The Fresno Bee*, Sept. 6, 1994: B1.

Smolens, Michael. "If Chacon Leaves Legislature, Area Hispanics Lose Their Loan Voice." *The San Diego Union-Tribune*, Feb. 9, 1992: A3.

The Farm Journal, "Rusty Areias, Bachelor of the year," January 1985.

Unz, Ron K. "Immigration Mockery." *English for the Children, a project of One Nation/One California*, [Online] Available: http://www.onenation.org/unz052195.html: 1997.

Uzelac, Ellen. "Jonestown Massacre: More Questions Than Answers A Look Back, 10 Years Later." *The Record*, November 15, 1988: A21.

Vellinga, Mary Lynne. "In Fall From Power Bid, Brulte Lands In Horcher's Office." *The Sacramento Bee*, June 7, 1995: A1.

Weintraub, Daniel. "Allen Fights The System; Politics: The Cypress Republican Is Challenging The GOP Power Structure." Morning Edition, *The Orange County Register*, May 11, 1995: B01.

Wiegand, Steve. "Lawmakers Tied Up In Jokes." *The Sacramento Bee*, Sept. 17, 1995: B1

"Will Orange County Rebound With Reform?" *The Cal-Tax News* (newsletter), Jan. 1, 1995.

Wolinsky, Leo. "From the Horror of Jonestown to State Capitol; Fate Plays Part in Assemblywoman Speier's Life." *The Los Angeles Times*, Dec. 14, 1986: 3.

Woolfolk, John and Zinko, Carolyne. ""Speier's Husband Dies After San Mateo Crash He Was Going To Work At Time of Car Collision." *The San Francisco Chronicle*, Jan. 26, 1994: A17.

Printed in the United States
4074

9 781591 130772